"For too long, we have allowed our daughters to bear the burden of bad theology about what it means to be female. Well, no longer! Sheila, Rebecca, and Joanna provide a practical, candid, and theologically astute guide for mothers and daughters that exposes harmful teachings circulating in churches today and helps women rediscover their truest selves as ones loved and cherished by God."

**Amanda W. Benckhuysen**, author of *The Gospel According to Eve* and director of Safe Church Ministry for Christian Reformed Church

"In this book steeped in research and wisdom, Sheila, Rebecca, and Joanna unwind the false, shaming gospel of outward appearance and point our daughters to a true and confident faith—one rooted in a good Father who delights in his beloved and deems her worthy of healthy esteem and relationships. But perhaps one of this book's greatest contributions will be the bold conversations it sparks between parents and daughters. If you have a daughter or are a daughter, your soul needs this book."

**Laura Barringer**, coauthor of *A Church Called Tov*

"Sheila Wray Gregoire, Rebecca Gregoire Lindenbach, and Joanna Sawatsky's invitation to raise girls who resist toxic teachings on sex, self, and speaking up is one that I'm gladly accepting! As a parenting educator and family-life coach, I have a special heart for helping parents who have been told damaging lies by the church about what it takes to be a "godly parent" that have led to disconnection and harm in their homes. Since mentoring our daughters about sex, self-esteem, emotional health, consent, firm boundaries, and bodily self-awareness is a requirement and honor for *all* parents, thank God for this book that alerts us to the dangers of mainstream Christian teachings and empowers us to be bold in our parenting in a way that honors Christ *and* our children. I'm extremely grateful for the research and solid advice presented in this book that give myself and the parents I support the courage to do things differently. I will be recommending it to *all* of my students at Fresh Start Family."

**Wendy Snyder**, founder of Fresh Start Family
and host of *The Fresh Start Family Show*

## Praise for *The Great Sex Rescue*

"This book is a groundbreaking look into what true, sacred biblical sexuality is intended to be and the root causes and ideas that damage a couple's intimacy in marriage. Going straight to Scripture, the authors dig deep into ideologies that draw couples away from God-designed intimacy, and they seek to construct a framework for sexuality that is truly rooted in Scripture and God's beautiful design, elevating sexuality and marriage to the glory and sacredness it was intended to have. This is a must-read."

**Rachael Denhollander**, lawyer, victim advocate,
and author of *What Is a Girl Worth?*

"This book is so incredibly powerful! If you've ever read a Christian book on sex and marriage, you owe it to yourself to read this one. Armed with extensive survey data and equipped with compassion and common sense, the authors dismantle the devastating myths long promoted by Christian leaders that have caused untold damage to generations of Christian women. Equal parts distressing and liberating, this book is desperately needed in this moment."

**Kristin Kobes Du Mez**, author of *Jesus and John Wayne*

"I cannot think of a more important book (outside of the Bible) that you must read. This book is the authentic gut-punch that the evangelical community needs. This exposes our historic dismal handling of sexuality and gives us a clear path forward to sexual maturity, wholeness, and health. I already want to read it again and will surely be telling my network to purchase this vital guide. Thank you for such a seminal work!"

**Andrew J. Bauman**, LMHC, cofounder and director of the Christian Counseling Center for Sexual Health and Trauma

*"The Great Sex Rescue* is exactly the type of book on sex I would want my college students reading. This next generation has been personally burned by bad Christian sex advice. Both women and men will benefit from *The Great Sex Rescue*, but I think young adults may benefit most."

**Dr. Heather Thompson Day**, author of *Confessions of a Christian Wife* and professor of communications at Colorado Christian University

# SHE
## DESERVES
## BETTER

# SHE
## DESERVES
## BETTER

### RAISING GIRLS TO RESIST TOXIC TEACHINGS
### ON SEX, SELF, AND SPEAKING UP

## SHEILA WRAY GREGOIRE,
### REBECCA GREGOIRE LINDENBACH, and JOANNA SAWATSKY

BakerBooks

*a division of Baker Publishing Group*
Grand Rapids, Michigan

Published by Baker Books
a division of Baker Publishing Group
PO Box 6287, Grand Rapids, MI 49516-6287
www.bakerbooks.com

Printed in the United States of America

Library of Congress Cataloging-in-Publication Data
Names: Gregoire, Sheila Wray, 1970– author. | Lindenbach, Rebecca Gregoire, 1995– author. | Sawatsky, Joanna, 1990– author.
Title: She deserves better : raising girls to resist toxic teachings on sex, self, and speaking up / Sheila Wray Gregoire, Rebecca Gregoire Lindenbach, and Joanna Sawatsky.
Description: Grand Rapids, MI : Baker Books, a division of Baker Publishing Group, [2023] | Includes bibliographical references.
Identifiers: LCCN 2022031101 | ISBN 9781540900838 (paperback) | ISBN 9781540903020 (casebound) | ISBN 9781493437757 (ebook)
Subjects: LCSH: Mothers and daughters—Religious aspects—Christianity. | Daughters—Religious life. | Daughters—Conduct of life.
Classification: LCC BV4529.18 .G735 2023 | DDC 248.8/431—dc23/eng/20221110
LC record available at https://lccn.loc.gov/2022031101

Some names and details have been changed or presented in composite form in order to protect the privacy of the individuals involved.

Baker Publishing Group publications use paper produced from sustainable forestry practices and post-consumer waste whenever possible.

23  24  25  26  27  28  29      7  6  5  4  3  2

To Mariana Grace, Talitha Jeannette, and Vivian Louise.
You deserve better, and by God's grace you'll get it.

# Contents

# 1

## She Deserves to Be Set Up for Success

### *Understanding How the Church Influences Your Daughter's Self-Esteem and Well-Being*

Sheila grew up with blue eye shadow, *The Brady Bunch*, and Abba records on repeat. The only thing higher than her shoulder pads were her bangs. She learned to play guitar using Amy Grant tunes while on summer missions trips as she dreamed of bringing Jesus to the nations. And she dated. A lot.

Joanna and Rebecca grew up in the era of *I Kissed Dating Goodbye*, when dating became anathema. They read Focus on the Family's *Brio* magazine until the pages wore out, sang BarlowGirl at the top of their lungs, and delighted that their teen heartthrobs wore purity rings.

All three of us writing this book grew up loving Jesus and attending youth group. But our experiences were separated by a generation (not so surprising since Rebecca is Sheila's daughter!). That generation saw a huge shift in the evangelical church, when youth groups and popular media embraced purity culture whole-heartedly. While evangelicals have always preached about waiting for marriage for sex, purity culture ramped it up several notches, emphasizing abstinence as the cornerstone of one's identity; hyperfocusing around sex, even though no one was supposed to have it; and some even declaring dating and kissing to be near sins.

Well, guess what? Purity culture worked. Girls who took purity pledges were much more likely to save sex for marriage than those who did not. And the younger the girl was when she took the pledge, the higher the odds were that she wouldn't "do it" until she'd said "I do."[1] But on average, those same girls who took purity pledges before puberty had lower self-esteem in high school (and they *still* have lower self-esteem today), and they knew less about how sex and their bodies worked in general.[2] They were also more likely to suffer from vaginismus, a sexual pain disorder long known to be more prevalent among conservative Christians.[3] So purity culture "worked" only if the sole metric for success was virginity until marriage. Yet if we also value future relationships, mental health, and spiritual wellness, then purity culture failed, big time.

I (Sheila) have been writing on sex and marriage for almost twenty years. When I started, I mostly toed the typical evangelical line, including spreading some of these purity culture messages myself. But as I listened to women's stories and read the memoirs coming out about the effects purity culture was having, alarm bells went off. My focus on my blog, and later my podcast, shifted to how we can identify the harmful things we used to believe and replace them with truth. At the same time, two important young women in my life were finishing their studies and looking for flexible work options at home to accommodate having babies. So our trio was formed: myself, an author and speaker; Rebecca, a psychology grad with psychometrics training; and Joanna, an epidemiologist and statistician. Through FaceTime calls frequently interrupted by nursing babies or toddlers who needed a sippy cup, we began trying to help people grapple with the fallout of bad teachings about sex in the evangelical church. In 2021, we released *The Great Sex Rescue*, which reported the results of our survey of over 20,000 women. Our survey is, to date, the largest study ever done on Christian women's sexual and marital satisfaction. And we uncovered that much of the traditional evangelical advice actually leads to worse marriages and sex lives for women—not better.

So how do we set up a new generation of young women to avoid the pitfalls that have been experienced by so many? That's what we're exploring in this book—and it starts with taking an honest look at where it all started.

### What If Youth Group Is Setting Up Your Daughter for Hurt?

Marriages aren't harmed only by what we are taught once we're married. For many Christians, their marriages were set up on a rough trajectory as early as youth group. We found in our survey that many common youth group teachings on sexuality actually led to worse marriages for those girls once they became adults.

And women are finally saying, "Enough." *The Great Sex Rescue* offered them a way forward. But it also left many with one big question: If the church has primed so many women for body image issues, sexual dysfunction, or even abusive marriages, how on earth are Christian moms supposed to raise their daughters? With the release of *The Great Sex Rescue* came a flood of emails from concerned moms:

- "How do I raise my daughter to have confidence in herself and have a solid faith when so many of our bread-and-butter youth group teachings might damage her twenty years down the road?"
- "Since I was harmed by purity culture teachings, how do I raise my daughter without passing my hurt on to her?"
- "What if the hypersexualized social media world my daughter is steeped in terrifies me, but the only alternative given by my church is a purity culture mindset?"

- "How do I raise a daughter to love Jesus when I feel like the church has pulled the rug out from under me in regard to my own faith?"

Whatever your concern, you're not alone. We've heard from countless moms (and other mentors of girls) about the complexities of raising a girl with high self-esteem, confidence in herself, and wisdom to pursue healthy relationships in our hedonistic selfie-obsessed social media culture.

Christian parents in the past were given a shortcut—don't trust the world, just trust the church! Christian book and music stores, Christian movies, Christian T-shirt brands—pretty much anything you could think of for your teen, there was a Christian substitute.

In the last ten years, that Christian bubble has popped. Parents today are woefully aware that the Christian subculture they so gladly embraced as adolescents did not provide the safety it promised. The sex abuse scandals, the devastation left in the wake of purity culture, and the mass church exodus these things caused have made it impossible to ignore any longer: the bubble may have kept some harmful stuff out, but it also allowed a different form of harm to grow unchallenged. Kids were protected from the lyrics in Nirvana or Alanis Morissette songs but not from sixty-year-old elders who blamed their lust problems on preteen girls.

Parents today wanting to raise Christian girls who stay with their faith and find their identities in Jesus are faced with two battlefronts: the excesses of the world and also unhealthy church cultures. What is a mom to do?

## Bad Fruit Is for Compost, Not Pulpits

The three of us believe part of our mission is to offer a new perspective on how we give advice in the church: *evidence-based teachings*. My (Sheila's) husband is a pediatrician. Before suggesting a new asthma treatment for a patient, he scours research. He wants to know what has been shown to actually work. He could just offer a regimen that "feels" right to him or that he could justify why it "should" work, but that would be irresponsible: nothing beats cold, hard numbers.

We don't actually have many evidence-based protocols for raising daughters in the church. Sure, we have a lot of *theology*, opinions, and cultural norms—but what's been missing is actual evidence of whether our methods work. That's what our team set out to fix with our surveys: we want moms, mentors, grandmas, aunts, and pastors to have a way forward when teaching girls about their worth and identity in Christ that is based on evidence, not just opinion. The three of us believe the words of Jesus that if a theology is true, it will bear good fruit. Talking about how to identify false teachers, Jesus explains in Matthew 7:17–20:

> So every good tree bears good fruit, but the bad tree bears bad fruit. A good tree cannot produce bad fruit, nor can a bad tree produce good fruit. Every tree that does not bear good fruit is cut down and thrown into the fire. So then, you will know them by their fruits. (NASB 1995)

We are called by God to do the work of examining the fruit of teachings. And if a teaching doesn't bear good fruit? We get rid of it.

That's what we're hoping to do with our research. After we surveyed 20,000 women and 3,000 men, we then set out to survey another 7,500 women specifically on their experiences and beliefs as teens. That survey of teenage experiences and the focus groups that went along with it form the backbone of this book and the majority of the charts in it, supplemented by results from our original 20,000-woman survey. We looked at how key parenting practices, experiences at church, and evangelical teachings in general affect girls' self-esteem, relationship choices, future marriages, and more. And we've got to level with you: a lot of what the church has been teaching our teenage girls has some really, really bad fruit.

## Good News—Attending Church Leads to Positive Outcomes!

Before we explain what that bad fruit is, though, we want to clear up something vitally important: going to church tends to be a very positive thing with lots of great fruit! Why do hospitals and militaries and nursing homes have chaplains? Spiritual health matters. Even Rebecca's psychology professors at her secular university were constantly touting the health and well-being benefits of religiosity, because the proof is widespread. People benefit from spiritual community, a sense of belonging, and purpose for life, and data (including our surveys) repeatedly bears that out.

Longitudinal research from the University of Texas found that religious involvement helps boost children's social development

### Understanding the Statistics in This Book

Strap in for a quick stats lesson with Joanna (I promise it's not bad!). We use numbers throughout this book because they are a beautiful way to tell a story. They offer us an opportunity to zoom out beyond our limited experience. Ultimately, statistics give us a powerful way to examine the fruit of teachings and ideas. In this book, we'll be sharing a lot of numbers with you, but we recognize that math isn't everyone's cup of tea, so I'll do my best to make this easy to understand!

Frequently when we were running our analyses, we separated our respondents into two categories: above-average self-esteem and below-average self-esteem. That way, we can see how being exposed to different teachings, situations, or ideas changes the odds of being in either self-esteem group.

Okay, but now I've used the word *odds*, and I'm not talking Vegas. So what am I talking about?

Well, if you've read *The Great Sex Rescue*, you'll know that I, like most public health nerds, am rather obsessed with odds ratios. Odds ratios speak to probability: how much more or less likely a person is to experience an outcome depending on whether or not they have a particular exposure. For example, in *The Great Sex Rescue*, we found that women who believed "all men struggle with lust; it is every man's battle" were 79% more likely to engage in sex with their husbands only because they felt they had to.

With odds ratios, you can't run analyses unless you have people who are in different groups, which means that our surveys had a very mixed bag of respondents—we had ultraconservatives, ultraliberals, and everything in between. Otherwise we would not be able to compare between groups! What made our surveys even more powerful is that we were looking at beliefs over time, so it was easier to see how certain beliefs may have actually contributed to causing future outcomes.

One really important question we frequently get about our results is whether we are dealing simply with correlation or if we have discovered a causal relationship, in which one thing leads to the other. There are a lot of ways to do what biostatisticians call "causal inference," but one of the simplest is time! If one thing happens before another and there is a statistical correlation, we can infer that the one that happened first is causally linked to the one that happened later. It's not perfect, but it's the best we can do without access to time machines (or a ton of funding to do prospective research).

and can help them become more psychologically well-adjusted.[4] The *American Journal of Epidemiology* released a study in 2018 that discovered a wide range of benefits of both church attendance and personal practice of prayer. Those who attended church at least once a week, compared to those who never attended church, were 18% more likely to be happier as adults, 28% more likely to be involved in volunteer work, and 33% less likely to do illicit drugs.[5] Put simply, faith is a force for good.

We weren't surprised, then, when we found that church attendance was a protective factor for high schoolers' self-esteem: women who rarely or never went to church in high school were 70.8% more likely to have below-average self-esteem during high school when compared with those who attended church once a week, and 81.2% more likely to have below-average self-esteem than those who attended church more than once a week (see the graphs in figure 1.1).[6] Church can be, and usually is, a powerful influence for good.

Except when it isn't.

## Bad News—Not All Churches Have a Good Influence

For our most recent survey, we measured the effects of several teachings that we found throughout evangelical resources for teen girls. These aren't Apostles' Creed–level teachings about the nature

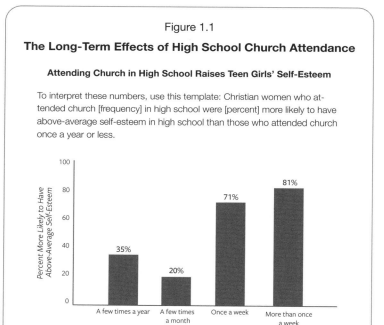

Figure 1.1

### The Long-Term Effects of High School Church Attendance

**Attending Church in High School Raises Teen Girls' Self-Esteem**

To interpret these numbers, use this template: Christian women who attended church [frequency] in high school were [percent] more likely to have above-average self-esteem in high school than those who attended church once a year or less.

Percent More Likely to Have Above-Average Self-Esteem

- A few times a year: 35%
- A few times a month: 20%
- Once a week: 71%
- More than once a week: 81%

*High School Church Attendance Frequency*

**Attending Church in High School Helps Build Happier Marriages Later**

To interpret these numbers, use this template: Christian women who attended church [frequency] in high school were [percent] more likely to have above-average marital satisfaction in adulthood than those who attended church once a year or less.

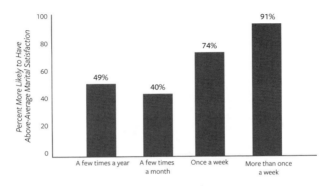

*High School Church Attendance Frequency*

**Attending Church in High School Sets Women Up for a Healthier Sex Life**

To interpret these numbers, use this template: Christian women who attended church [frequency] in high school were [percent] more likely to have an above-average sex life in marriage than those who attended church once a year or less.

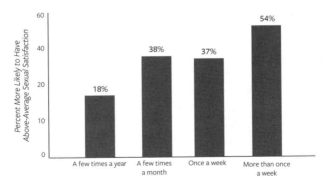

*High School Church Attendance Frequency*

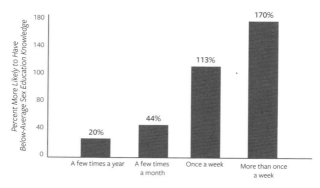

**Church Attendance Is Also Correlated with Insufficient Sex Education**

To interpret these numbers, use this template: Christian women who attended church [frequency] in high school were [percent] percent more likely to have below-average knowledge of sex education vocabulary terms in high school than those who attended church once a year or less.

Key finding: Church attendance yields good fruit—but there are still some bad apples.

of God or the means of salvation, but rather denominational differences in concepts like gender hierarchy, the nature of sexual sin, and what healthy identity looks like (see figure 1.2).

If you're reading this book, you probably already are suspicious of many of the things you may have been taught. After all, while each harmful teaching we measured was believed in high school by an average of 74.1% of our respondents, today that number falls to just 19.1%. However church leaders may think or feel about it, deconstruction is happening. And we think we have a hint about why. *All these messages caused real harm in the past—and they are still causing harm today* (see figure 1.3).[7]

The self-esteem impact of these teachings is so strong that there

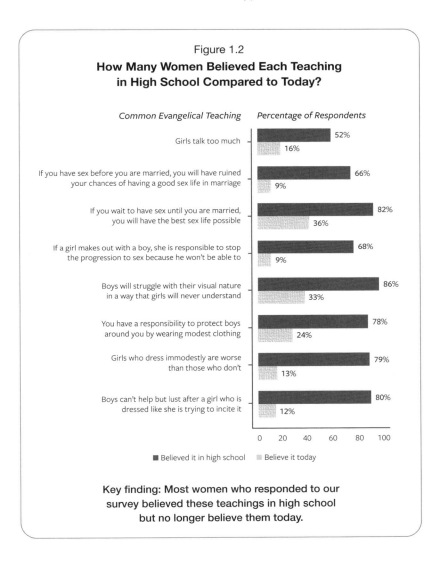

Figure 1.2

**How Many Women Believed Each Teaching in High School Compared to Today?**

*Common Evangelical Teaching*     *Percentage of Respondents*

Girls talk too much — 52% / 16%

If you have sex before you are married, you will have ruined your chances of having a good sex life in marriage — 66% / 9%

If you wait to have sex until you are married, you will have the best sex life possible — 82% / 36%

If a girl makes out with a boy, she is responsible to stop the progression to sex because he won't be able to — 68% / 9%

Boys will struggle with their visual nature in a way that girls will never understand — 86% / 33%

You have a responsibility to protect boys around you by wearing modest clothing — 78% / 24%

Girls who dress immodestly are worse than those who don't — 79% / 13%

Boys can't help but lust after a girl who is dressed like she is trying to incite it — 80% / 12%

■ Believed it in high school   ■ Believe it today

**Key finding: Most women who responded to our survey believed these teachings in high school but no longer believe them today.**

is no statistically significant difference between the self-esteem of Christian high schoolers who rarely if ever attend church who *don't* believe these teachings and those who attend church more than once a week but *do* believe the teachings.[8] All the gains in self-esteem from church attendance are lost if the church is toxic in its teachings. *What kind of church we attend matters.*

Okay . . . but is self-esteem really that important? If the main thing we want is for our daughters to know Jesus as their Savior, isn't *that* more important than self-esteem?

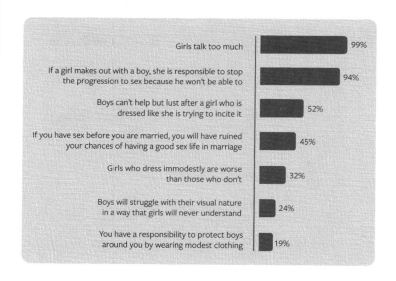

Figure 1.3

**The Effects of Common Evangelical Teachings on Teenage and Current Self-Esteem**

**High School Self-Esteem**

To interpret these numbers, use this template: When girls believed [teaching] in high school, they were [percent] more likely to have low self-esteem as teens.

| Teaching | Percent |
|---|---|
| Girls talk too much | 99% |
| If a girl makes out with a boy, she is responsible to stop the progression to sex because he won't be able to | 94% |
| Boys can't help but lust after a girl who is dressed like she is trying to incite it | 52% |
| If you have sex before you are married, you will have ruined your chances of having a good sex life in marriage | 45% |
| Girls who dress immodestly are worse than those who don't | 32% |
| Boys will struggle with their visual nature in a way that girls will never understand | 24% |
| You have a responsibility to protect boys around you by wearing modest clothing | 19% |

*Believing common evangelical teachings about marriage and sex as a teen is correlated with lower self-esteem in high school.*

While that's a common question, we think it misses the mark. First, it assumes you have to choose between Jesus and healthy self-esteem—but many women went to churches that preached Jesus and that boosted their self-esteem. They got their cake and ate it too! And second, what if healthy self-esteem is actually necessary for the kind of abundant life Christ desires for us?

Our survey measured how low self-esteem affected a girl's future marital and sexual satisfaction,[9] and the results weren't pretty.

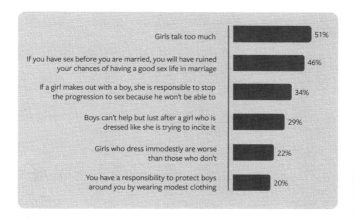

**Current Self-Esteem**

To interpret these numbers, use this template: When women believed [teaching] in high school, they are [percent] more likely to have low self-esteem today.

| | |
|---|---|
| Girls talk too much | 51% |
| If you have sex before you are married, you will have ruined your chances of having a good sex life in marriage | 46% |
| If a girl makes out with a boy, she is responsible to stop the progression to sex because he won't be able to | 34% |
| Boys can't help but lust after a girl who is dressed like she is trying to incite it | 29% |
| Girls who dress immodestly are worse than those who don't | 22% |
| You have a responsibility to protect boys around you by wearing modest clothing | 20% |

*Believing common evangelical teachings about marriage and sex in high school is correlated with lower self-esteem today.*

Key finding: Many of the messages given to our teenagers in evangelical contexts lower their self-esteem, and those effects often persist into adulthood.

This is serious stuff, leading to outcomes we would never want for our daughters.

But positive self-esteem? That leads to all kinds of benefits (see figure 1.4)!

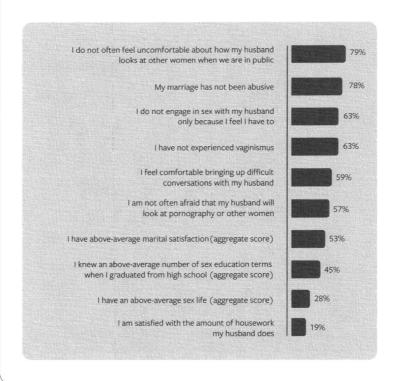

Figure 1.4

### The Effects of High Self-Esteem

**High Self-Esteem in High School**

To interpret these numbers, use this template: Women who had high self-esteem in high school were [percent] more likely to report [outcome variable].

| | |
|---|---|
| I do not often feel uncomfortable about how my husband looks at other women when we are in public | 79% |
| My marriage has not been abusive | 78% |
| I do not engage in sex with my husband only because I feel I have to | 63% |
| I have not experienced vaginismus | 63% |
| I feel comfortable bringing up difficult conversations with my husband | 59% |
| I am not often afraid that my husband will look at pornography or other women | 57% |
| I have above-average marital satisfaction (aggregate score) | 53% |
| I knew an above-average number of sex education terms when I graduated from high school (aggregate score) | 45% |
| I have an above-average sex life (aggregate score) | 28% |
| I am satisfied with the amount of housework my husband does | 19% |

But here's something else: we didn't actually write the questions we used to measure self-esteem—they were part of something called a "previously validated data set." That means that other researchers have already proven that this measure of self-esteem really works. Here's where things get cool (and why we like the evidence-based model so much): There is already a whole body of research using these same questions to measure totally different

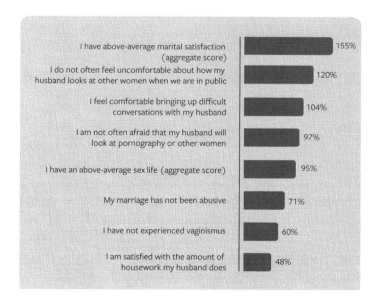

**High Self-Esteem Currently**

To interpret these numbers, use this template: Women who have high self-esteem currently are [percent] more likely to report [outcome variable].

| | |
|---|---|
| I have above-average marital satisfaction (aggregate score) | 155% |
| I do not often feel uncomfortable about how my husband looks at other women when we are in public | 120% |
| I feel comfortable bringing up difficult conversations with my husband | 104% |
| I am not often afraid that my husband will look at pornography or other women | 97% |
| I have an above-average sex life (aggregate score) | 95% |
| My marriage has not been abusive | 71% |
| I have not experienced vaginismus | 60% |
| I am satisfied with the amount of housework my husband does | 48% |

**Key finding: Self-esteem is a powerful protective force. That's why Jesus calls us to love our neighbor as we love ourselves.**

outcomes. And researchers have already found that negative self-esteem leads to:

- higher rates of body dissatisfaction,[10]
- greater likelihood of becoming a victim of domestic violence,[11]
- higher rates of engaging in aggressive behavior themselves.[12]

We don't need to reinvent the wheel; we already know that poor self-esteem leads to all this bad stuff. When you read in this book, then, about how something—whether it be a teaching, an attitude, or an experience—lowers self-esteem, recognize that the impact goes beyond whether a girl thinks she's pretty. It's interconnected with every part of her life.

### Are You Ignoring the Undertow?

When Rebecca turned eighteen, I (Sheila) took her to Mexico to celebrate. One day we decided to swim along the shore from a rocky outcropping to a dock. The sun was shining, the view was breathtaking, and I really wanted some exercise. So we dove in and began swimming. It was harder than I thought it would be, but I made it to within twenty feet of that dock. And then, no matter how hard I pumped my arms and my legs, I couldn't move any farther forward. Rebecca made it to the ladder, but she wasn't strong enough to pull me against the ocean currents.

Happily, I hadn't even gotten to full-blown panic before a burly man watching from the beach jumped in, swam to me with a flutter board, and towed me the rest of the way to the ladder. I think he was used to clueless tourists underestimating the current.

Now, I'm a strong swimmer. I love distance swimming. But I had no idea how strong that current was. Later that night, as Rebecca and I discussed my near miss, she reminded me of something her lifeguarding teachers always told her. The people with one of the highest risks of drowning are lifeguards because they think they can handle the situation. They're more likely to take reckless risks because they have an overinflated sense of trust in their own skills.

It's all too easy, as a parent, to become that reckless lifeguard and ignore the currents that could drag your daughter out to sea. Think of this book as the big burly man towing you back to the ladder. What makes this book different is that we want to look primarily not at the risks *outside* the church but instead those *inside*. We've heard so much about the risks outside. But it's made us ignore the threats that are right inside our church walls.

- "Sure, my church says some stuff about women that I don't agree with, but my daughter is confident in herself, so she'll be fine."
- "I don't agree with the leadership on how they discuss modesty or sex in the youth group, but we're a strong family, so I'm sure she'll be able to see through it."
- "Other churches may be unhealthy, but I know the people in my church—everyone is so godly, that would never happen here."

In this book, we'll look at the messages that our daughters often hear from the thirty-three-year-old mom of two leading her small group, from the Instagram influencer with millions of followers, from her twenty-five-year-old newlywed youth pastor. But these messages are very much like those invisible currents: they're in the water, but they can be hard to identify. When we reviewed Christian messages about sex and marriage for *The Great Sex Rescue*, we chose the bestselling evangelical sex and marriage books to locate the messaging. But there aren't that many bestselling books or popular magazines aimed at Christian teen girls today! Today, instead of poring over every edition of *Brio* magazine, girls follow five hundred different social media accounts.

The messages that were spread in books and magazines to teen girls in the early 2000s are still everywhere in evangelical culture because they are the teachings your daughter's mentors, Sunday school teachers, and youth pastors grew up with. The evangelical church knows that a lot of the messages from the 2000s are harmful—but evangelical leaders never actually tore the rotten stuff out and started over. Instead, they just cloaked it in politically correct language.

These teachings we found to be so harmful to our young girls are still all over our daughters' Instagram and TikTok feeds. However, for the three of us writing this book, this presents a tricky situation. When we reviewed marriage resources for *The Great Sex Rescue*, we focused on the bestselling authors in the niche: people who had deliberately pursued positions of spiritual authority and in turn had become the most influential voices in that space.

For our teenagers, though, the most influential voices are not necessarily bestselling authors with power and prestige—they are other young girls and young women who are influential simply because they are *popular*. They don't have fancy degrees. They haven't spent a decade trying to become a spiritual authority. They simply post about their lives and their faith, and people like them and follow.

They are a product of the harmful environment; they're not working to perpetuate it. There's a difference between someone who's popular who happens to be wrong and someone who has sought and garnered power and authority *with the intent* to share their message—a message that we now know causes harm. Influencers are famous because of who they are, but then there are people who are famous because of what they teach.

Quite frankly, it does not feel fair or kind to critique the eighteen-year-old who is simply parroting back what she heard in youth group. In this book, then, when we call out harmful teachings, we're going to quote the big-name authors who shaped the culture. It's not because their books are bestsellers among teens today—though they likely influenced you if you grew up in evangelicalism! Rather, going back to the root helps us identify harmful messages that are still everywhere and allows us to become familiar with the phrasing that is often used to spread them. Then, when your daughter sees her favorite nineteen-year-old social media influencer spread one of these teachings, she knows how to spot it.

Whether you, like Rebecca, escaped from purity culture without major hang-ups or battle scars or, like Joanna, got stuck in the muck of bad teachings and an unhealthy evangelical culture, we want to empower you to imagine a better church for your girl—so that she is healthy *because of* church, not *in spite of* church.

Evangelicalism has taught us to ask, "Do I agree with this? Is this proper doctrine?" But what if our litmus test for truth was less about ticking doctrinal boxes and more about looking like our Savior and bearing good fruit? After all, if something is of Christ, then it should not cause harm. This is the journey we'd like to invite you on—a journey along the road less traveled, where hopefully you will find a much richer relationship with Jesus in the process.

### How to Use This Book

The core of this book is really for you, Mom. Each chapter looks at how a certain category of harmful teachings or experiences correlates with your daughter's future well-being while outlining what she should know instead. Then, at the end of the chapter, you'll find conversation starters and exercises to work through with your daughter. If you have older teens, your daughters may want to read the whole book themselves! But for those of you with younger girls who may not be ready for some of the heavier content in the body of the book, the interactive sections are a great way to have these conversations with your daughter in an age-appropriate way.

Do you remember the parable of the sower and the seeds? The sower goes out and spreads seeds on the soil, but not all the seeds thrive. Some are immediately eaten by birds before they have a chance to sprout. Some sprout but wither in the sun. And then some grow well but are choked out by weeds.

You're already building good soil for your daughter. That's why you're reading this book—you love her, and you are trying your best to be the best mom you can be for her. Now it's time for some serious weeding.

# 2

## She Deserves a Big Faith

*Defining Our Faith by Fruit, Not Fundamentalism*

One Easter Sunday back when I was in university, I (Rebecca) vividly remember the praise team concluding the celebratory service with a rousing chorus of "Hosanna." As the voices swelled, a swarm of kindergarteners flooded the aisles, dancing in pure joy. One little girl scrambled up to her dad, who was leading the praise band, and twirled holding on to his hand. Isn't that what our relationship with God is meant to be—to be able to dance with reckless abandon with the Father?

Those little girls are now preteens and teenagers, and they likely don't run up onto stage to dance with Dad anymore, because that would be embarrassing. But don't we want our daughters, no matter what age, to have that childlike faith marked by authenticity and trust in their good, good Father? We want, as the apostle Paul prayed over the Ephesians, for our daughters to know "how wide and long and high and deep is the love of Christ" (Eph. 3:18). We're sure you want your daughter to grow up to be a wise, strong, confident woman of God. You want her to, as Jesus declared, "have life, and have it to the full" (John 10:10). That doesn't mean, though, that church involvement automatically churns out healthy, well-adjusted, lifelong believers. If the equation were that simple, we all would have figured it out by now. So let's take a closer look: *Why is it that religiosity tends to bring about these positive outcomes?*

Well, religion takes you out of the self-focused *me* mentality that we all—especially teenagers—too naturally have as our default. Simply believing in a higher power means that you're here for a reason, you're not the most important being on this planet, and you have a purpose in this life—this isn't all about you, but you still matter. Our decisions, the consequences of those decisions, and how our decisions affect others are more often talked about in religious homes and during religious services than they might be in nonreligious settings or families because religious people believe serving God is the first priority for the family.

Additionally, families who are well-connected in religious communities and go to church frequently are more likely to have a solid social support network of people gathering around shared beliefs. You can make friends with similar convictions more easily. Your peer group growing up is more likely to have the same boundaries you do in terms of what behaviors are inappropriate and what are fine. If your family falls on hard times, you're more likely to have a hand to help you up.

But there's one more big reason that we can easily overlook when we talk about how religion actually acts as a protective factor for our kids, building up their resilience against the hardships of life: hope. Simply put, *Jesus gives us hope.* As your child wades through the rocky waters of adolescence, starts questioning everything she knows, and tries to sort out how to navigate as an adult in this incredibly complex world, she has an anchor, a rock, a safe resting place in Christ. This may explain why studies have found that personal devotion to faith is a greater predictor of positive outcomes than simply strict adherence to religious beliefs, especially when it comes to teenagers.[1]

Although you likely don't have to be convinced that a personal relationship with Jesus is good for your daughter, I hope this comes as a relief: your daughter is, according to psychological research, capable of having a very real and impactful faith life even at a young age. She is capable of truly knowing and believing in God in a way that will shape her life, shape her choices, and shape her view of the world for the better.

We moms just need to make sure we protect her from tricky teachings that may throw her off course.

Did you ever take a logic and critical thinking class? If you did, you may recognize the term *red herring*. It comes from an 1807 story about a man who used a smelly smoked red herring to distract a hound who was sniffing out a rabbit, causing him to lose the scent trail, and it is used to describe arguments that mislead or distract from the original point.

When it comes to her spiritual development, far too many red herrings may be thrown in your daughter's path. These red herrings act as tricky teachings that pull her away from Christ. We don't want to put up obstacles to our children's faith, but we know from both research and Jesus' own words that we can: "Let the little children come to me, *and do not hinder them*, for the kingdom of heaven belongs to such as these" (Matt. 19:14, emphasis ours). Interesting how Jesus doesn't say "force your children to come to me" but rather "let them, but don't get in the way." Jesus calls our children to him—but sometimes we push them in directions that make them veer off course, even if that's the last thing we ever meant to do.

You are raising a daughter in a time in church history when there is a lot of upheaval, and the church is changing. In fact, it's very likely that your daughter is going to ask questions about what it really means to follow Christ, and she may have real moral or ethical issues with the church she is surrounded by. So how do we raise daughters who will chase after Christ, even if it means adopting a faith that looks different from what they're used to? How do we help our daughters build up a faith that will stand strong even if the church lets them down?

This is such a tough subject for many of us—because we're scared. We're scared our kids will grow up and not love Christ. And we're scared it'll be because we didn't do enough. So it's tempting to want to find a one-size-fits-all faith equation that fits together like a piece of Ikea furniture: pull the pieces out of the box, find the Allen wrench, and assemble according to the instructions. Do it right, and she'll be able to take that Lagkapten desk with her when she leaves for college. It's likely why books like *Mama Bear Apologetics* are so popular—because it's comforting to think that as long as we can give our girls the right arguments, as long as they can out-argue the atheists, then they'll stay in the church.

But a relationship with Jesus isn't strengthened by devastating your debate opponents. It isn't strengthened simply by knowing more. A relationship is a deep knowing—it requires *internal evidence*, not just *head knowledge*.

We invite you to imagine a faith for your daughter that embraces and encourages her to celebrate the internal evidence of Christ in her life. John Wesley wrote a beautiful series of letters in 1749 that includes this excerpt discussing the difference between head knowledge (traditional evidence) and one's personal experience of Christ (internal evidence):

> It is generally supposed that traditional evidence is weakened by length of time, as it must necessarily pass through so many hands in a continued succession of ages. But no length of time can possibly affect the strength of this internal evidence. It is equally strong, equally new, through the course of seventeen hundred years. It passes now, even as it has done from the beginning, directly from God into the believing soul. Do you suppose time will ever dry up this stream? Oh no! It shall never be cut off.[2]

Your daughter is capable of experiencing Christ in a profoundly real way, as Wesley describes. But too often we allow fear of the "other" and fear that they won't follow God the "right" way to distract us from our heart's real cry to "know [Christ] and the power of His resurrection" (Phil. 3:10 NASB 1995).

So let's talk about what gets in the way.

### Tricky Teaching: There's Only One "Right" Way to Be a Christian

When I (Rebecca) was around sixteen years old, my Baptist youth group decided to focus that night's sermon on explaining why Catholics were not actually Christians. While my youth pastor explained how everyone in that room knew Jesus more than any Catholic ever could, all I could think about was my Catholic friend Lucy. I laughed to myself. "Well, Lucy's totally a Christian—she has just as good of a relationship with Jesus as I have, and frankly, she's way more loving and far less judgmental than the youth leader giving this talk."

That pastor tried to convince me that Lucy, who prayed with me and talked with me about what God was doing in our lives, was less of a Christian than the boys who shared his theology but were heavily into the party scene and watched pornography openly at the back of the room during youth group sermons. It seemed bizarre that these people would be elevated as spiritual leaders over my clearly Spirit-filled friend simply because she didn't have the "right" doctrine—even though our church's particular doctrine had existed for less than three hundred years.[3]

Doctrine is important, yes. But Jesus clearly states, "By their fruit you will recognize them" (Matt. 7:20), and, "By this everyone will know that you are my disciples, if you love one another" (John 13:35). When we place doctrinal alignment above how people act, it cheapens what it means to follow Christ. We want to challenge you to think about how you can live in the tension of holding to your doctrinal beliefs without allowing those beliefs to eclipse the fruit of the Spirit in importance. Many churches define being "Christian" as being on the right side of different debates:

- conservative versus liberal
- six-day creation versus evolution
- infant baptism versus adult baptism
- charismatic versus reformed
- Calvinism versus Arminianism
- a gendered approach to leadership versus a giftings approach to leadership

And that's just a few of the arguments that cause us to focus more on head knowledge than on the working out of our faith. We know that we are saved through faith alone, but faith without works is also dead! So why are we so quick to exclude Christlike people based on the wrong head knowledge and so quick to accept those with bad works if they tick all the right theological boxes?

The quickest way to make your daughter run away from the faith is to show her that the Christian walk is all about being in the "right crowd" rather than living a life characterized by radical transformation into the likeness of Jesus (Rom. 8:29) as we serve one another (James 1:27). Your daughter will meet many people in her life who do not agree with you, your church, or even your denomination but who also love Jesus. Will that be a challenge to her faith, or will it be a cause for celebration that she's found good community among people of all stripes who love God?

My youth leader was not the first to judge people's faith based on outward shows or allegiances, and he won't be the last. Even in the New Testament we see infighting among congregations about the circumcision issue—can you really be a Christian if you are uncircumcised? To us, it seems silly—of course circumcision has nothing to do with salvation because it's not a matter of the heart! But we make the same mistake today with how we slap the label

"Christian" on someone or something that claims Christ but shows no evidence of it.

Now, many of you may read that and think, "Whoa, wait—the Bible says that we are saved by simply believing in Jesus!"

Certainly evangelicalism tends to define Christianity by whether you've said the sinner's prayer. And we writing this book believe that it is by grace we are saved through faith alone, not by works (Eph. 2:8–9). But we need to live with the tension that the same Jesus who said that we simply need to believe in him to be saved also told the parable of the sheep and the goats (Matt. 25:31–46). Many of the goats knew all the right theology, but they failed to actually live it out. On the other hand, the sheep were surprised to be praised—they didn't feel worthy. But Jesus welcomed them and called them faithful. The faith Jesus proclaims in the Gospels is about more than doctrinal alignment.

Maybe it's politics, maybe it's denomination, maybe it's even as simple as how someone dresses—teaching your daughter that our faith is judged by signaling which club we are a part of distracts from the real message of the gospel like a big, smelly fish.

### Tricky Teaching: A Christian Girl's Faith Is about Staying a Virgin and Then Getting Married

One weekend while doing research for this book, I (Sheila) filled up my Kindle and my tea maker, grabbed my reading glasses, and curled up in my yellow chair to read the evangelical books on the Christian market aimed at teen girls: *Lies Young Women Believe, Every Young Woman's Battle, And the Bride Wore White,* and *Passion and Purity.* Earlier I had read *When God Writes Your Love Story* and *For Young Women Only,* and these messages were still in the back of my mind too.

Reading these books all in a row was a jarring experience, and to illustrate it, I developed some word clouds comparing the frequency of common words that appeared in both the New Testament and these books to see how that frequency differed (see figure 2.1).

Looking at these word clouds leads one to wonder if the evangelical church's approach to teenage girls has more in common with a sex cult than the Bible. The preoccupation with the sex life of teen girls, rather than with any other aspect of her life, is astounding. How does a girl show that she loves God? She doesn't have sex before she's married.

When we compare the common words in the New Testament with the common words in Christian books aimed at girls, we notice a big discrepancy (as figure 2.2 shows, using just ten of the

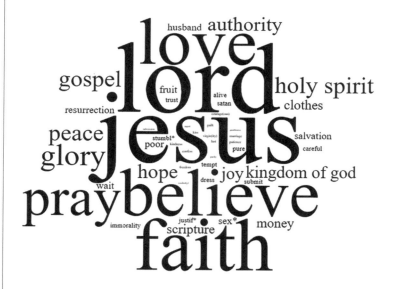

Figure 2.1
**New Testament**

*The results for each of these words in both word clouds include the base word along with any permutation of the word with a suffix added.

fifty words we measured for comparison). In the New Testament, we read about the Holy Spirit, the kingdom of God, and the gospel much more than we do sex, modesty, lust, or even temptation. But the inverse is true for our girls' resources. Ironically, the girls' resources that are so focused on warnings against sin don't prioritize the same dangers that the Bible does—the lure of wealth is far more emphasized in Scripture than in our resources.

It's concerning to us that the bestselling evangelical books aimed at teenage girls have revolved around boys, relationships, and sex. Simply put, we could not identify any bestselling Christian books for teen girls that *don't* lead with sexual purity as the primary marker of their faith. Elisabeth Elliot, in *Passion and Purity*, admitted, "It is, to be blunt, a book about virginity."[4] It's quite a contrast with

**Christian Materials for Teen Girls**

a bestselling secular book we found aimed at teen girls—*The Teen Girl's Survival Guide*.[5] Boys and dating certainly come into the discussion, but they are more like minor characters in a bigger story about self-esteem, healthy relationships, and healthy boundaries. Christian girls, though, are told that sexual purity and getting married someday is the main plotline of their story.

Although both boys and girls are told to abstain from sex, this virginity-focused approach to faith seems more heavily targeted to girls. Dannah Gresh, founder of Secret Keeper Girl events and books (now rebranded True Girl), hosts a mother-daughter event

---

Figure 2.2

**Words with Highest Frequency Difference between Christian Books for Teen Girls and the New Testament**

**More Common in Teen Books**

| Word | Rank in Books Aimed at Christian Teen Girls (out of 50) | Rank in the New Testament (out of 50) |
| --- | --- | --- |
| sex* | 2 | 24 |
| tempt | 11 | 34 |
| virgin* | 19 | 39 |
| lust | 24 | 45 |
| modest* | 27 | 49 |

**More Common in the New Testament**

| Word | Rank in Books Aimed at Christian Teen Girls (out of 50) | Rank in the New Testament (out of 50) |
| --- | --- | --- |
| Holy Spirit | 37 | 8 |
| gospel | 40 | 10 |
| kingdom of God | 47 | 14 |
| money | 42 | 16 |
| resurrection | 50 | 19 |

*This word's results include the base word along with any permutation of the word with a suffix added.

---

aimed at "talking about true beauty and modesty."[6] Their boys' event, though? It's branded "Born to Be Brave." Considering these events side by side, it would seem that boys are encouraged to please God by doing brave things; girls are encouraged to please God by not doing shameful things.

This message reduces girls' faith to something self-focused and small. Being self-controlled when it comes to sex is one of the fruits of living out a life of service to God, absolutely. But we have to be careful not to mix up the emphasis: we submit our sexual desires to God's will *as a result of* our love for God, not *as our primary way* to love God.

The greatest commandment given to our girls is not that they keep their legs shut. The greatest commandment given to our girls is that they love the Lord their God with all their heart, soul, mind, and strength, and that they love their neighbor as themselves.

### Equipping Your Daughter for a Big Faith

If you had asked me (Sheila) at sixteen what it meant for me to live out my faith for God, "staying a virgin until I'm married" wouldn't have crossed my lips. Yes, I was planning on staying a virgin until I was married (and, for the record, I did, but I don't think I deserve brownie points for that), but I didn't spend my life obsessing over it, nor did I feel that it defined my faith. Instead, I would have told you about the huge burden I felt about sex trafficking in East Asia, and how I was watching documentaries and starting letter-writing campaigns to embassies to change laws to try to help. I would have told you about feeling convicted at the age of twelve to start tithing my babysitting money, and how I researched different charities and started sponsoring a child through World Vision when I was only a child myself. I would have told you about praying for the girls from my high school who were going into the Toronto Morgentaler abortion clinic literally right next door to my church (Knox Presbyterian), where we often gave coffee to the police who were stationed there to protect those using the clinic. I would have told you about the Operation World prayer book that I had recently bought, about the unreached nations of the world, and how I was trying to pray through the book, one country a day. I would have told you that the things that haunted me most, that kept me up at night and drew me to prayer, were the stories I had read of the Holocaust and of slavery and of the persecution of Christians on the other side of the world. I asked myself, "Would I have hidden Jews during the Holocaust? Would I have been part of the Underground Railroad before the American Civil War? And if so, am I missing the equivalent today?" I would have told you that I wanted to make the world a better place.

If we raise girls who practice spiritual disciplines, who are a part of the same "group" as we are, and who successfully remain virgins, but as a result their faith is entirely about outward signaling rather than a deep, aching desire to serve those around them, then have we really taught our girls to love God? Have we introduced them to the hope, grace, love, and faithfulness of our Savior, to the joy that comes from serving him? Or have we given them a false gospel based on outward appearance—even if the outward appearance is good and looks very, very Christian?

In Luke 18, after Jesus talks about the two biggest commandments, the rich young ruler says to Jesus, "I've done all of this my whole life. I've got you covered." And Jesus doesn't contradict him. The rich guy likely was living a life in which he was crossing every *t* and dotting every *i*. (If they had *t*'s and *i*'s in Aramaic. I don't think they did.) So Jesus gives his final challenge: "You still lack one thing. Sell everything you have and give to the poor, and you will have treasure in heaven. Then come, follow me" (Luke 18:22). To Jesus, living a life focused on loving the Lord your God will mean that we care about the rest of the world—it means that we love. As the apostle Paul said so well in 1 Corinthians 13:

> If I speak in the tongues of men or of angels, but do not have love,
> I am only a resounding gong or a clanging cymbal. If I have the

gift of prophecy and can fathom all mysteries and all knowledge, and if I have a faith that can move mountains, but do not have love, I am nothing. If I give all I possess to the poor and give over my body to hardship that I may boast, but do not have love, I gain nothing. (vv. 1–3)

Living out a life of holiness doesn't matter if that holiness doesn't stem from love for the world and love for Jesus. It's tempting to follow the red herrings—but as we work through this book together, let's remember our goal: to raise girls who live out of love rather than fear or pride. Brave, it turns out, is not just for boys.

### Rescuing Your Daughter's View of Loving God

One of the women in our focus groups is now a pastor working with youth and young adults. In closing her interview, she told us her philosophy for ministry: "The order is belong, then believe, then behave. We want people to belong, even before they believe, and only after that do we talk about how to behave. But for so many of us, we have to behave before we even believe or belong."

If we get the order wrong, if our daughters feel they have to behave before they know where they stand or even what they believe, we can make them feel that Christianity is really just an act, and potentially one that they don't perform very well. That's the opposite of the genuine relationship we want our kids to have with Jesus. How do we, as moms, get the order right? How do we prepare our daughters to enter a world—even a church—where there will be roadblocks to a genuine, grace-filled, loving relationship with Christ?

We've talked about the red herrings that are the big-picture obstacles the church might put in your daughter's path. Remember how we said the problem with red herrings is that a dog on the track of a scent gets distracted by a big, smelly fish? Well, our goal as moms is not to make sure the world is emptied of big, smelly fish. That's never going to happen. Instead, let's teach our daughters to discern between what's a red herring and what's the voice of the Shepherd.

Jesus' words are so comforting as we raise kids to love him: "[The shepherd's] sheep follow him because they know his voice. But they will never follow a stranger; in fact, they will run away from him because they do not recognize a stranger's voice" (John 10:4–5). Your daughter's faith does not need to become a casualty of the tricky teachings in her path. She, too, can hear the voice of the Good Shepherd and follow gladly when he calls her. And he's calling her to a bigger faith than following the instruction manual, memorizing the right scripts, and staying in her little box.

## MOTHER-DAUGHTER
### SECTION

Want to work through the principles in this chapter with your daughter? Here are some exercises to read through and do together to have those conversations.

### What You Need to Know

Picture a girl named Hannah. She sings in the youth group worship band, teaches Sunday school every other week, wears a purity ring, and always dresses modestly.

Seems like a pretty great kid, right?

What if I told you that there are several kids who refuse to step foot in a youth group that Hannah goes to because they know her from school, and she is the meanest girl in their homeroom? She is judgmental, she teases people (but always in a sneaky way that the teachers don't notice), and she has a holier-than-thou attitude that makes the people around her feel like garbage.

Sometimes the things that we think most make a person a Christian are not actually the things that matter. It's like judging a cake by the frosting. If the base is made out of dirt, you can't hide the taste of dirt with a really great icing.

One of the reasons the religious powers didn't like Jesus much is that he tore down *legalism*. Legalism is when we make rules that determine if someone is "good" or "bad" based on things that don't actually matter—it's a tool people use to create "in" and "out" crowds.

For example, your grandparents may have grown up in a church that told them playing cards were from the devil and Christians didn't play Crazy Eights. This rule isn't actually in the Bible, but it was an easy way to categorize people into "Christian" or "not Christian." Sometimes the way that we categorize people is by whether they do the right things, and sometimes we categorize people based on what they believe. You might hear Christians saying that to be a Christian you have to vote a certain way, get baptized a certain way, or even believe the earth was created a certain way. But as you grow up, you'll likely meet Christians on different sides of all these things! Faith is about a living relationship with Jesus, so that means there's room in the church for a lot of different people with a lot of different viewpoints as long as we're all pointed at the same person: Christ.

## ⟨?⟩ Q&A

Look at the word clouds on pages 40–41 and the charts on page 42.

DAUGHTERS

What do you notice in the differences between New Testament writings and the popular evangelical books for teen girls? Which words do you hear more in your youth group? Which words do you think best describe your faith?

MOMS

Which five words from those word clouds do you want to most describe your daughter's faith?

MOMS

Growing up, did you have rules about what it meant to be a "good Christian" that we don't have today? Tell your daughter about them.

James 1:27 says, "Religion that God our Father accepts as pure and faultless is this: to look after orphans and widows in their distress and to keep oneself from being polluted by the world."

DAUGHTERS

Based on this verse, what are the two elements of the Christian life?

DISCUSS TOGETHER

Is there one that we're better at as a family? Is there one that our church is better at? How can we get better at the other? What would it look like? What one thing can we do differently in the month ahead to live out the *other* part of the verse?

## Spot the Tricky Teaching

Pick two of the following scenarios and see if you can spot any tricky teachings. For each scenario you go through, work through these questions:

DAUGHTERS

What message are they giving about what makes you a Christian? How could this be a problem? How could this be changed to be healthy?

MOTHERS

What do you want your daughter to know if she hears someone saying this?

### Scenario 1

Your pastor is giving a sermon on the decline of moral conviction in your country as an election is coming up. He says, "Any real, true believer is going to be on the Conservative side in this election.[7] This is the most important election in our time. We need to pray that the enemies of God don't win."

### Scenario 2

Your church has brought you to a big youth rally. The speaker is telling the girls how their virginity is the most precious gift they have to one day give to their husbands, and they should pledge to remain virgins to honor Jesus and to honor their future husbands. They announce that girls who pledge to remain virgins should come up to the front to get a ring. Two of the girls from your youth group are hanging back, and your youth leader tells them they should go forward.

### Scenario 3

Your youth leader is handing out pledge cards to read the New Testament in eighty days. He is saying that if you have time to watch Netflix and text your friends you have time to read the Bible. He says that Jesus is sad when you don't want to spend time with him. He says that if you love Jesus, you'll devote time before school to start every day with him.

### Scenario 4

Your friend Jessie is angry that she was passed over to lead the small group study for your school's Christian group on campus. "I just can't believe it. Fatima and Kallie have both been Christians for only like two years, and everyone knows Kallie's not a virgin. It's ridiculous. I've been in church my entire life; I know the Bible better than either of them. It should have been me."

# 3

## She Deserves to Be Heard

*Why Emotional Health Isn't Attained by Just Telling Her to "Be Joyful in the Lord!"*

If you peeked into my childhood bedroom on July 22, 2009, you would have seen fourteen-year-old me (Rebecca) running my tongue over newly braces-free teeth, with my hair in a side-ponytail, curled up in my puffy pink chair in the corner of my purple flower-power bedroom.

My RelientK album playing in the background on my bright pink boombox, I furiously scribbled in my green journal with a black lab puppy on the front.

Look over my shoulder, though, and you might be surprised to see what that pink, bubbly, fourteen-year-old version of me was writing:

> The atmosphere is poison
> The smells of medicine, smells of the sheets,

Remind her of what is soon to come.
The room reeks of death.

This was the third of my four-part cancer poem series I wrote for no apparent reason between July and August of that year.

Teenage angst is a beast. Research confirms that, compared to adults, adolescents tend to experience more frequent emotional highs and lows, and they feel those peaks and troughs more acutely.[1] Their brains are dealing with so much complexity for the first time, and it can be overwhelming. In fact, studies have shown that teenage angst actually *is* far more intense than the emotions we experience in adulthood. When your teen says, "You just don't understand how I feel!" in an emotional outburst, they're kind of right—you may have experienced similar angst when you were fifteen too, but statistically speaking, it's unlikely you have experienced it anytime in the last ten years. As our kids grow into teenagers, they start to experience what psychologists have termed *adolescent egocentrism*, which means that our kids become focused on themselves in such a way that they find it hard to differentiate what *they* think about themselves from what *others* think about them. This is why the zit on picture day is such a big deal—because teenagers really do have a hard time believing that other people are not as focused on their zit as they are. They're not just being melodramatic; they really do feel like they're living life under a microscope. Psychologists posit that this may be one of the main reasons for the steep decline in self-esteem in adolescence and the corresponding increase in self-consciousness.[2]

Perhaps this also helps to explain why mental illness is so common among teenagers. Data from the National Institute of Mental Health found an overall prevalence rate of major depressive episodes of 17% among American youth aged twelve to seventeen.[3] Girls had a much higher rate of depression than their male peers, with 25% of girls experiencing at least one major depressive episode compared to 9% of boys. Additionally, "adolescent girls with higher (vs. lower) emotional frequency, intensity, and instability and lower emotional clarity are at an increased risk for mood and anxiety disorders."[4] It also seems that in later adolescence, girls in particular can experience negative emotions more frequently than positive ones. Adolescent mood swings may seem melodramatic and humorous in hindsight, but your daughter is in the thick of it. Life, quite frankly, can feel a bit too much.

## Adolescent Angst Is Emotional Training Wheels

Likely because of my own literary pursuits, I (Rebecca) adore the Canadian podcast *Grownups Read Things They Wrote As Kids*. The podcast episodes are the "best of" stories read at live events all across Canada where adults bring childhood journals, poetry, short stories, or anything else they wrote when they were younger and read it, publicly, in front of a room full of strangers.

There's something so therapeutic about listening to a fifty-seven-year-old financial assistant recite his ninth-grade poem about his first heartache, or a thirty-two-year-old successful entrepreneur read a journal entry about how her life was over in the eighth grade when Jared saw a tampon fall out of her backpack. It's comforting to be able, as an adult, to look back and laugh at our adolescent selves—the angst, the heartache, the excitement—and know that, in the end, we grew, we survived, and it was all quite silly.

But it can be easy to forget that for that fourteen-year-old, life truly felt over when their crush went to the homecoming dance with someone else. It can be easy to laugh about the embarrassment of a tampon falling out of a bag—but we forget that when we were thirteen, if that had happened, we would have woken up in a cold sweat for weeks.

However, your daughter doesn't need to be left adrift in a sea of emotional turmoil. Adolescence is a prime time for learning coping strategies and improving emotional health so that when she reaches adulthood, she is ready for the "real world." Experiencing huge, overwhelming emotions about things that are objectively not life-ending means we get to test-drive emotional regulation before something that actually does have long-term consequences happens (getting laid off from work, failing a course you needed for your med school application, having a partner cheat on you).

But here's the kicker: not all coping skills we learn are helpful. Anxiety is actually a coping skill—it's just a maladaptive one! If you're obsessively concerned about getting a low grade, you're more likely to study more, go to class, do the assignments, and as a result get a good grade. But you could have achieved the same result by developing self-control rather than relying on panic and terror.

Religiosity can be a positive coping skill. By allowing us to reframe the world so that we aren't at the center of it but rather are put back in our "place," it reminds us that the world doesn't sit on our shoulders. Everything's not going to come crashing down if we don't perform perfectly. We have a purpose, we have a calling, but we're not the "main character" of the bigger story.[5]

This is why we can't just push big teenage emotions aside and say, "She'll grow out of it" with a chuckle. We have to listen and engage so that our daughters reap the benefits of this time of having "emotional training wheels" before the stakes increase. If we're not listening to our kids, not allowing them to feel their adolescent emotions, it's like buying a bike with training wheels but then locking it in the shed until we're ready to pull out the two-wheeler. We're going to end up with far more scraped knees. We want to make sure our daughters grow up with *healthy* coping skills, not *maladaptive* ones.

But even beyond that, your daughter needs to be heard *because she matters*. Her emotions may be inconvenient to your family life, frustrating when they seem out of proportion to reality, or heartbreaking when watching her feel so sad is killing you inside. Unfortunately, some of the "Christian" messaging around emotions can actually make it harder for our daughters to express themselves, and harder for us to hear them.

## She Should Know: Your Feelings Should Not Be Ignored

In my (Rebecca's) first year of university, Haribo Sugar-Free Gummi Bears were released. You get to snack on candies without the sky-high sugar content! Sounds great, right?

Turns out, no. Apparently sugar substitutes, such as Marlitol, can wreak havoc on the intestines. Reviews started pouring in on their Amazon page about the horrifying effects these tiny, colorful bears were having on people, mostly in the form of uncontrollable, projectile diarrhea. The reviews went viral:

- "Be sure to also buy a tub of OxiClean with this to get the blood and diarrhea stains out of your underwear, clothes, furniture, pets, loved ones, ceiling fans."
- "After three hours of a pelvis-shaking Gummy Bear assault, I was spongy and weak, surprised that I had any bones left. I cursed Haribo with the little strength I could muster."
- "If you think it's a fart . . . it's NOT."[6]

Our girls are raised in a culture where singers croon about how if something feels good right now, it can't be bad. Consumers of Haribo Sugar-Free Gummi Bears beg to differ. Pursuing what makes us happy in the moment, ignoring future consequences for ourselves or others, is a really bad idea.

But just because hedonism is bad doesn't mean that pleasure is bad or that we can't trust our emotions. Just because something that makes you happy can be bad doesn't mean that what makes you happy is always bad. It doesn't even mean that your emotions are a bad measure of whether something is healthy or not; it just means they can't be the *only* measure. We don't like the taste of rotten meat for a reason—it's bad for us. So just because we can't trust our taste buds about Haribo Sugar-Free Gummi Bears doesn't mean that we should ignore what our taste buds tell us altogether, because usually our taste buds are right.

But the church can go too far to the other side, drumming into your daughter the prophet Jeremiah's words that "the heart is deceitful above all things, and desperately wicked" (17:9 NKJV). She can't trust her feelings; she must act only on knowledge and faith.

But if Jeremiah really felt that emotions couldn't be trusted, he wouldn't have written Lamentations. Far too often, emotions are pitted against a healthy Christian walk with God. We are told our feelings are waiting to sabotage us with lies and deceit. Marc Alan Schelske, in his book *The Wisdom of Your Heart*, explains instead how emotions are our early warning signs of what's happening so that we can take stock and make decisions. When we are emotionally healthy, our emotions become our litmus test for the world. They're our "spidey-senses" that something isn't quite right. They tell us this relationship isn't good for us, this job environment is toxic, this university degree just isn't the right fit. Yet, as Schelske explains, we're often told to ignore those warning signs. "Ignore the emotion, and it would go away. That was often called living by faith. We were taught to keep the proper sequence: faith, fact, feelings, in that order. There was no encouragement to stop and reflect on the feelings we were having."[7] When we're advised to ignore feelings, though, and live only by faith and logic, we can end up doing great harm.

Your daughter is going to wrestle with big questions, emotions, and feelings in her teen years. As a mom, it can be really tempting to tell her to "conceal, don't feel," as Elsa's parents do in the movie *Frozen*. But your daughter needs to know that you love her—all of her, even the messy parts. She needs to know that she doesn't need to clean up before she's welcomed at your table.

## She Should Know: Struggling with Mental Health Doesn't Mean You Did Something Wrong

Picture an overwhelmed, anxious fifteen-year-old. How do you think being told "anxiety is a belief issue"[8] would affect her? Because that's what she would read in *Lies Young Women Believe*, and our already anxious girl might wonder if she has failed God. That same girl might hear something similar watching "5 Tips for Overcoming Crazy Girl Emotions" on the Girl Defined YouTube channel, run by Bethany Beal and Kristen Clark. In their video, Beal and Clark explain: "If our hearts and thoughts are in a godly place, our emotions will be peaceful. . . . Our emotions are a reflection of what's going on in our hearts. . . . Our emotions are a dictator of where our heart is." Listing the fruits of the Spirit, they conclude, "[The fruits of the Spirit] result in awesome emotions. If that's what's on the inside, the emotions will be stable on the outside, not like a hurricane. The opposites of the fruits of the Spirit are things like anger, anxiety, worry, things the Bible actually calls sin."[9] Read the Prophets, though, and you won't exactly see accounts of people who were emotionally placid—but you will see a *lot* of hurricanes of emotion.

Hearing that we need to take every thought captive and confront our depression and worry and focus on gratitude may work wonderfully for the stressed-out thirty-five-year-old who gets a bit grumpy sometimes. But for the fifteen-year-old who feels isolated and alone and wonders how she can get up in the morning? When you're dealing with all-or-nothing thinking, this advice, when not paired with an acknowledgment of how deep and debilitating depression can be, can cause shame, as we've heard from these mothers:

- "My daughter *asked* to stop going to church because of the predominant views taught in youth group about mental health (all depression/anxiety is a spiritual problem). She loves Jesus and seeks to know God/understand how she was made by him uniquely and perfectly. To be told she isn't yielding to God or knowing who she is in Christ as a result of autism and related anxiety was as un-Christlike as it comes. I stay home on Sundays with her now."

- "My children were told during a chapel service at their Christian school that it was a sin against God to feel anxious or depressed. One of them was in therapy at the time for issues that were in part aggravated by the school environment. My children are no longer at that school."

These moms protected their kids. But it's an embarrassment to the gospel that our Christian spaces can be so cold and unfeeling toward those in our midst who need the most compassion.

## Tricky Teaching: You've Given Satan a Foothold

If denying the emotions and accusing the girl experiencing the emotions aren't working, we do have a third tool available: blame it on Satan. Now, we are not saying that spiritual warfare or demonic influence doesn't exist. But much Christian rhetoric to teenagers especially is very demon-focused. When we used the search function in the ebook format of *Lies Young Women Believe*, which focuses heavily on emotions and mental illness, we found more instances of the name "Satan" than we found of "Jesus." We think that's a problem.

And yet, this devil-focused view of psychology is firmly entrenched in many areas of evangelicalism. Many of us are raising our girls in churches that promote counseling services that reject evidence-based approaches to handling mental illness and emotions and instead label inconvenient emotions "demonic." The popular biblical counseling book *Soul Care*, for instance, gives a textbook description of intrusive thoughts and labels them "demonization."[10]

### The Effects of Telling Kids They Don't Feel What They Feel

It would be irresponsible of us if we didn't touch on the subject that poses the most danger to some of our kids: how we deal with sexual orientation. In *Lies Young Women Believe*, girls struggling with big questions about their sexuality are told, "So here's what we've got to keep in mind: feelings aren't facts. Our feelings can fluctuate wildly, and are often tied to changing circumstances rather than reality. In fact, the Bible reveals that the heart—including our feelings—apart from the grace and indwelling Spirit of God, is deceitful and wicked (Jer. 17:9). The most important thing about your sexuality is not how you feel but what God says is true."[11]

Telling someone, "You don't feel what you think you feel," or training someone to systematically doubt and mistrust their own instincts is a form of psychological abuse called *gaslighting*. When we consider the fact that LGBTQ+ youth in the church have a seven-times-higher suicide rate than those outside of it, this kind of advice becomes doubly alarming. If you are afraid that your child is not straight, it may be tempting to simply brush off their "feelings" as untrue. But gaslighting your child won't make them straight—though it may contribute to a higher likelihood that they will want to die.

As explained in a study put out by The Trevor Project, religiosity is protective for straight kids when it comes to suicide—they make fewer attempts on their lives if they believe in God. However, for LGBTQ+ youth, being religious doesn't decrease their risk at all. Rather, if they are in religious circles that speak negatively about the LGBTQ+ community, they are *more* likely to attempt suicide.[12] Let that sink in: Being a Christian makes it less likely that teens will attempt suicide—unless they are gay. A study out of the University of Texas found that the more important faith was to a gay, lesbian, or bisexual student, the more likely it was that they were suicidal.[13] We need to wrestle with that, because telling these children "Your feelings aren't real" is having earth-shattering, permanent effects.

I (Joanna) suffered for years with crippling fears of demonic forces because books like this threatened that although people like me weren't possessed, we were indwelt by a demon.[14] When people already have extreme anxiety and intrusive thoughts, telling them it's a demon in your brain simply feeds the anxiety and strengthens the obsessions. I didn't need more fantastical threats—I needed help.

The church must be careful that its desire to explain away difficult things with spiritual language does not cause it to further victimize the people who need help the most. It's absurd and deeply damaging that *Soul Care* teaches that demons literally sexually assault rape survivors instead of calling these experiences by their actual name: PTSD flashbacks.[15] With so many churches influenced by works such as this, parents need to be alert and not simply assume that the youth pastor, small group leader, or biblical counselor at their church is equipped to counsel their daughters.

Using demons or a lack of faith to explain away extreme emotions, mental health issues, or even an unwanted sexual orientation is arguing in bad faith, because it's an irrefutable pat answer. You can't definitively prove it is *not* a demon or that you *do* have enough faith (how would you even do that?), so others have the right to ignore your problem, shame you for your problem, or label you "under bondage." Yes, our spiritual health impacts our mental and psychological well-being. But if all mental illness were caused by a lack of faith or a demon, would that mean that medications like Zoloft are a substitute for belief or that therapies like EMDR are equivalent to an exorcism? Because Zoloft and EMDR are very effective.

### What If There's Actually Something Wrong—and It's Not with Your Daughter?

Interpreting anxiety and depression as signs that something is wrong with your *daughter*, rather than signs that your daughter's *situation* is untenable, means we treat the symptoms and not the root. Why do we do this? Because it's hard to hear your daughter. You might have to deal with things that you're not ready to face. But what happens if you train your daughter to only deal with the symptoms and not do the hard work of getting to the root? She'll learn not to listen to herself either.

- Maybe she keeps trying to make friendships work, even with people who treat her badly.
- Maybe she stays in a university program that is killing her soul because she thinks she needs to learn to work harder.
- Maybe she pushes through her anxiety or depression, thinking, "I should be able to handle this," instead of realizing there's no shame in having struggles or needing help.

If your daughter is systematically taught that negative emotions mean she's done something wrong, how is she supposed to recognize when her emotions are warning her that something around her is toxic? The problem has already been identified, and it's all within her. So instead of trying to fix the situation or fix the danger, she retreats into herself and blames herself.

## She Should Know: Happy Isn't the Only Good Emotion

Did you learn the children's song "If You're Happy and You Know It"? We sang it in nursery Sunday school every week, but I (Sheila) didn't realize until joining a moms' group at a school in downtown Toronto that the song actually has emotions other than "happy." The chorus encourages people to clap their hands if they're happy, stomp their feet if they're angry, cry boo hoo if they're sad, shout hooray if they're excited! But in my church growing up, we just said "happy" for every action—and we left out the "cry boo hoo" part entirely. So we had little four-year-olds with huge smiles plastered on their faces clapping their hands, stomping their feet, and shouting "amen" because they were so darn "happy."

Happy is good! Happy is fun! Happy is a lot more pleasant than sadness and rage. But when we emphasize forced joy over authentic emotional experience, we're left unable to properly deal with big feelings.

Recently, a well-known pastor posted on Twitter about the issue of worry with a hypothetical situation. It went something like this:

What if I'm late to work?
Well, maybe I'll lose my job.
So?
I might not be able to provide for my family.
So?
We might lose our house.
So?
We could become homeless.
So?
I might become ill due to my homelessness and die.
So?
I'd be with Jesus.

In the space of 240 characters, the scenario escalated from being late to work to being dead. Yoinks. I (Joanna) asked him if he'd say, "So what?" to me if I'd been tearful about my cancer diagnosis, which came when I was a brand-new mommy. Of course not! Because it would be horrible and mean. He deleted the tweet within minutes of my reply.

While that tweet was a stellar example of toxic positivity, more insidious examples are all around us, likely all over your daughter's Instagram home page:

- God never gives you more than you can handle.
- "God is good, even when you don't feel like He is."[16]

- "The more you trust Christ with your future, the more His peace will fill your heart."[17]
- He knows the hairs on your head! Don't you think he's got this sorted?

Many of the platitudes are well-meaning. Many even quote Scripture! But they all shut down empathy and don't allow space for real intimacy and vulnerability. Every time we throw a platitude at our daughters when they're confused, hurt, or anxious, we communicate to them that they don't get to be heard, because it makes others uncomfortable. (Sounds an awful lot like Job's friends, doesn't it?)

There's actually a term for using religious language to avoid dealing with uncomfortable emotions: *spiritual bypassing*. Psychotherapist John Welwood, who coined the term, describes spiritual bypassing as the "tendency to use spiritual ideas and practices to sidestep or avoid facing unresolved emotional issues, psychological wounds, and unfinished developmental tasks."[18] Instead of truly listening to the person's pain, we provide distance from unresolved feelings using God-language. In practice, that means we make God sound indifferent to our pain, which God would never be.

Spiritual bypassing focuses on spiritual platitudes—which may even be true—but ignores the deeper truth of God's compassion for us. It might be helpful for your daughter to meditate on "his eye is on the sparrow" when she is feeling stressed out. But telling her "you don't need to be stressed because his eye is on the sparrow" is invalidating. Shutting down someone's feelings is not shepherding their emotional health. If your daughter is crying over her Wheaties on picture day because she woke up with a zit on her nose and you tell her, "Jesus can handle that," you're spiritually bypassing her. Yes, it is true, but she already knows that, and besides, it's unkind and unhelpful.

Your daughter needs to know that her experiences are valid and real even if they're immature and inconvenient. You can validate what your daughter is going through while also calling her to maturity. You can say, "I recognize this feels like the end of the world, and it is *not* how you want picture day to go, but you still do need to show up for that school picture. But why don't we google some quick remedies together before you have to leave for school!" And remind her that the zits will not always be this bad.

Perhaps one of the reasons the church so often falls to platitudes instead of addressing big feelings is because of a limited view of evangelism. We have a responsibility to be a witness so others will turn to Christ, and why would they want to do that if Christians are unhappy? We learn from a young age that *the world is always watching, and if you're not a good witness, you might be the reason someone goes to hell.* So smile! It looks good on you.

### Is the Church DARVOing Girls?

When we looked at the messaging to our girls around emotional health in the church, a familiar but unsettling pattern arose. There's a concept in psychology called DARVO that describes the common tactics used by abusers to control their victims (and the victims' allies). It stands for Deny, Attack, Reverse Victim and Offender.

Now let's look at the teachings girls may be taught in church:

1. You don't feel what you think you feel (Deny).
2. If you do feel that way, it's your fault because you don't trust God enough or you allowed a demon to have a foothold (Attack).
3. If you show that you're feeling that way, you're going to be a bad witness and you're going to hurt the church or even potentially threaten someone's salvation (Reverse Victim and Offender).

The DARVO manipulation strategy is so effective because it systematically chips away at a person's self-confidence and their ability to trust themselves. If you don't want to deal with something uncomfortable, just erase the person experiencing it! Then the problem goes away. Of course it won't go away for the person in crisis, but at least they'll be quiet about it, because they'll think they are the problem. They won't want to draw attention to it anymore.

While writing this book, we talked to many women about how high school experiences shaped their faith. This mentality—that a Christian should always be happy because we need to be a good witness—was mentioned multiple times by the women who left the church or struggled with their faith in high school and early adulthood. Flor was raised in a churchgoing family, but she also was a victim of abuse as a child. At home, she couldn't talk about the abuse without her mother exploding in an angry outburst. Flor often felt punished for talking about what happened to her, so she learned to keep things bottled up. Unfortunately, the church she attended unwittingly affirmed this decision.

Flor explained, "In the church, you have to kind of live in this fever where because of the gospel, you feel you have to forget yourself, to die to the self, and present a joyful, happy front even if you're hurting. It's not important to be honest as much as it's important to look healthy, prosperous, all good, and then maybe others will want to come to Christ." Flor did a fantastic job of keeping up the act, and everyone at school felt she was a happy, put-together, good little girl. "It was strange," Flor said, "because I realized that my friends at school were able to be honest with what they were going through—they were actually addressing the depression, they could talk about the abuse—and they thought life was so easy for me because I just put on this happy face. But I was so scared that if I talked to them about it, I would be ruining my witness because I'd be admitting that Jesus doesn't make life perfect."

Eventually, the pressure was just too much for Flor. She figured that the only real difference between her and her non-Christian friends was that they didn't have to plaster on a fake smile when they were miserable, and so she'd rather be real. She left the church and got caught up in the party scene and a toxic romantic relationship. After a few years, she hit rock bottom and felt God calling her back to him. She had tried her family's form of Christianity, and that hadn't worked; she had tried the world's way of numbing pain, and that hadn't worked; so Flor decided to try again with God, but this time refusing to wear a fake smile.

"The biggest thing I realized when I came back to the faith was that God is the God of Abraham, the God of Isaac, and the God of Jacob. He was the same God but had totally different relationships with each of those men, which meant there was room for me to have a faith and a relationship with God that didn't look like other people's faith—and yes, mine might look a little less happy sometimes, but that was okay. God is big enough to be the God of hurting people too." Flor ended our conversation with this: "I grew up thinking that we are Christians, so we have to be perfect or it's all in vain. But actually, you find hurting people in the church, and I needed to learn that it's okay to be hurt."

Additionally, believing that a good Christian keeps a veneer of perfection makes her a perfect victim for abusive spouses:

- From Erika, whose husband would physically force sex on her: "I just wanted to save face, I had gotten married early, I came from the perfect Christian family—it was just too much of a failure if I got divorced so young."
- From Dawn, a woman in one of our focus groups: "While this was happening—while he was forcing me to act out his porn fantasies and forcing me to do any and all sex acts he craved while he systematically abused and harmed me—I was still posting on Instagram and Facebook about what an amazing servant-leader husband and father he was. I was waxing poetic about him to my friends. I was saying all the things 'good Christian wives' said because I couldn't bear the thought that my marriage had failed. I

was keeping up appearances—when I finally divorced him and told my friends what was going on, the reaction was all the same: we had no idea."

We are concerned that a "keeping up with the Joneses" mentality about spirituality and religious markers may mean that teen girls grow up believing it's more important to project a picture-perfect image than to speak truth and have their pain heard.

## Our Daughters Need God as Their Safe Space

When I (Sheila) was a little girl, before the days of kidnapping fears, I was allowed to take a short walk to the mall on Saturday morning and hand over my quarter in exchange for a chocolate bar, to let my mother sleep in for one more hour.

Those solitary walks were the favorite part of my week. I talked with God nonstop. I told him what had happened since our last chat; I confided what I was scared of; I celebrated what I was looking forward to. And I felt God. He was my safe space.

Growing up after my father walked out on us, I needed that safe space. I needed to know that even though important people failed me, God never would. He cared. He listened. And he delighted in me.

That's why messages like Elisabeth Elliot's "Better to stick with what God was saying to me than what my heart was saying"[19] can be so tricky. They make it sound like God doesn't really care about your heart. Such messages seem to imply that God doesn't want to hear you; he only wants you to hear *him*. And the stakes are high— we're told we're at war. Nancy DeMoss Wolgemuth and Dannah Gresh say, "If your generation is going to win the battle Satan is waging against it, it will begin with you hiding His Word in your heart and being able to speak it accurately to those who are parroting Satan's lies in our culture. If you aren't filling your mind and heart with God's Truth, you will end up believing Satan's lies."[20]

Now doing your devotions and reading your Bible aren't safe spaces either! They're done out of fear of failure. Even in this, God doesn't want to know us for the sake of loving us. He wants us to know him so that he can win the culture wars. This kind of faith turns your daughter into a pawn to be used. And when your job is to be used, your emotions get in the way of the goal.

Religiosity is a protective factor in future well-being, but as we told you earlier, fear-based messages hurt. When God is your daughter's safe space and she knows that he truly hears her and cares for her, your daughter's well-being increases. When God instead becomes a source of threat, where if she is authentic she will disappoint him and where every bad emotion is a sign that she's failed, well, is it any wonder that anxiety plagues so many of our girls?

## Be the Mom Who Pays Attention

We know you're a parent, not a mental health professional. We don't believe you need to become a pediatrician or a psychologist to be a "good enough parent." But here's the ask: be a witness to your daughter's life.

Both Rebecca and Joanna have experienced anxiety disorders, and both were at their sickest in their teens and early twenties. When I (Joanna) was about thirteen, my favorite Scripture passage was Psalm 13. It reads:

> How long, LORD? Will you forget me forever?
>     How long will you hide your face from me?
> How long must I wrestle with my thoughts
>     and day after day have sorrow in my heart?
>     How long will my enemy triumph over me?
>
> Look on me and answer, LORD my God.
>     Give light to my eyes, or I will sleep in death,
> and my enemy will say, "I have overcome him,"
>     and my foes will rejoice when I fall.

But I trust in your unfailing love;
   my heart rejoices in your salvation.
I will sing the LORD's praise,
   for he has been good to me.

I shared my comfort verses with adults in those years, and now, from the vantage point of my thirty-year-old self, I'm surprised no one saw my choice of favorite verses as a neon sign on my forehead flashing "OCD" (with which I was later diagnosed). I remember feeling forgotten by God and wondered how long I'd have to deal with thoughts that didn't feel like mine. Unfortunately, none of the grown-ups picked up on what my favorite Scripture passage revealed about my mental state. While I clung to the promises at the end of the psalm like a life raft, I wish someone had helped me get to safe harbor.

I found my way to shore myself, and I've forgiven those who didn't see me. But I sometimes wonder how much of my life could have been different if someone had taken the time to notice me and truly hear and help process my emotions and experiences. On the other hand, when sixteen-year-old Rebecca started showing signs of depression, she got help. Sheila and Keith weren't perfect parents, but they were *good enough.*

The National Institute of Mental Health states that among adolescents who experience a major depressive episode, only 41.6% will receive any treatment. It might be easy to say, "Okay, but maybe it's just that the majority of depressive episodes aren't that bad," but the stats remain steady even for kids with debilitating depression that causes them severe impairment (46.9%).[21] It's tempting to just ignore it and hope it goes away, and most parents do. But this could be a chance to offer your child an easier path, the way Rebecca's parents did for her. If you are concerned, you should contact your primary care provider. Mental illness in teenagers is common. It's perfectly fine to err on the side of caution and ask your doctor for a referral.

We are both doing well today. We both still have mental health struggles that impact our daily lives. But now when we have big feelings, we know we haven't failed Jesus and we don't have to plaster on a fake smile to please him.

My (Joanna's) daughter has a children's psalter with adapted psalms for young children. One psalm ends with this simple phrase: "Already, in my heart, I'm saying thank you for listening."[22] We may not be able to fix the angst, but we can notice, and we can listen. And that can be enough.

## MOTHER-DAUGHTER
### SECTION

### What You Need to Know

Adolescence is a really intense time emotionally. In fact, research has shown that it's not just in your head—you really *are* experiencing higher highs and lower lows than the adults around you! Your brain is learning how to cope with big emotions right now so that when you're an adult and have to take care of yourself and potentially others, you will have the tools you need to make good decisions even if things are stressful or hard.

If you're going to learn those tools, you're going to have to learn to work through your emotions today, as a teen. You might meet people who, in different ways, shut down what you're feeling and want you to be happy all the time, even if it's fake. But God wants to know the real you. He shows a wide range of emotions in Scripture, and you're allowed to show emotions as well!

Let's work through these exercises to help figure out healthy ways to talk about big feelings, mental health, and healthy coping skills.

## 🔍 *Spot the Tricky Teaching*

We're going to play detective for a bit and spot some tricky teachings. Remember, tricky teachings always have a grain of truth, but they are wolves in sheep's clothing! They are harmful because they're not *the* truth but only *partial* truth.

Here are a bunch of things that you may hear in church circles:

- "Anxiety is a belief issue."[23]
- If you're depressed, you don't have the fruit of the Spirit. Joy is a fruit of the Spirit, so good Christians can't be depressed!
- The heart is deceitful and wicked. Strong emotions will lead you astray.

Now let's dissect these tricky teachings! For each one, ask:

1. What is the truth in this?
2. What is the tricky part of this teaching?
3. How would hearing this affect someone struggling with anxiety or depression? What about someone whose parents are getting divorced? What about someone trying to recover from an eating disorder?

Brainstorm together other Christian-sounding messages that punish people for their feelings.

Bonus: Go to Instagram and find some there! How would you change those messages to sound more like Jesus?

## ❓ *Q&A*

Let's talk about ways to cope with sadness, anxiety, or anger.

### MOMS

What helps you calm down or re-center when you're experiencing big emotions? Are there coping skills you've found helpful?

**DAUGHTERS**

Think back to the last time you felt really sad and over-whelmed. Did you go to anyone to talk about it? Did you feel like you were able to cope with those big feelings, or did you feel like you were drowning? What can your mom do to make it easier for you to go to her when you are feeling overwhelmed?

Now let's take a look at your family environment.

**DISCUSS TOGETHER**

Is home relaxing for you? What's your favorite way to relax?

**DISCUSS TOGETHER**

Do you feel that your family environment or schedule makes you more stressed out? Would any of the following help?

- reducing family commitments so there's more time to recharge
- getting therapy for siblings/parents so that the family as a whole is more emotionally healthy
- having a more consistent eating and sleeping schedule
- reducing contact with certain friends/extended family members who bring chaos

Sometimes when life is stressful, children can accidentally end up carrying some of that emotional burden in their family.

**MOMS**

Did you ever feel like your mom or dad put too much on your shoulders?

**DAUGHTERS**

Is there anything that stresses you out when your mom talks about it?

## What Would You Do?

For each of the following scenarios, work through how you would talk to a trusted adult about what's going on, and even create a code word you and your mom can use that says, "I'm not okay right now!"

### Scenario 1

You just can't stop getting angry. Everything your siblings do ticks you off, and although you want to be happy and calm, you just can't seem to stop snapping at everyone around you.

▶ PROMPT: Your parent says, "If you keep talking to your brother like that, you're losing your cell phone for the rest of the week." What do you do?

### Scenario 2

You're carrying a heavy course load, volunteering at church, and working a part-time job. You feel constantly overwhelmed and like you just want to cry, but you're terrified that if you stop doing any of these things, people will be disappointed in you or you won't be able to get into your dream college.

▶ PROMPT: You get a slightly lower grade on a test than you were hoping for and you can't stop sobbing. You're panicking, your heart rate is through the roof, you can't catch your breath. What do you do?

There are some things that are nonnegotiable that need to be brought to an adult's attention. For example:

- disordered eating behaviors
- self-injury such as cutting or burning of the skin
- suicidal talk or violent intentions

Let's role-play how you can go to an adult in a safe way if you notice any of these things happening.

### Scenario 3

You are in school and you hear your friend throwing up in the bathroom after lunch. You know she's not sick with any stomach bugs, and you've also seen her restricting her food other times as well.

▶ PROMPT: She notices you are there and says, "It's not a big deal. Promise you won't tell anyone." What do you do?

Moms, who would you want her to tell?

# 4

# She Deserves to Be Respected

*Teaching Girls to Draw Bold Boundaries*

Shel Silverstein's *The Giving Tree*, a classic children's book, is a heart-wrenching tale of sacrificial love depicting the friendship between an apple tree and a little boy. Over the boy's life, the tree gives and gives so that the boy can be happy—apples to eat, a place to play, branches to build into a house, and a trunk to carve into a boat. The book ends as the little boy, now an old man, simply needs a place to sit. And there is the tree, with only a stump remaining, offering him the perfect spot to rest.

As much as this book is lauded, we want you to remember this: *your daughter is not a giving tree.*

What would have happened if the giving tree had just said no to the little boy when he wanted to hack off her branches? That boy could be baking apple pies with his grandkids today! Instead, all that's left of her is a stump. She had the potential to bless generations of the little boy's family, but she was completely spent because he took everything from her in pursuit of his own happiness.

The Christian walk is a selfless one—we don't get to live convenient, comfortable lives if we're following Jesus. We are called to carry our crosses, to turn the other cheek, to love our neighbors as we love ourselves. What can get tricky is raising our daughters to be able to recognize when it is a time to put their own desires on hold for the sake of another, and when it is time to tell the little boy to buzz off and get that saw away from their branches.

## Boundaries Are for Her Good

I (Rebecca) loved my job as a lifeguard when I was a teen, largely because of my amazing colleagues—teens who had little in common with those I knew from youth group. Every single week someone would invite me to a party, saying, "There's going to be drinking, so I know you'll say no, but I just wanted to let you know." Like clockwork, I'd smile, thank them for the invitation, and say, "No, thank you, but I'll see you Monday!"

I'm quite proud of high school me in those scenarios. What allowed me to have wonderful friendships with friends with lifestyles different from mine, though, was the concept of *boundaries*.

Everyone knew my boundaries. They weren't a secret. I wasn't ashamed that I didn't date people who didn't share my faith. I didn't drink, I didn't smoke, I didn't swear because I had simply chosen differently for myself. People around me could choose to do those things, and I would not berate them, judge them, or laugh at them for it. But they also knew that I would not participate. And my friends respected my beliefs and my convictions because while I was firm in what I wanted for myself, I didn't try to control what choices *they* made.

Boundaries can be separated into two types: those that don't affect other people and those that do. Boundaries based on convictions tend not to affect others. Rebecca's choosing not to go to parties didn't mean that the other teens she worked with had to abstain from alcohol—it affected only her. The only way these types of boundaries ever affected the people around her was she was almost impossible to beat in "Never Have I Ever." She could always just pull out "Never have I ever said a swear word" and everyone would groan and put down a finger, leaving her the undisputed champion.

The church is quite good at encouraging young people to have these kinds of "stand up for your convictions" boundaries. It's likely one of the reasons religiosity leads to so many positive outcomes—we give kids the encouragement they need to say no to harmful actions like doing drugs, drinking, and engaging in sexual promiscuity. And the proof is in the pudding: religious kids have less sex,[1] do less drugs, and drink less alcohol.[2]

But while the church excels in encouraging our daughters to stand up for their convictions, it can falter in teaching our girls the second type of boundaries—those that *do* affect others. It can fail to teach our girls to stand up for themselves.

Our research for *The Great Sex Rescue* revealed that many teachings prevalent in the evangelical church today lead to unhealthy marriages and dissatisfying sex lives. These teachings cover a wide variety of topics from gender roles to pornography addiction, but the harmful ones all have one thing in common: *they limit a woman's ability to stand up for herself.* In one way or another, each downplays a woman's experiences, needs, convictions, or safety in order for her to placate her husband or keep up appearances of a "good Christian marriage."

Our daughters deserve to grow up with the strength to stand up for themselves and the courage not to allow others to mistreat them. And yet, the church has too often failed to teach well about this second type of boundary: a boundary that allows you to stand up not only for your convictions but also for yourself.

## She Should Know: She Is Not Less Important than Anyone Else

If you attended Sunday school or summer camp, you were likely taught the mantra "J.O.Y.: Jesus first, Others second, You third." This was the Christian way to live—seeing ourselves as less important than the people around us. This saying became so popular that it's the basis of a popular children's Sunday school song, teaching kids as young as three that their proper place is last.

Being others-oriented is an excellent, praiseworthy thing. The Christian walk is predicated upon a call to selflessly love and serve others. But if your daughter is trying to live out this J.O.Y. lifestyle, what is she to do when dealing with people who are making her uncomfortable?

- A girl from your daughter's youth group who doesn't have a ton of friends is texting your daughter for hours every day, and it's taking a toll on her.
- A shy, socially awkward boy is in love with your daughter and keeps asking her out even though she turns him down every time. It's beginning to feel like harassment.
- A close friend of your daughter's is leaning on your daughter for emotional support during a family crisis, refusing to talk to anyone else, and it's causing your daughter to experience anxiety and lose sleep because she feels responsible for her friend's well-being.

How do you draw boundaries in these situations if you're supposed to put yourself last? We're supposed to emulate Jesus, who literally died for us, so how do we have any right to say no when the consequences aren't as dire?

Our daughters need to know *why* Jesus sacrificed himself for people. Or perhaps, they need to know what were *not* the reasons he sacrificed himself.

- He didn't die to spare our egos.
- He didn't die so that we don't have to face our problems head-on.
- He didn't die so that our feelings aren't hurt.
- He didn't die so that we don't have to seek medical or psychological help from trained professionals.
- He didn't die so that we can avoid facing the consequences our actions have on other people.
- He didn't die so that we can avoid learning social skills and continue to make people uncomfortable.
- He didn't die so that we can avoid facing the truth.
- He didn't die so that we can mistreat the people around us.

Jesus died for us because there was something greater he was offering, not because he wanted us to avoid any and all discomfort. And Jesus gives us many examples of when he himself drew boundaries for his own well-being:

- Throughout the Gospels, Jesus asked people to keep his miracles secret, because he'd be mobbed if the word got out (Matt. 8:4; Luke 5:14–16; also Mark 1:43–45).
- In Mark 8, Jesus sends the crowds away of his own volition instead of waiting for them to leave when they wanted to.
- Matthew 8:18 says, "When Jesus saw the crowd around him, he gave orders to cross to the other side of the lake."

Jesus was capable of healing every person and feeding every stomach, but he didn't. There were probably parents of sick children who were angry that Jesus didn't heal their son or daughter. There were likely paralyzed beggars who felt disappointed when Jesus got into a boat and sailed away. Jesus even acknowledged that crowds were coming to him for food, but he did not give them any (John 6:25–59).

If our idea of Christian selflessness is that we always take care of everyone else's needs before we take care of our own, we are expecting more of ourselves than Jesus did of himself. *And he was God.* God's desire is not that you—or your daughter—destroy yourself in pursuit of someone else's happiness. Your daughter needs to know that she gets to be an equal part of the equation when she makes decisions.

The J.O.Y. mentality distorted the biblical concept of humility, in which we do not consider ourselves to be *higher* or *more important* than anyone else, and replaced it with an extreme version. Rather than loving our neighbors *as* we love ourselves, we are told to love ourselves *less* than we love our neighbors.

Now, frankly, many teens are inherently selfish and could use a reminder that the world does not, in fact, revolve around them. The J.O.Y. overcorrection may help self-obsessed teens find a healthy middle ground. But what if your daughter is naturally empathetic? What if she's a people-pleaser? What is this kind of girl apt to do when she is facing an awkward boundary situation? She's likely going to look for any excuse not to have to set that boundary so she can escape the discomfort—and J.O.Y. gives her exactly the way to do it: bury her own needs for the sake of avoiding conflict.

In church circles, our daughters will hear that a good Christian girl puts herself last. She keeps the peace at all costs—even when the cost is herself. Our church leaders tell her to imitate Jesus by giving up her rights, but they often fail to remind her that she's to love her neighbor *as herself*—meaning that others shouldn't be able to get away with more than she allows herself to.

## She Should Know: Truth Should Not Be Sacrificed for Peace

Focus on the Family's *Brio* magazine for teen girls published a script for a skit about a girl and a grudge. After Susan gets into a fight with her mom, she finds herself with a small green friend, her grudge. Over time, she feeds the grudge, and it grows until it leaves her bloodied and bitten and scratched. The school nurse informs her the only way to get rid of the grudge is to let it go. Susan obediently complies, and the skit ends with this:

> But no matter how [the grudge] begs you, never, NEVER budge!
> And whether you were right or wrong . . . don't ever hold a grudge![3]

Yes, petty grudges are self-sabotage, but telling girls that *even if they're right* they should always let it go without also advising them to talk to the person who wronged them? That's blatantly against Jesus' own advice in Matthew 18:15–17 about speaking directly to the one who hurt you. This type of teaching frames proper conflict resolution and even peacemaking as a sin or, at the very least, as less holy than being willing to let someone walk all over you.

In *Passion and Purity*, Elisabeth Elliot recounts the story of her romance with her first husband, Jim, one of five missionaries killed in Ecuador in 1956. For decades, this couple has been revered by our evangelical culture, their story portrayed as one to emulate. However, after Jim confessed that if he were ever to marry, it would be to Elisabeth since she was the only woman for him, he spent his final year of college kissing multiple other women, devastating Elisabeth. Her response? To forgive and forget: "What more could I expect? Jim Elliot was a man. Men are sinners. That was the simple truth. He was my ideal, but I had to come to terms with the truth. He had disappointed me. Hadn't I disappointed him many times?"[4]

Forgiveness is good, but note how she downplayed the significance of what Jim had done: *"Hadn't I disappointed him many times?"* The J.O.Y. mentality tells your daughter to trade *truth* for *peace* by downplaying her hurt and overstating her flaws in order to avoid difficult conversations or decisions. This line of thinking trains her to ignore truth that may lead to conflict and instead adopt a false narrative about the relationship.

Magdalena and Kyle grew up together; their parents were close friends. Everyone rejoiced when their relationship became romantic in their senior year of high school. When the two left for separate colleges, they vowed to make the long-distance relationship work. Within the first two weeks of being apart, Kyle had already made out with another girl. He called Magdalena crying and apologizing, and when she talked to her parents about his betrayal, they convinced her to give him another chance. "We all make mistakes," her dad said. Her mom warned, "Do you really want to start a long-term, potentially lifetime relationship with judgment and with a lack of grace?"

Magdalena and Kyle dated for another year until Kyle eventually ended it. Magdalena was angry, hurt, and mad at herself for wasting a year of her university life on a cheater. When her friends had asked her why she was still with him, though, she had made the same excuse we see in *Passion and Purity*: "I'm not perfect either." Our daughters need to know that they don't need to attain perfection before they are allowed to make some waves.

Are we teaching our daughters to disregard the hurt others cause them with the logic "everybody sins"? Are we teaching them that if they have ever wronged someone, even in a small way, that gives that person permission to wrong them tenfold?

Rather than teaching our daughters to rationalize away the sins of others or to downplay their own hurt in order to maintain an appearance of unity, let's teach our daughters to stand up and speak truth—even if the truth is uncomfortable. Anti-abuse advocate Sarah McDugal explained to us in an interview how she's implementing this with her own children:

> I teach my kids that they have to be able to live "conscience first." If your friend does something really dumb and you feel you have to go along with it because you don't want to get teased, that means you can't put your conscience first. And if you can't put your conscience first without there being a punishment, it's not a safe relationship.

What this comes down to, according to McDugal, is whether the relationship is mutually respectful.

We need, as parents, to take real steps to train our girls to be okay with other people disagreeing with them, but also to expect as a baseline to receive respect in the midst of disagreement. If you can't express that you're afraid of something, that you don't like something, or that you disagree, is that a safe relationship? No! And our girls need to have permission to act on that.

Your daughter needs to feel secure in her permission to do things like:

- speak up firmly and say no when a boy is sexually harassing her at school, even if it has social consequences.
- limit the time she spends talking to a friend who is draining her emotional energy.
- leave a friend group that makes her feel as if she isn't good enough, pretty enough, or popular enough.

Don't let the J.O.Y. mentality teach your daughter that she is worth less than other people or that she should bury truth in exchange for false peace. But even more than emotional safety, let's teach our girls that their physical safety matters too.

### She Should Know: God Does Not Ask for Human Sacrifice

Joe White, the founder of Kanakuk Camps, branded his camps with the slogan "I'm Third." It had the same meaning as J.O.Y., and they ran with it: "I'm Third" week at camps; "I'm Third" discipleship groups; small group discussions called "I'm Third All Year"; and their slogan "God First, Others Second, I'm Third."

The camp also made national news for covering up sexual abuse.[5]

We think there's a connection here. Teaching children to see themselves as the least important grooms them for evil, predatory people, whether that grooming was intentional or not. And all too often, Christian leadership has shown girls—and, in the case of

Kanakuk, boys too—that their physical and sexual safety can be sacrificed for "the greater good."

A reader of my (Sheila's) blog shared this story:

> Our pastor and his wife were hosting a huge dinner for their daughter's friends and dates for homecoming. His daughter told him she didn't want to include a particular friend, because this friend was dating a boy from school who had acted physically inappropriately with her best friend and other girls among their friend group. The pastor/dad argued with his daughter about inviting the teenage predator, because he wanted his home to be "welcoming for the sake of the gospel." The pastor/dad ended up not inviting the teenage predator, and hosted at a restaurant instead of his house as a compromise, but it was obvious he was still really torn up over the decision. And I thought, "for the sake of the gospel TO WHOM?" Clearly not to his own daughter and all of her friends, who had justifiable reasons for not feeling safe around this young man. Clearly not to the unfortunate girlfriend, who needed to be told that she was a precious child made in the image of God and deserved better than this. And clearly not to the young man himself, who needed to learn that actions/sins have consequences, and a consequence of mistreating girls/women is that you no longer get to be around them.

Often girls are told in subtle ways that drawing boundaries around personal safety means failing to live for the sake of "the gospel." Is this the message that we want to give our girls—that Jesus cares so little for them that he's fine that they experience trauma if it means someone else hears about him?

This is not a fringe experience either. Far too many evangelical circles have made themselves unsafe for girls because they ask girls to put their safety on hold for the sake of making predators comfortable. For example:

- Multiple women in our focus groups reported that as teens they were assaulted by a boy in the church youth group. In

the case of all but one, leadership did nothing when they
reported it.

- "We used to attend church regularly until we were kicked
out and threatened with the law after my teenage daughter reported sexual abuse by a thirty-four-year-old man on
the pastor's leadership team" (survey response).

- "My youth group experience as a teenager was very damaging. Several youth workers, volunteers, and staff had inappropriate relationships with teen girls. While they may not
have been criminal (but likely were), they were certainly
ungodly. The church did not deal with these issues, besides
to send one man on to another church" (survey response).

- The world watched as the news broke about Josh Duggar's molestation of his sisters, which his parents had kept
hush-hush. When interviewed, Jim Bob Duggar downplayed the trauma his daughters endured, saying, "This
was not rape or anything like that. This was like touching
over the clothes. There were a couple instances where
he touched someone under the clothes, but for like a few
seconds." Michelle said, "I know that every one of us have
done things wrong. That's why Jesus came!" The couple
ended the interview declaring that "we want to be an advocate for protecting juvenile records."[6]

- In our survey of women's experiences as teenagers, 18.7%
of respondents reported being sexually harassed at church
before they turned eighteen. Of those who were harassed
as minors, 10.2% received unwanted sexual attention from
their pastor, 20.3% were harassed by a youth leader or Sunday school teacher, and 47.4% were harassed by another
adult in the church.

This erasing of women's boundaries for the sake of predatory
men has even happened in our own personal circles. When Rebecca

was fifteen years old, there was an eighteen-year-old young man attending the youth group who gave off a distinctly predatory vibe. However, even after some of the girls expressed their fear of this young man to the youth leader and gave their reasons for why they found him dangerous, the youth leader simply chastised the girls for being judgmental. Instead of being concerned about safety, the leader told the girls to prioritize the boy's opinion of Jesus. The girls were told to "accept" him even though he was "weird." (The girls had no problem with "weird." It was "dangerous" they were concerned with.)

During youth games in which the kids ran around playing "man-hunt" with the lights off, other teenage boys who understood the threat decided together to create a buddy system with the girls to make sure they stayed safe. These high schoolers protected the other children better than the adults did.

Yes, we are called to sacrifice ourselves for the sake of others. But that does not mean we sacrifice our daughters' safety and well-being so that sexual predators can be in the praise band. Jesus did not die so that we can go on hurting others, and if you are in a church environment that is trading your daughter's safety for someone else's salvation, that is not a church that is valuing her emotional health, her physical safety, or her sexual safety the way that Jesus does.

### DARVO and Safety

**Deny**—"He's a good kid and he deserves to be included."
**Attack**—"You need to learn to accept people you think are weird—don't you think you're being a little judgmental?"
**Reverse Victim and Offender**—"He needs Jesus; do you think gossiping about him like this will help him come to the Lord?"

## She Should Know Women Who Model Boundary-Making

This harmful J.O.Y. teaching can be reinforced in the adult relationships that your daughter sees modeled all around her—most especially in your own relationship with her father (or father figure) if she has one. One of the big teachings I (Sheila) try hard to fight

---

### Be Your Daughter's Excuse!

Your daughter is going to be faced with socially tricky situations in which she wants an easy "out"—you can be that for her! Drawing boundaries does not always mean there needs to be a confrontation. Sometimes the best way to avoid a tricky situation is by leaving in the safest, quickest, easiest way you can. Here are some creative "outs" other moms have given their daughters:

- **Use a code word.** If she calls you "mother" instead of "mom," for example, you know she really wants you to say no to the request. Other common code words are "pretty please," "Mumsy," "chill out for a while," and the like. Any regular-sounding phrase that you never use as a family will work.
- **Give her a secret way to ask you to come to her rescue.** Texting you a specific emoji or phrase means that, magically, in a matter of minutes, Mom or Dad will call and suddenly need their child to return home immediately. This way, if she's uncomfortable and wants to leave, she has a way out without causing embarrassment or escalation in what may already be a dangerous situation.
- **Be willing to be her "stick-in-the-mud."** Are your daughter's friends pressuring her to watch a TV show she's really uncomfortable with? "Sorry, Mom said I can't." Are her friends wanting to go somewhere on Saturday and she'd rather not because of other kids in attendance? "Oh, Mom is making us have a family night." And then always back her up! (Note from Rebecca: I pulled this one a lot.)

---

against is the "Duck" principle, which goes something like this: *God is trying to teach your husband something. Maybe God wants to knock your husband over with a 2 x 4! But if you're standing between God and your husband, trying to be your husband's Holy Spirit, God won't be able to get to him. You need to duck, stand back, and let God do his work.*

It sounds super spiritual, doesn't it? And it's a very intoxicating message to believe: *You don't actually have to do anything but trust. Let God do it for you.* So we don't advocate for ourselves. We

---

## Honor Your Daughter's Preferences— Even in the Small Things!

To draw a boundary, your daughter must be able to voice what she actually wants—which requires knowing what she wants! The ability to understand her own preferences, then, is a building block for her developing healthy boundaries. Giving your daughter opportunities to figure out what she truly wants when it doesn't matter that much will help her identify what she truly wants when it does matter. Encourage her to speak up and name what she wants.

- For moms of young kids: Limit playdates with children your child simply doesn't enjoy being around, even if you really like their parents!
- For moms of older kids: Allow your daughter to have a say in her spiritual community, whether that means switching youth groups, summer camps, or even churches if necessary.
- Rather than operating as a "majority rules" family, give each member a chance to choose things like restaurants, outings, or even vacations.
- Give your daughter a choice of which extracurriculars she is involved in, and listen to her if she hates something you loved. (Note: some activities that are safety-based may be necessary nonnegotiables, like swimming lessons or driver's ed.)

don't say anything when we're being hurt. We don't rock the boat, because it's God who will eventually vindicate us. We don't *need* to draw boundaries, because we can let God take care of it and rest easy knowing whatever happens was simply meant to happen.

When you've done all you can do, yes, you do have to leave things in the hands of the Almighty. But God is not an excuse for passivity. It's such a temptation to leave things undone by taking the "God will prove me right" shortcut, and too often our church culture encourages our girls to do just that. But a shortcut will not bode well for your daughter in the long run.

If our daughters are trained to believe that their needs and beliefs matter less than other people's, they are more likely to end up with a husband who treats them poorly. In our survey of 20,000 women, we found that married Christian women who believe that their needs matter less than their husband's had worse marital and sexual satisfaction outcomes than those who do not. In fact, they are:

- 9.32 times less likely to be satisfied with the amount of closeness they share with their husbands during sex,
- 2.26 times less likely to frequently orgasm during sex,
- 3.61 times more likely to have sex only out of a sense of obligation.

*Lacking intimacy, feeling unseen, disappointing sex lives.* That's not the future you want for your daughter. But this is the fruit of the "God will vindicate me" argument! When we don't know how to advocate for ourselves, and when we don't draw boundaries and stand up for our worth in our relationships, it's terrifically easy for us to be taken advantage of.

What impact could it have on a daughter who is hearing at church that she is supposed to be selfless, who is being taught to consider everyone else as more important than herself, and who also sees her female role models being treated like second-class citizens in their marriages, families, or even churches? How will she learn that she is of infinite worth? How will she feel equipped to speak up if in the future her husband dismisses her opinions, needs, or desires as secondary to his own?

You are reading this book because you want to raise a daughter who is empowered, confident, and bold to walk into God's calling for her life. We know that many moms reading this haven't experienced that for themselves, which is why they want it so desperately for their daughters. But could it be that one of the gifts your daughter needs from you is that you expect the same goodness for yourself as you do for her? Can you show your daughter, through the example of your own life, that Jesus really wasn't lying when he said that he came that we may "have life, and have it to the full" (John 10:10)?

### Check-In: Does Your Family Model Good Boundaries?

- When was the last time I changed my behavior because my child confronted me about how I had spoken to her or treated her?
- When was the last time my child saw me speak up for myself?
- Have I allowed my child or my spouse to hurt me and let it go unresolved in order to maintain family peace?
- Have I shown my daughter that I think she is *capable* of having and keeping boundaries?
- Do I get accusatory when she tells me that her friends are doing things I don't approve of?
- Do I often assume my daughter did something that it turns out she did not?
- Do I check my kids for signs of alcohol use, sex, drug use— even though they have not done anything to suggest they might be doing those things?
- Do I give my daughter age-appropriate opportunities to earn my trust without me hovering or micromanaging?

We believe that your daughter was put on this planet because she has a unique and wonderful purpose for her life. We believe she is a gift, a treasure worthy of being cherished by those she meets.

We also believe that for you.

So let's move on into how we, as moms, can teach our daughters how to draw healthy boundaries—and maybe take some of these lessons to heart for ourselves too.

## MOTHER-DAUGHTER
### SECTION

### What You Need to Know

As a teen, I (Joanna) believed that keeping my mouth shut and not standing up for myself was how I could show Jesus' humility. When a teammate of mine was rude to a competitor, I didn't ask him to apologize, even though I worried that his behavior reflected badly on me. I didn't trust myself enough to speak up. But I also knew that the situation wasn't right.

Another situation was so serious that I couldn't use that old trick—and so I used my voice. One of my best friends went through a phase where he drove recklessly. I felt terrified when I was in the vehicle with him, and as the car accidents piled up, I became increasingly concerned that he would hurt himself or someone else. I knew that I couldn't live with myself if he died and I hadn't told him I was worried, so I marched into his room one day when I was visiting and I told him that if he was killed by a drunk driver, I would mourn the tragedy of his death. But if he died because he was being an idiot, he would be leaving me to remember him as . . . *an idiot kid who threw his life away.* I begged him not to.

Not surprisingly, my friend became very angry and threw me out of his room. Nevertheless, I was proud that I was able to put aside caring about what other people might think, even in conflict, and didn't care that I had caused a conflict and a rift—because I'd said what I needed to say as best I could.

Today, my friend is a devoted husband and father and a very conscientious driver. He pulled me aside years later and thanked me for calling him out. He said that my words really made him think and, along with a scary car accident, convinced him to change.

You deserve to know that when God looks down on your life, he's not angry at or disappointed in you for standing up for yourself. He doesn't want you to suffer so that someone else can skate by.

He wants you to *live*. And that can mean using your voice and drawing a bold boundary.

Boundaries exist so that you are treated the way Jesus wants you to be treated. As Christians, we are called to live sacrificial lives. We are called to love our neighbors as we love ourselves. But that does not mean that you matter *less* than your neighbor—it just means that you don't act selfishly.

There are two main categories of boundaries we want you to talk about: boundaries of conviction and boundaries of protection.

> **Conviction boundaries** are pretty easy to understand: things you simply won't engage in (e.g., underage drinking, cheating on tests, participating in bullying) because you consider them sins or they are illegal.

> **Protection boundaries** are more subjective: these are standards you need to maintain your emotional or physical health (e.g., not riding in a car when certain people are driving, personal preferences for which TV shows you watch, or even blocking mean or rude people on social media).

Conviction boundaries are pretty simple because they don't tend to affect others (e.g., if you choose not to go to a party because there's drinking, everyone else can still go). Protection boundaries can seem mean to the people who are affected by them. Maybe it offends your friend that you're not willing to get in the car if he's driving—but if he drives unsafely, it is not mean to impose consequences on his actions, even if he doesn't like it. It might feel rude to block a friend who sends you unsolicited messages with inappropriate content—*but it is not rude to protect yourself.*

## Spot the Tricky Teaching

Time to put that detective hat back on and tackle some more tricky teachings. Here are two teachings you may hear in Christian circles:

1. J.O.Y.—Jesus first, Others next, You last.
2. Jesus gave up everything—even gave his own life—because he loved you and wanted to save you. And he asks us never to think of ourselves but to give up everything for others.

Remember, tricky teachings always have a grain of truth! What is the truth in each of these messages?

Now consider how those teachings would affect the person in these scenarios:

- A girl babysits for a single mom who's in need of childcare but constantly gets home far later than promised and often pays her less than they agreed on.
- A girl at a youth group is feeling threatened by a boy in her small group, but she knows he's not a Christian yet and doesn't want to be the reason he's not allowed to come anymore.

DAUGHTERS

How could these messages cause harm to the girl in each of these scenarios? How can these messages go off course?

### MOMS

Have you ever been hurt, or seen someone else hurt, by messages like these? If so, tell the story to your daughter.

Brainstorm together other "Christian-sounding" messages that tell people they're less valuable than someone else. How would you fix these messages so they are healthy and Christlike?

 **Q&A**

### DAUGHTERS

Is there some situation in which you think your mom doesn't have good boundaries? How would you rather see her treated?

### MOMS

Is there some situation in which you think your daughter doesn't have good boundaries? How would you rather see her treated?

### DAUGHTERS

When was the last time you stood up for yourself? Did you find it easy or difficult?

### MOMS

When was the last time you stood up for yourself? Do you find it easier to stand up for your daughter than to stand up for yourself?

**What Would You Do?**

Pick two of the following conviction boundary role-play scenarios and two protection boundary role-play scenarios to do together (or do them all if you'd like!). Start with the prompt, and then continue the conversation.

*Conviction Boundaries*

### Scenario 1

A new girl who is quite socially awkward starts attending youth group. Your friends are laughing at her behind her back, saying cruel things that you know would hurt her if she heard.

▶ PROMPT: Your friend asks, "Oh my gosh, have you seen this?" and shows you a photo on the girl's Instagram feed that your friend finds cringey.

### Scenario 2

Your friend is really struggling in a class you have good marks in. He knows he's going to fail and have to redo the course over the summer. He begs you to "help" him with his final assignment—but he really just wants you to do the work for him.

▶ PROMPT: Your friend says, "Please, I'm desperate—I really can't do this course again, and it's just one assignment. I just need to pass or I'm going to get in huge trouble."

### Scenario 3

A friend invites you to a party where you know the parents are okay with teenage drinking and you really feel uncomfortable about going, but you find out everyone in your youth group is going anyway.

▶ PROMPT: Your friend asks, "Who's giving you a ride to the party? Do you want me to find someone to pick you up?"

*Protection Boundaries* ───────────────────────────────

### Scenario 4

You've been friends with two girls for five years, but in the last few months they've changed. Whenever you're with them, you feel nerdy and excluded, and they've been using you as the butt of their jokes recently. You realize you just don't like hanging out with them anymore, and you want to "break up" as friends.

▶ PROMPT: Your friends say, "Are you coming over this weekend? We're going to binge-watch that new Netflix series!"

### Scenario 5

A girl from your youth group is texting you at all hours of the day. She doesn't have any other friends. You want to make her feel included, but she's taking up so much of your time.

▶ PROMPT: You're trying to finish a homework assignment due the next day when you receive a text saying, "I'm so BORED. What are you doing?"

### Scenario 6

A classmate whom you don't like keeps asking you out and declaring his love. You've tried to let him down gently on a few occasions, but he is seriously not getting the hint.

▶ PROMPT: You receive a text saying, "You looked so hot at school today. I dream about you every night."

### Scenario 7

Your best friend's parents are going through a divorce. She's really upset, and you sometimes worry that she may even be suicidal. She's become withdrawn and will talk only to you.

▶ PROMPT: You receive a text at 1 a.m. saying, "They're fighting again. I can't take this. I hate them."

# 5

## She Deserves the Whole Story about Dating

### Why a One-Size-Fits-All Approach Won't Work

I (Rebecca) grew up in the era of the anti-dating purity movement. I was taught at thirteen that I wasn't supposed to date, and when I was old enough to start dating, I would do so only with the intention of marriage—a model evangelicals called "courtship," popularized by Josh Harris's book *I Kissed Dating Goodbye* (he has since disavowed the book). In this mentality, high school was not for dating because you couldn't get married anyway, so you're just inviting heartbreak. At fourteen, my favorite band was BarlowGirl, and my favorite song was their hit "Average Girl" (I'm pretty sure I could still play it on the guitar if I tried).

"Average Girl" was our anthem. God would bring our husbands along when the time was right. We sang at the top of our lungs that we weren't dating, we were waiting for our prince. We didn't have to write our love stories or make anything happen, because God was writing the love story for us. All we had to do was *wait*.

For many of us, the flawed early 2000s logic of "don't date until you can marry the guy or you'll get your heart broken" fell apart pretty quickly. The house of cards toppled for me when I realized that not dating wasn't sparing me of heartache—it was just stopping guys who were flirting with me from making any real commitment. I still got my heart broken, but the guy got off scot-free because, well, "we weren't dating." By the time I was sixteen, our family had ditched the "I kissed dating goodbye" mentality and accepted a more nuanced position.

For others, the realization didn't come so early. The *I Survived I Kissed Dating Goodbye* documentary studied the results of this anti-dating movement. It included testimonies from unhappy single women who had waited for their prince only to realize in their thirties that passively waiting at home is not an ideal strategy for finding a mate, and from others who had married unhealthy marriage partners because they were never taught what healthy dating relationships looked like.[1] It's a sobering reminder of the consequences of claiming to have biblical truth about a concept that doesn't even appear in Scripture.

Of course, the whole "no dating" culture of the 2000s didn't happen out of nowhere. Generation X and Boomer parents grew up in the decades when adolescent sexual activity and teen pregnancies were skyrocketing.[2] We often think that teen trends are steadily getting worse, but in fact it is more likely that Sheila's peers were drinking, having sex, and doing drugs in the 1980s than it is that Joanna's and Rebecca's friends were in the 2000s. In the 1990s, youth crime, delinquency, and pregnancy rates continued to climb, comprehensive sex education classes were introduced to high schools, and Christian parents were left scrambling, terrified that a more comprehensive understanding of sexuality would continue to increase the rates of teen sexual activity.

Purity culture did not set out to hurt a generation of Christian teens; it set out to save them. And purity culture, it seems, did work to stop kids from dating. Millennials who grew up in the midst of purity culture had fundamentally different dating experiences than their parents or grandparents before them. Their grandmothers were more than twice as likely to have been allowed to date in high school than they were (see figure 5.1).

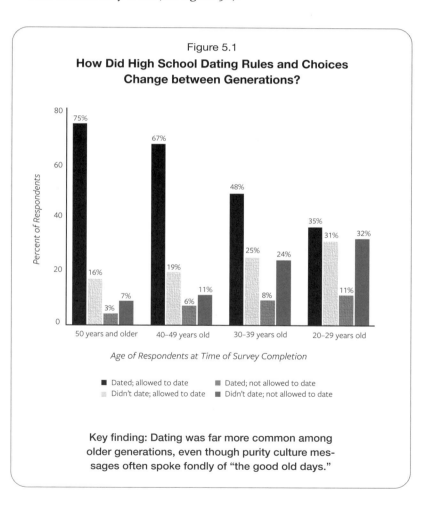

Figure 5.1
**How Did High School Dating Rules and Choices Change between Generations?**

*Age of Respondents at Time of Survey Completion*

■ Dated; allowed to date    ■ Dated; not allowed to date
▨ Didn't date; allowed to date    ■ Didn't date; not allowed to date

**Key finding: Dating was far more common among older generations, even though purity culture messages often spoke fondly of "the good old days."**

For the last few decades, rules around dating and relationships have been the defining feature of teen evangelical culture. So let's do something different. Let's measure what actually works and what doesn't so that you, as a family, can make an informed choice about how to handle teen relationships instead of claiming to know the one "biblical" way forward.

## So . . . What Dating Rules Are Best?

That depends on how we measure "best." For years, the only measure that mattered was whether kids stayed virgins until they were married. Frankly, we think this is a rather heartless measure when it comes to our precious daughters. I (Sheila), as the mom of two daughters who have now been married for a combined ten years, can tell you that their well-being, happiness, and safety are far more important to me now than any virginity status on their wedding day. I want my girls to thrive, and I'm sure that's what you want too. So let's expand our list of desired outcomes: we want daughters who have high self-esteem, who choose good marriage partners if they marry, who are more likely to marry if they want to marry, and yes, who abstain from sex before marriage. Now, what is most likely to get us to those outcomes?

Let's start with high school self-esteem effects. The group of our survey respondents with the highest self-esteem was women who were allowed to date in high school but who had chosen not to. Then there was a small drop with those who were allowed to date and who chose to. But the next two drops? Those were large. Third place was those who weren't allowed to date and didn't, and dead last were women who hadn't been allowed to date but went against their parents' wishes and dated anyway.[3]

But what if we turn from self-esteem and look at girls' chances of marriage? In this case, it's not about whether you were *allowed* to date as much as it is about whether you actually *did* date. Those who were allowed to date and dated were most likely to end up married;

those who dated even if they weren't allowed to were next most likely to marry; and then those least likely to marry were those who never dated. It makes sense—those who have boyfriends in high school show that they are the kinds of people who will attract relationships.

That doesn't mean, though, that dating in high school means you'll marry *well*. Those least likely to marry an abuser are the girls who were allowed to date but didn't, and those most likely to marry an abuser are *also* those most likely to marry *at all*—those who dated and were allowed to date.

What if we look at the traditional evangelical measure of success with dating—that she saves sex until marriage? In this case, purity culture worked. Those who were not allowed to date and didn't date in high school were most likely to save consensual sex until marriage; in contrast, those who did date were the least likely. Take a look at how all of this plays out for all our variables as shown in figure 5.2.

There is no exact formula that will always work for every daughter or always lead to all the best possible outcomes, but we do know that rules overall make things worse. Rather than setting up rules about whether they *can* date, then, let's help our girls make good decisions about the timing of dating, deciding if they even want to date, and whom to date.

This leaves parents who grew up with rigid rules with a formidable task. As one mom explained to us, "I struggle with changing my thought process from how I was taught as a teen to a more balanced view as I raise my own teens. Avoidance is not the key, but often I don't know what to tell them about healthy relationships. I don't want them sleeping around, but I don't want to give them sex-phobia either!"

We understand the struggle. There are some serious downsides to teenage dating that our daughters need to know. We certainly don't want to do a pendulum swing in the other direction where we're sending our eleven-year-olds out to collect boyfriends. So let's see what *else* the data shows.

## The Effects of Various Dating Rules and Dating Choices in High School

When we looked at dating in high school, our findings told a complicated story. We looked at those who were allowed to date and those who were not allowed to date based on whether or not they actually dated. Then we ranked those four groups (allowed to date and dated, allowed to date but didn't date, not allowed to date but dated, not allowed to date and didn't date). We looked at how each group fared with high school self-esteem, current self-esteem, being in a marriage that is not abusive, ever getting married, and saving sex for marriage. Each group is ranked from best to worst below (with ties noted).

Figure 5.2

**High School Self-Esteem**

Best: Allowed ☑ Dated ☒
Second: Allowed ☑ Dated ☑
Third: Allowed ☒ Dated ☒
Worst: Allowed ☒ Dated ☑

**Current Self-Esteem**

Best(tie): Allowed ☑ Dated ☒
Best(tie): Allowed ☑ Dated ☑
Worst(tie): Allowed ☒ Dated ☒
Worst(tie): Allowed ☒ Dated ☑

**Marriage Is Not Abusive**

Best: Allowed ☑ Dated ☒
Second(tie): Allowed ☒ Dated ☑
Second(tie): Allowed ☒ Dated ☒
Worst: Allowed ☑ Dated ☑

**Ever Marrying**

Best: Allowed ☑ Dated ☑
Second: Allowed ☒ Dated ☑
Third: Allowed ☒ Dated ☒
Worst: Allowed ☑ Dated ☒

**Saving Sex for Marriage**

Best: Allowed ☒ Dated ☒
Second: Allowed ☑ Dated ☒
Third: Allowed ☑ Dated ☑
Worst: Allowed ☒ Dated ☑

Key finding: There is no one-size-fits-all approach when it comes to teens dating.

- Not allowed to date: Most likely to save sex for marriage, but less likely to get married; more likely to have low self-esteem, and still just as likely to marry an abuser. Plus, if she does remain single, the low self-esteem of adolescence is more likely to continue to adulthood.
- Allowed to date and choosing to date: More likely to marry, but also more likely to marry an abuser.
- Allowed to date but choosing not to date: Highest self-esteem in both adolescence and adulthood, least likely to marry an abuser, most likely not to have multiple sexual partners, but also less odds of getting married overall.

### Age Still Matters When It Comes to Dating

We met Ellie in one of our focus groups. When Ellie was twelve, she fell in pure, innocent puppy love with the boy next door. Telling us about him, she laughed and said, "He was the first guy I French-kissed. After it happened, I was so freaked out I ran straight inside and told my mom, 'I just kissed him like a grown-up—I don't know what happened, but it felt really good!'" Ellie laughed. "That's when the no kissing until fifteen rule started in our house."

I think most of us moms would have a mini–heart attack if our twelve-year-old came running to us, pigtails flying in the wind, declaring their excitement at having "kissed him like a grown-up." But what about at fifteen? Eighteen? Twenty-five and engaged? Rather than paving the way for parents to have nuanced conversations with their kids about wisdom and readiness, so many of the resources we grew up with offered legalistic rules or pat answers, like *don't make out at all, never be alone together,* or *don't do anything with him you wouldn't do with your grandpa.*

So let's talk about what purity culture had right: First, dating at a very young age introduces our kids to big issues earlier than they may be ready for them. It doesn't take a rocket scientist to put the logic together that dating makes it more likely you'll have sex because you'll have more opportunities! Additionally, no matter where one might fall on the sexual boundaries question, it seems pretty uncontroversial to feel that making out at thirteen is less wise than making out as an engaged twentysomething.

But this all comes down to a larger point: dating when very young can make adolescence even more complicated for your already confused child. All of us find puberty and the teenage years difficult—we're figuring out who we are; we're learning how to cope with adult realities; we're grappling with big moral and social issues that can cause a lot of introspection and inner turmoil. It's a lot for anyone to handle, but throw a significant other into the mix and suddenly your child isn't just carrying their own struggles and worries; they're also having to deal with the complexities of a romantic relationship with another person in the same confusing boat.

I (Joanna) dated in high school and found myself overwhelmed by the challenges my boyfriends faced, even after we broke up. One of my former boyfriends suffered a severe mental health breakdown after I chose to end the relationship. Rebecca's husband, Connor, had an ex-girlfriend attempt suicide after he broke up with her. Both Connor and I have worked through the challenges of the teen dramas we lived, but it was still far more than any sixteen- or seventeen-year-old should have had to handle.

So let's approach it this way: if your daughter wants to get married one day, she's going to have to learn how to date. How can you equip her with the information she needs to avoid unnecessary stress when she's too young but also develop the social skills and experiences needed to join the dating world when she's ready, whether that's at fifteen or twenty-two? Let's start at first principles.

## She Should Know: God Is Not a Husband Vending Machine

*Brio* magazine had a recurring segment called "God said . . . I said" in which readers "listened in" on an intimate conversation between a girl and God. Aside from the obvious theological implications of putting literal words in God's mouth, much of the advice given to girls from the "God" character was problematic.

> "God": I would *love* to help you [find your future husband], but I need you to do your part. . . . I need you to give Me total control of your love life . . . let Me write your love story. Trust Me to bring the right man into your life. I want to relieve you of all that pressure.
>
> Girl: But I still have to be on the lookout, right?
>
> "God": No. You don't have to do anything except be totally in love with Me.
>
> Girl: You mean . . . I don't even have to *look* for him?
>
> "God": No. That's My job. *Your* job is to trust Me. . . .
>
> Girl: This sounds too good to be true. . . . I don't even have to *look* for him?
>
> "God": All you have to do . . . is be totally in love with Me.[4]

It sounds romantic, doesn't it? Like a fairy-tale princess, locked up in a tower, so swept up in love for God that she can rest easy knowing that now it's all on God's docket—and all she needs to do is pray more and *trust*.

This "princess in the tower" model of romance and relationships is not just a relic of bygone days of purity culture. Christian channels such as Girl Defined, popular among conservative Christian crowds, are currently promoting this. A caption from a recent Instagram post by the sister duo reads:

Maybe you've done all the things. You've gotten to know him. You even have a friendship with him. You know for a fact that he's an amazing godly guy. He seems awesome in every way . . . minus the fact that he hasn't asked you out. Ahhh that's the hardest place to be. . . . My advice, be patient, and trust God. Don't manipulate the situation. . . . Ask God for the strength to trust this area of your life to Him. Pray Proverbs 3:5–6 and meditate on it. . . . Open up your hands and surrender your crush. Trust that God wants what's better for you than you even want for yourself. Try focusing on serving God.[5]

This all sounds very holy. But is it even biblical? There's no biblical warning against women being forward in pursuing a relationship. Ruth was forward with Boaz and was called a righteous woman. And yet, we keep telling our young girls that if they want to get married, the best thing they can do is finish another devotional.

The "princess in the tower" model of dating is a lie. Regardless of how romantic it seems, if your daughter wants to get married someday, a strategy involving getting someone's phone number is likely to be more effective. When we talk about "bad dating outcomes," we often mean breakups, unplanned pregnancies, or dysfunctional marriages. But what if an overlooked bad outcome is unwanted singleness?

Now, there are many women who choose singleness. That's not who we're talking about here—if your daughter chooses singleness, more power to her (and the apostle Paul especially commends her in 1 Cor. 7:34). However, the fruit of "princess in the tower" dating theology was that many women who desperately wanted to find a husband and longed to start a family were left *less* likely to achieve these things because of a false belief about God. Girls who did not date in high school, regardless of if they were allowed to or not, were less likely to get married than those who did date. How many single women today are single not by choice but because they were sold a lie about what will bring a mate? How many girls were passed over by the boys in their youth groups, college Christian groups, or churches because when a guy was looking for a partner, there were other girls flirting, chatting him up, and giving him signals they were interested? Feeling relaxed and easy around the opposite sex is a learned skill. Girls who are open to dating—even if they don't choose to date—are often hanging out with boys as friends, getting used to talking to guys, and honing their flirting skills. Girls who believed they should never date but should wait often avoided social situations with guys because it would seem forward or demonstrate a lack of faith, and so they never learned the skills they needed to start dating.

Yes, some women might marry a man God literally drops on their doorstep. But in a highly competitive dating scene, where Christian women outnumber Christian men in many if not most spaces, staying home to prayer journal and read devotionals is simply not an effective strategy for finding a mate—and our stats show that. You can't just focus hard enough on God that he will owe you a prince delivered to your doorstep. God is not a husband vending machine.

"You don't need to worry about this right now—trust God with your love life" may be a great message for a thirteen-year-old whose primary concern should be figuring out who she is. But for older teens or even young adults who are at a stage when it may be appropriate to start searching for a lifelong partner? It may be time to let your little girl grow up. If marriage and motherhood are large priorities for your daughter, then talking openly about the possible repercussions of taking herself out of the dating scene for several years in her twenties is worth considering. Is spending several years on the mission field, teaching English in Asia, backpacking across Europe, or working on a cruise ship productive to her goals? Is studying abroad wise? It may very well be for her. But count the potential cost, and don't teach her that if she does everything right, God *will* bring her a husband. That can feel soothing when you're young, but it's a hard reality to wake up decades later and realize you built your life, your decisions, your whole youth on a lie.

## She Should Know: Breaking Up Isn't a Sin

I (Joanna) had to be assigned a high school breakup as Spanish class homework. I knew I was going to have to break this boy's heart, and I couldn't bear to do it. My teacher reminded me, kindly, that if I didn't even like him, it was time to no longer be dating him. Her reminder to advocate for myself came at just the right time. Dating was taken so seriously in our evangelical subculture that breaking up felt like a sin—dating was a promise, so breaking up was an admission I had lied. I had taken a piece of his heart I could never give back. Without help from that teacher, I truly don't know how much longer I would have stayed in a relationship I wasn't happy with.

Teenagers have all sorts of reasons for dating that are bound to end in heartache. I was a lonely teenager—and I didn't like that. I chose to date starting in tenth grade with the primary motivation of fixing my loneliness. It was comforting to feel special and to know someone saw me. Some teens choose to date as a social stepping-stone to higher status, and some simply because they like the rush of romance. However, choosing to date for any reason other than genuine interest and compatibility will lead to a relationship with a best-before date.

But what if you're told that if you date someone and don't marry them, you've "used" them and sinned against them? That's what many of us were taught—if you shouldn't date unless you think you can marry the person, then breaking up feels almost like a divorce, even if you're ending the relationship because you never should have dated them in the first place.

If one of the big dating outcomes we want for our girls is that they marry someone of good character and who is a good match for them, then we need to ditch the idea that you can date someone only if you can picture yourself accepting a ring. After all, compatibility and character often aren't revealed until after you've been dating for a while—and if bad character is revealed, then you *really* don't want your daughter to marry him! When we make dating more of a commitment than it is, we take away girls' freedom to walk away when they have doubts. It's harder to break off an engagement than a two-week relationship, but when we talk about dating as if it's already an engagement, it lends that difficulty earlier.

## She Should Know: The First Date Isn't a Proposal

If you can date only someone you think you can marry, not only does this make breakups harder, but it also raises the stakes on accepting dates, as these single women told us:

- "I was told not to settle for anything less than 'the best.' I worked at a camp in my early twenties with a lot of great guys who I would never consider dating because they weren't as spiritual as another guy there. I was friends with all of them, though, but always turned them down. They are now all amazing husbands and fathers. Looking back, I'd tell my younger self to give them a chance, go out for coffee, etc. It seems like the church pushed you to know the guy was marriage material before going on a date."
- "I was told to not even think about boys until I was ready to get married. This created a twisted mindset that I can't even consider wanting to date a man unless I want to marry him. I am now thirty-four and have never been on a date."

We hate to think that this advice could end up preventing our girls from marrying if they want to, but that's what's happened to far too many women. Picture this: Mark and Stacy, two single people in their midtwenties, are set up for a coffee date by a mutual friend. The date is going well, they're clicking and really enjoying themselves, but then Mark mentions he grew up playing hockey.

Stacy's face goes cold, and she asks, "Would you want your kids to be in hockey someday?" He laughs and says, "Of course! I had an awesome time with my high school team, and I still play in a rec league on weekends!" After that the conversation feels more stiff and forced, and after about twenty more minutes, she thanks him for a lovely time and says she's really got to run.

Later, Stacy explains to a friend, "It's a shame. Mark seemed really great, but I could never marry someone who wanted to have our kids in hockey because I don't want my kids in contact sports. The risk of concussion is too real."

The problem with the "date because you want to get married to each other" philosophy is that it doesn't account for the fact that relationships cause us to grow and change, so we might reject people prematurely. Maybe Mark would have empathized with Stacy's concerns about concussions and decided there were lots of other activities his kids could do that would have the same benefits. Maybe Stacy would have changed her mind and been completely comfortable having her kids play in less competitive, less injury-prone leagues. Maybe they would have ended up having kids who hated hockey and it never would have become a problem at all.

What if Stacy missed out on a great guy because she was so focused on if she could *marry* him today, she didn't actually give herself a chance to get to know him? There is a big difference between saying "the purpose of dating is to get married" and saying "the purpose of dating is to *discover* whom you want to marry." The first adds a ton of pressure; the second is actually more akin to what previous generations did. The generation of women dating in the 1940s through 1960s didn't even subscribe to this courtship model of relationships—rather, they would date a bunch of people and then, when they wanted to become more exclusive, they'd "go steady." They might go to the drive-in with Bobby on Monday night, grab milkshakes with Fred on Thursday, and dance with four different guys at the sock hop on Saturday, and that was perfectly normal. Dating was allowed to be fun while they figured out what they wanted.

Getting to date before you actually enter a relationship adds an extra step to the mix: it lets you ask, "Do I like this person?" before you ask "Are they a good marriage candidate?" Because frankly, there are a lot of people who would make excellent spouses—for someone else. The important question is not only if they are marriage material but rather if they are marriage material for *you*. And you typically can't answer that on the first date. When dating becomes a discovery process rather than a destination on-ramp, it removes the pressure and allows you to make an informed decision.

### She Should Know: Jesus Is Not a Jealous Boyfriend

Because teenagers are naturally intense, it is very easy for them to get swept up in high school love. To try to prevent this, many Christian resources have given messages that, whether intentionally or not, ended up instilling a good dose of spiritual guilt. Girls are told repeatedly that obsessing over a crush means they're not putting God front and center. It's ironic since, as we remember from the word clouds in chapter 2, girls are simultaneously being told that the most important thing they can do is get ready for their future husband.

Now remember: red herrings work on the bloodhound because the scent smells good—it distracts because it smells like something the dog should be following. Very few tricky teachings are going to be 100% false. We want our daughters to remain strong in their convictions, we want our daughters not to embarrass themselves by being so obsessed with love that they lose reason, and we want our daughters to pursue God above all else.

But believing that a girl must acutely feel that she loves God more than her boyfriend takes something good—keeping God at the center—and defines it in a way that causes guilt over normal and God-designed human emotions. Reading through 2 Chronicles simply is not as butterfly-inducing as a "good morning" text from the cute guy from homeroom. And you know what? The Bible is all right with her attention being split. Paul lays it out clearly: If you're single, you can be wholly devoted to God, so unless you really want to get married, stay single. If, however, you want to get married, the expectation is that you will have less time and energy to devote to God—*and that is still a good thing* (1 Cor. 7:32–35). Paul doesn't say that the unmarried love God more; it's just that if you're part of a couple, you will have less time and energy to spend on specifically kingdom-related stuff.

Focus on the Family's *Brio* magazine, though, ends an otherwise balanced article on finding "the one" with this instruction from editor Susie Shellenberger: "Girls, here's my prerequisite for marriage . . . It's not simply 'Are we in love?'. . . My prerequisite is, 'Can this man and I together do more and be more for God than we can separately?' If not, I shouldn't even consider marrying him."[6] The idea that you must find a partner with whom you can do *more* for God than you could alone asks more of our daughters' teenage relationships than Paul expects of full-fledged adults in the congregation at Corinth.

Dannah Gresh tells her own story of her courtship with her now-husband, Bob, in *And the Bride Wore White*. She broke up with him for nine months at one point because she felt that he was interfering with her spiritual life. She explains, "Instead of looking up the Bible verses when the pastor encouraged us to do so in church, I had opted to keep holding Bob's big, warm hand. And my roommate . . . had given me a kind confrontation about how I was allowing my friendship with Bob to squeeze out my friendship with her and just about everyone else. Our last few dates had included some passionate kissing. My journal had become full of him and not God."

So she had held his hand instead of looking up Bible verses; she had been praying and journaling about her relationship; she'd kissed him too much; and she hadn't spent as much time with her roommate. It could very well be that God wanted Dannah to put her relationship on the altar and take a step back. *But what she is describing is very normal and healthy behavior that pretty much everyone who dates will experience.* When you date, your prayer life may shift. You won't have as much time with friends as you did before. Frankly, we can't figure out how someone is supposed to spend just as much time with friends and with God and with volunteer work once they add dating to the mix.

Perhaps that's why books such as Elisabeth Elliot's *Passion and Purity* present a model of romance that seems incredibly stressful. She repeatedly advises her young readers to be willing to put love "on the altar" for the sake of Christ so that Jesus may always be preeminent.[7] We have no problem with putting God first, or with choosing singleness, but we want to caution against an unbalanced emphasis. Elliot explains about her own relationship with Jim: "We talked again about marriage, puzzling over the thought that for us it might amount to an admission that Christ was not sufficient."[8] The desire to marry is portrayed as an admission of spiritual weakness rather than as a normal, healthy human emotion. After all, God is the one who created marriage in the first place, so surely couples can be passionately in love and this need not displace their love for God.

In preparation for writing this book, I (Sheila) read through many of the books aimed at teen girls. And the overarching feeling that I had in reading them all was that if I had to follow what these authors were touting as healthy, I would end up a paranoid mess. What they were peddling was fear, not peace.

In *Passion and Purity*, Elliot describes spending years obsessing over whether she was devoted enough to God, because if she loved Jim and wanted to marry him, that was proof that she was failing to put Jesus first. Her whole life was about wondering, "Do I love God enough?" Gresh's courtship with her husband, as Gresh describes it, shows something similar, with the author recounting many instances of concern that her overwhelming happiness with this great guy was a sign that there was something wrong with her spiritual life. Christian theology should show us a Jesus who speaks over us with love as a joyful parent does, not a Jesus who, like an abusive and controlling boyfriend, resents us for having things that bring us joy.

Yes, talk to your daughter about how to keep her head when emotions are flying and about how to ascertain if being with someone is making her more or less Christlike. But don't let her define enjoying a healthy relationship as failing Jesus. No one would tell a new mom of twins who used to get up in the morning to do devotions and now chooses to sleep that she's somehow spiritually failing—we accept that she's just in a stage of life when she will have less time and energy to devote to spiritual discipline. We need to be able to have that conversation around dating and love as well.

When Adam was in the garden, and God dwelt there with him, God still said, "It is not good for man to be alone." Adam had closer contact with God than we experience today, and God *still* gave him another person to meet that particular need: community. It's not wrong for us to long for intimate relationships, because God never intended to fully fill our need for other people.

But above the spiritual guilt this teaching can create, we have another critical concern: What if this emphasis on hyperspirituality inadvertently pushes girls to choose unfit romantic partners? Would you want your daughter to date a boy who treated her as second place to his prayer routine, his devotions, his volunteering with the church? Or would you want your daughter to date a boy who truly loves God but is also wholly devoted to her? Perhaps he does shorter devotions than before he dated her because now he spends lunch period with your daughter instead of studying on his own. Perhaps he stops volunteering as much with the praise band so that he can spend time with his girlfriend instead of spending all Sunday putting up and tearing down the stage setup. But they pray together, they encourage each other in their walks with Christ, and she's not lonely and left wondering when or if he's going to call her back. Church leadership may be far less impressed with this young man—but isn't he a better, more emotionally healthy option for your daughter?

Ada Cecilia Pfautz was married to A. W. Tozer, who was arguably one of the most influential Christian theologians of the last one hundred years. His desire was to pursue God above all else, and he lived this out every day by choosing simple living over hedonistic pleasure. He never purchased a vehicle; he gave away most of his money; and he was known to spend countless hours cloistered in his silent office, where he would meditate on Scriptures, pray, and write. He was truly, unequivocally, and wholly in love with his Creator. In fact, much of what we consider "good Christian" spiritual practices can be tied back to Tozer's own individual faith walk, which he explained in his book *The Practice of the Presence of God*.

In an article for FathomMag, though, Sarah Bessey tells us the rest of the story:

> After Tozer died, Ada remarried a man named Leonard Odam. Later, when she was asked about the difference between her marriage to The Great Man of God and her current husband, she candidly said, "I have never been happier in my life. Aiden (Tozer) loved Jesus Christ, but Leonard Odam loves me."[9]

*Aiden loved Jesus. Leonard loves me.* Ouch.

As Bessey shows, Tozer's personal dedication to Christ meant that his wife and children were effectively emotionally and physically abandoned. Tozer chose to give away so much money that the family lived in poverty, and it was Ada, not Tozer, who carried the burden and the anxiety of that decision. He spent so much time secluded away from his family that his children described their mother as a single parent. His choice not to purchase a car didn't affect him very much because he could conveniently use trains to get to his various work locations, but his wife was left walking in the snow with their seven children during harsh winters.[10] Tozer

115

loved God—but his intense devotion to the spiritual realm made him, frankly, a bad father and husband in the material realm.

It's appropriate to tell an eleven-year-old who's spending hours every day writing in pretty cursive letters how her name would look if she was married to twelve-year-old Brett to maybe redirect her efforts. But the seventeen-year-old who's dating a truly great guy, who's racked with anxiety and guilt because she thinks about her boyfriend more often than she meditates on the Psalms, and who feels that being this happy means she's failing God—maybe she just needs to be told to calm down a bit. Even God doesn't expect that much of her.

### She Should Know: If a Relationship Feels Hard, She May Need to Reevaluate

I (Rebecca) have always found listening to the homily during wedding ceremonies very telling—perhaps a bit more telling than the pastor anticipated. One wedding stands out as having the most uncomfortable wedding sermon ever. The groom and the bride stared lovingly into each other's eyes while the pastor spoke these words:

> You're going to wake up one day and the beautiful young woman in front of you is going to be an angry, middle-aged cobra of a woman and you're gonna wonder, "Where is that beautiful woman I married?" You're gonna wonder, "Is this really worth it?" And you [he turns to the bride] are gonna roll over in bed one day and you're not gonna see this man that you so love and admire today—you're going to see the jerk who keeps leaving underwear on the bathroom floor. One day you're gonna wake up and the romance will be gone, and you'll want to just knock each other out with a baseball bat. But you know what? Marriage is hard. But it's worth it.

I couldn't help but wonder—has anyone checked to see if this man's wife is okay?

He drove the message home: feelings of love will fade and be replaced by bitterness, disappointment, and frustration. But their job as a couple was to recognize that just as we disappoint and frustrate Christ and he never leaves us, marriage is a way to be an example of selfless servitude even when we want to run screaming the other way.

That's a depressing view both of how Christ sees us and of marriage. No one is contesting that marriage can be difficult. But a marriage can be difficult for different reasons:

1. Because life, in general, is just hard.
2. Because marriage is often paired with kids, in-laws, and other related things that simply add more complexity to life.
3. Because there is something wrong with the relationship.

The mantra "marriage is hard but worth it" can be a calming and grounding message for couples in options (1) or (2). You're dating a really, really great guy whom you love and who is so, *so* good to you—but he has trauma or abuse in his background that he wants to work through more before you can get married. Or you've had to work through communication issues because your life circumstances have you dating long-distance. These are examples of how relationships can be hard but worth it. A couple has a child with severe medical complications that threaten to tear apart the marriage because of the stress—yes, the marriage is really hard right now, but if they stick it through to the other side, that relationship can be a soothing balm and comfort.

But are these issues marriage issues or just life issues? What happens when our daughters hear teachings like *marriage* is hard when what we really mean is *life* is hard, even if you're married? Then our kids grow up and choose mates expecting the relationship to feel like a bit of a slog, expecting to be disappointed, expecting to have to muscle through when it should feel natural.

With that expectation, what kind of mate is a girl likely to pick? Even if young women are able to weed out the abusive, lazy, or immature men, how many times have they married men who are excellent people but not excellent matches for them? One commenter recalled seeing this almost play out for the worse in a friend's life:

> I once listened to a friend in a Bible study go on and on about how hard her dating relationship was, but she knew marriage would be hard and she shouldn't expect it to be easy and it was better that they figure that out now and be prepared for it to be hard. . . . And finally, the much older, wiser, happily married leader of our group said, "Yes, marriage can be hard, but you should also find someone you enjoy being with."
>
> And it was like it hadn't occurred to my friend that that was allowed. That even if the guy was nice and honorable, she could still break up with him just because she didn't think being married to him would be enjoyable. And that makes sense if you've been told over and over that marriage will just stink no matter how much you love each other at the beginning.
>
> They broke up the same year. My friend is now happily married to a man she has FUN with, and it's a delight to see her so happy.

Marriages may have rough patches, yes, even healthy and happy ones do. But overall, barring any unforeseen life events, your relationship should make your life *easier*, not *harder*. And the person you choose to spend your life with should be someone whose company you genuinely *enjoy*.

All the tricky teachings in this chapter have given our daughters an incomplete picture. They give our daughters a glimpse into truth, but they obscure the full picture. Yes, God is in charge of his plan for your life—but no, that doesn't mean you don't have to actually get out there and look for a boyfriend if you want one. Yes, the ultimate purpose of dating is marriage—but that doesn't mean you have to know if you can say "I do" before the first date. Yes, God should be preeminent in your life—but that doesn't mean you're not allowed to fall in love. And yes, marriage can be difficult—but that doesn't mean you should choose one that's *guaranteed* to be difficult.

It's time we stop using pat answers and shame tactics with our daughters. Here are a few quick and easy ways to start to help your daughter see past the tricky teachings and make real, informed decisions for herself about dating.

## MOTHER-DAUGHTER
### SECTION

Dating can be exciting and exhilarating and make you feel really grown-up and loved. It can also be complicated, stressful, and heartbreaking. It's up to your family what rules, if any, you have for dating. We're not going to tell you what you should or shouldn't do. But no matter what you decide to do, talking to your mom about it is so important!

### What Would You Do?

Instead of telling you "what you should know" or working through specific Q&As, we want you to work through these five common dating scenarios together so you can decide together what the best choices would be.

## Scenario 1

Tyler is really cute, really funny, and really popular. He makes your heart flutter when you're near him. He asks if you want to hang out this weekend. What would you, or should you, say in each of the following scenarios:

- You're eleven.
- You're fourteen, but he's eighteen.
- You're both sixteen.
- He goes to your youth group, but he also goes to a lot of parties where you know there are alcohol and drugs.
- He's really nice to you now, but two weeks ago he acted like you didn't exist.
- He's the kind of person who makes everyone feel safe, and he has been your friend for some time now.
- He has dated seven different girls in the last three months.
- He drives recklessly.

## Scenario 2

You've been best friends with Declan since you met him at a sophomore debate competition in the state capital last year. You have inside jokes, you like all the same music, and you can talk about important stuff. Plus, flirting is really fun—and it's always great to hear how pretty he thinks you are. But he's very hot and cold. Some days he'll text you nonstop, and other times you won't hear from him for almost a week. You've developed serious feelings for him, but even though he tells you you're amazing and would make a great girlfriend, he's never actually asked you out. You don't want to text him too often and scare him off. But this has been going on for months now and you have no idea how he feels about you.

- What should you do?
- How long would you be willing to wait for someone to make up his mind? Do you think someone having to make up his mind about you is a red flag?
- If your best friend were in this scenario, what would you tell them?

## Scenario 3

A classmate of yours has a super big crush on you and you know it. You're not interested in him, but he's fun to hang out with, and the attention is really, really nice. He also has his own car, he's a really responsible driver, and he is always available for a ride when you ask—which is super convenient for Mom and Dad too. However, you have no intention of ever dating him.

- What should you do?
- How can you make sure that you're not leading someone on? What are some good boundaries to have with friends who may be interested in you? How do you make expectations clear and not build up false hope?

## Scenario 4

You're seventeen years old, and you're pretty sure no one has ever had a crush on you, let alone anyone you've also liked. You desperately want a relationship, but you have a very hard time getting guys' attention or talking to them.

- If this were your friend, what would you say to her?
- If you're someone who does have people interested in you, how can you be considerate to friends in different situations who may be lonely?
- Moms, what do you want your daughter to know if this is her?

## Scenario 5

You've been dating Paul for six months now, but you realize it's just not working. You don't have things to talk about, you don't have much in common, and the initial attraction has fizzled out. However, your mom really loves him, his mom is already planning the wedding, and he's part of your core friend group. He's not in a great place emotionally, and his mom tells you how grateful she is that you're in his life. But you're not happy in this relationship.

- Role-play what breaking up might look like.
- What if he tells you he'll kill himself if you break up with you? What should you do?

# 6

## She Deserves to Be Protected

### *Identifying Red Flags for Toxic People*

*The Paper Bag Princess* by Robert Munsch is a Canadian anti–fairy tale. In this classic picture book, Princess Elizabeth uses wit and trickery to rescue her betrothed, Prince Ronald, from a dragon that burned down her castle, leaving her with nothing to wear but a paper bag. Upon his rescue, Ronald—the epitome of princely decorum—scoffs at the sight of Elizabeth and demands she change into something more appropriate. Elizabeth rightfully points out that although he looks very princely, he is, in fact, a bum. The book ends as she dances away into the sunset with the closing line "and they didn't get married after all."

How tragic would the story of the Paper Bag Princess have been if, after Ronald was a complete snot-head upon his rescue, Elizabeth looked herself up and down and said, "Yeah, you're right. I do look a mess. I'm sorry I offended you by rescuing you while wearing a paper bag. I should have cleaned myself up first."

And yet, how many girls stick around even after someone reveals that they are, in fact, a bum?

## Does Your Daughter Have Discernment When It Comes to Tricky People?

As your daughter grows into adolescence, part of her development process is learning with whom to align herself. And frankly, she's likely to be quite awkward at it at first. For a parent who is used to having almost sole influence on your kids' lives, it can be terrifying to see your daughter idolizing that girl in class who you know is bad news, or crushing on the last boy you would want her to be interested in.

Part of parenting is using our influence over our kids to teach them who is and who is not a safe person to attach themselves to. Part of that is teaching our daughters how to respect and maintain boundaries, as we discussed in chapter 4. But another, perhaps even less talked about skill that our daughters need to learn is *how to identify tricky people*.

It may feel easiest to just protect your daughter from all this—have rules about whom she can and cannot hang out with, find an amazing church and stick her in all its activities, and then rest assured that no one "bad" will get through the cracks. Unfortunately, that doesn't work. How many of us have stories of how the golden child in youth group was actually the worst behind closed doors? Additionally, many youth groups have serious problems with misconduct even among the leadership. In fact, 15.6% of our survey respondents reported that while they were in youth group, a leader in their church engaged in inappropriate sexual contact with someone in the congregation. Half knew about it in high school and half found out later.[1] Being in a church where there are inappropriate sexual relationships makes it more likely that a girl will have below-average self-esteem in high school, even if she doesn't learn about the actual misconduct until after high school is over. When the water we swim in is toxic, it has effects, even if we don't know all the sordid details.

When teens are exposed to inappropriate sexual relationships in church, they are:

- 26% more likely to end up in an abusive marriage[2]
- 50% more likely to have below-average self-esteem in high school[3]
- 17% more likely to have below-average self-esteem now[4]
- 24% more likely to experience sexual dysfunction[5]

Simply finding your daughter a youth group and washing your hands of the matter is not nearly enough to keep her safe from

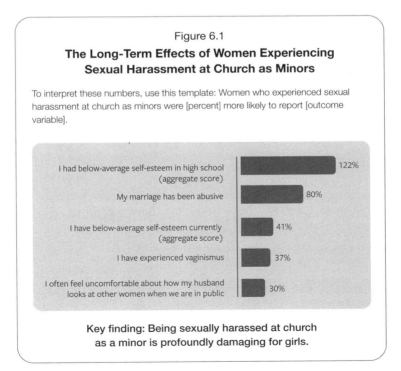

Figure 6.1

**The Long-Term Effects of Women Experiencing Sexual Harassment at Church as Minors**

To interpret these numbers, use this template: Women who experienced sexual harassment at church as minors were [percent] more likely to report [outcome variable].

| | |
|---|---|
| I had below-average self-esteem in high school (aggregate score) | 122% |
| My marriage has been abusive | 80% |
| I have below-average self-esteem currently (aggregate score) | 41% |
| I have experienced vaginismus | 37% |
| I often feel uncomfortable about how my husband looks at other women when we are in public | 30% |

**Key finding: Being sexually harassed at church as a minor is profoundly damaging for girls.**

toxic, tricky people. Youth groups that look great on the outside can still have serious issues she may need to navigate.

Does your daughter have the skills she needs to identify who is safe and who is not? Will she be able to identify when her interpersonal conflicts cross over from normal squabbles to bullying and boundary crossing? If your daughter wants to get married someday, is she learning the skills she will need to identify who will make a good and loving husband—and who will not? Let's talk about the truths your daughter needs to know to foster her intuition and discernment about safe communities and safe people.

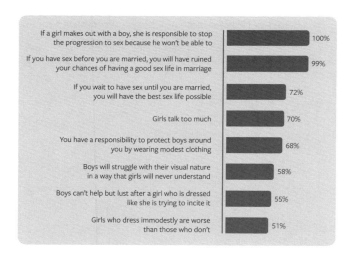

Figure 6.2

**Women Who Experienced Sexual Harassment at Church as Minors Were Primed for Toxic Teachings**

To interpret these numbers, use this template: Women who experienced sexual harassment at church as minors were [percent] more likely to believe [teaching].

| Teaching | Percent |
|---|---|
| If a girl makes out with a boy, she is responsible to stop the progression to sex because he won't be able to | 100% |
| If you have sex before you are married, you will have ruined your chances of having a good sex life in marriage | 99% |
| If you wait to have sex until you are married, you will have the best sex life possible | 72% |
| Girls talk too much | 70% |
| You have a responsibility to protect boys around you by wearing modest clothing | 68% |
| Boys will struggle with their visual nature in a way that girls will never understand | 58% |
| Boys can't help but lust after a girl who is dressed like she is trying to incite it | 55% |
| Girls who dress immodestly are worse than those who don't | 51% |

Key finding: Sexual harassment makes it more likely that girls are in an environment where they believe toxic and dangerous messages.

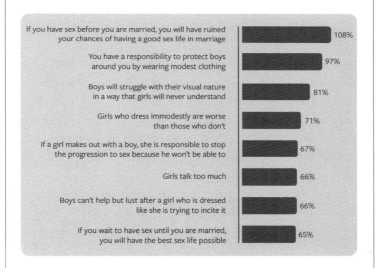

Figure 6.3

**When Teenagers Are Aware of an Inappropriate Relationship between Church Leaders, They Are Primed for Toxic Teachings**

To interpret these numbers, use this template: When teenagers are exposed to inappropriate relationships between church leaders, they are [percent] more likely to report believing [teaching].

| Teaching | Percent |
| --- | --- |
| If you have sex before you are married, you will have ruined your chances of having a good sex life in marriage | 108% |
| You have a responsibility to protect boys around you by wearing modest clothing | 97% |
| Boys will struggle with their visual nature in a way that girls will never understand | 81% |
| Girls who dress immodestly are worse than those who don't | 71% |
| If a girl makes out with a boy, she is responsible to stop the progression to sex because he won't be able to | 67% |
| Girls talk too much | 66% |
| Boys can't help but lust after a girl who is dressed like she is trying to incite it | 66% |
| If you wait to have sex until you are married, you will have the best sex life possible | 65% |

Key finding: Being exposed to an inappropriate relationship between church leaders primes teenagers to believe toxic teachings.

### She Should Know: Her Ultimate Submission Is to God Alone

Abusive family members, toxic friends, and dangerous organizations all have one thing that unites them: they attempt to control other people. That's the opposite of how Jesus told us to live:

- "Jesus called them together and said, 'You know that the rulers of the Gentiles lord it over them, and their high officials exercise authority over them. Not so with you. Instead, whoever wants to become great among you must be your servant'" (Matt. 20:25–26).

- "Submit to one another out of reverence for Christ" (Eph. 5:21).
- Whole passages of Scripture are focused on removing class and power differentials from the congregation in the church so that everyone can worship on equal footing (Gal. 3:28; 1 Tim. 2:9–10; the whole book of Philemon).

In God's family, there's no first and second place. We may have different roles or giftings (1 Cor. 9; 12), but the body requires each member. In following Christ, we do not seek power over others; rather, we aim to tear down hierarchy as a way to revere the *imago Dei* in ourselves and in others. Yes, we can and should respect authority, but respect is *earned*. And respect doesn't mean blind obedience or an immunity from criticism.

Some of you reading this may believe in a power hierarchy in marriage in which the husband is in the decision-making role and has authority over the wife. You may be teaching this to your daughter. But here's something you may not realize: 78.9% of couples, including the majority of couples that claim to believe this, *do not actually act it out.*[6] Instead, they make decisions together. And if the husband does make the final decision, even if he consults with his wife first, they're 7.4 times more likely to wind up divorced.[7]

Parents who believe in a power hierarchy, even if they do not practice it and actually have a healthy marriage, can unwittingly groom their daughters to fall prey to abusers because they've given the abusers an out: just claim Christian male headship.

Anti-abuse advocate Sarah McDugal told us how this became a reality in her marriage. Sarah's parents are the epitome of a healthy relationship—they celebrate each other's strengths and help carry each other's weaknesses. Sarah's mom is a bubbly, effervescent people person. Her dad is the quiet, steady type who takes a while to come out of his shell.

Growing up, Sarah didn't watch her family struggle with uneven power dynamics. Her mother and father both could voice their opinions and preferences in full confidence that they would be honored and respected by the other. However, when it came to personality, "My mom was 'shinier' than my dad," Sarah explained. "But my dad was perfectly happy to see her do the things that made her happy, even if it meant she outshone him."

However, even though Sarah's parents modeled a healthy relationship, Sarah was steeped in a culture that disapproved of their family dynamic. "I remember comments from people at church about how Mom must wear the pants in the house," Sarah told us, "and my mom crying because she felt so woefully misunderstood. It impacted me greatly to see people assuming that because my mom was a bigger personality than my dad, she must be controlling him or usurping his rightful authority as a man. I remember, even from a young age, wanting to make sure I didn't experience that kind of judgment."

During high school, Sarah was the typical devout evangelical teenager, reading every Christian book on dating she could find. She read things like:

- "Sin has impacted us negatively . . . in a desire to resist a husband's leadership" (Nancy DeMoss Wolgemuth and Dannah Gresh, *Lies Young Women Believe*).[8]
- "Since the early days of creation, women have had a love/hate relationship with men, wanting a man's love but resisting the idea that any man should have authority over a woman" (Shannon Ethridge and Stephen Arterburn, *Every Young Woman's Battle*).[9]
- "God has designed that men be given the position of authority, and women the position of submission. It is

generally then true that a man, whether he be married or single, must think of himself as someone who has been given by God a responsibility for authority in one sense or another. And a woman, whether she is married or single, must recognize the fact that in general, as a woman, she must have a spirit of submission to all men" (John MacArthur).[10]

From messages like these, Sarah learned that her job, as a woman, was to make sure she never outshone the men around her, to make sure she was submissive and quiet, and to make sure that when she married she didn't usurp her husband's God-given authority as a man.

When Sarah met a charismatic theology student who seemed larger-than-life, she thought, "Here's a man who is 'big enough' to lead me." But in her quest to find a Christian leader, Sarah found herself in an abusive relationship that turned into an abusive marriage. Her Christian resources, though, had set her up to see this dynamic as godly—a godly man will require that you obey him, and a godly woman will know her place.

Sarah explained to us, "If it had just been my parents' example influencing me, I would have had a much better opportunity to find a healthy mate. My odds would have been much, much better if I had not also been reading Christian dating material. It was books that were supposed to set me on the right path that instead set up abusive relationship dynamics as the norm." If you have a healthy marriage but you are using the same words and terms and theology to describe it as abusers use to justify their abuse, your daughter may follow your words, not your example.

Look at the influences in your daughter's life. Even if you have a healthy marriage yourself, is your daughter being exposed to Christian leadership that demands obedience and fights for control? Is she being exposed to teachings that will train her to look for domineering men as romantic partners? Is her still, small voice telling her to stand up for herself being encouraged in your church environment, or are the leaders in her life telling her that she needs to stay silent and obey?

## She Should Know: Not Everyone Who Claims to Be a Christian Has Good Character

Todd was very unlucky in love. A sensitive and kind soul, he also happened to be the "it guy" at the Christian camp where he worked. All the girls wanted to date him, and for good reason.

Unfortunately, he kept dating girls who would later cheat on him.

Each time he'd introduce a new girlfriend to his friends, his friends would notice red flags about her—she was materialistic, she was a bit of a mean girl, or she just seemed vapid and shallow. Because Todd met these girls at camp, the relationships would inevitably turn long-distance, and after a few months of dating, they'd break up after he found out that they had been flirting with other guys, kissing someone else, or worse. But every single one of these girls had two more things in common other than their unfaithfulness: they said they were Christians, and they came from strong Christian families.

When Josie was seventeen, she met Brian at a summer youth group pool party. They didn't get along at first—Josie found him abrasive—but he flirted with her and, unsurprisingly, she enjoyed the attention. Over the summer they saw each other more and more and started texting. He was popular at church, he seemed to really know his Bible, and he liked her. By September, they were dating. By December, Josie realized she was in an abusive relationship, but she didn't know how to get out.

Looking back, Josie sees the red flags she missed. He was popular at youth group because he was a funny guy, but he only ever made jokes at the expense of others. If anyone teased him in response, he'd act angry and hurt. He would tell Josie that he liked how smart she was, but then he'd point out all the ways he was still smarter than she. He'd shower her with affection and praise, only to subtly cut her down so she was even more desperate for his approval. On dates, they always did what he wanted to do—Josie learned to enjoy all his favorite shows and watched his favorite movies countless times, but he rarely watched one of her recommendations, and when he did he'd complain that it was "girly and lame" and expect some sort of payback for doing her such a big favor.

Yasmine's friendship with Melanie had similar dynamics. In tenth grade, the two girls were the closest of friends. Yasmine admired Melanie as a Christian role model—Melanie came from a great Christian family and her parents were on all the leadership teams at church. Melanie knew her Bible inside and out, and she was the golden child at their youth group. Melanie had a confidence and certainty about the answers to the messiness of life that Yasmine yearned for. Yasmine had become a Christian only in junior high, so she relied on friends like Melanie to help her make sense of her new faith.

Soon, however, Yasmine started realizing that whenever she left Melanie's house, she felt deflated. Melanie would say horrible things about other kids in their class and scoff at Yasmine if she protested. When she and Yasmine went shopping, Melanie would laugh at Yasmine's choices, cuttingly declaring, "There's no way you're going to fit into something like that." Yasmine had curves while Melanie was straight up and down, and Melanie didn't let her forget it. When Yasmine spent time with other friends, Melanie would give her the silent treatment or else send a barrage of passive-aggressive texts that made Yasmine feel guilty and ashamed. But Yasmine didn't feel free to question Melanie because, after all, Melanie was such a good Christian girl. Everyone said so. This toxic friendship continued for over ten years before Yasmine realized Melanie was a bully.

Todd, Josie, and Yasmine all missed red flags because they were so focused on Christian virtue–signaling that they didn't look for *character.* And it makes sense—many parents' only real instruction for choosing a boyfriend or a best friend is that the person is a Christian. But this appeared to apply to Melanie, who was actively hailed by church leadership; to all of Todd's girlfriends, who were leaders at a Christian camp; and to charismatic Brian. All too often, our advice to teenagers on how to identify healthy people and our warnings against unhealthy ones don't adequately address the *heart* of the person but merely make sure they check off a list of virtue-signaling behaviors.

Take a look at these examples:

- *Brio* magazine, in an article warning girls about missionary dating, includes the fact that a boy's parents have been divorced as a warning sign against dating him.[11] Whether a person's parents are divorced does not dictate their character.
- One of our blog readers told us, "When I was seventeen, I really wanted to go to a bonfire with a bunch of friends, but it was at a house where the parents didn't go to church. On the same day a TWENTY-FIVE-year-old man from our church had asked me out. My mom refused to let me go to the bonfire and told me I needed to go out with the twenty-five-year-old simply because he went to church. The man from church ended up being a pill-popping abuser who eventually ended up sexually assaulting me. The whole reason I was even put in the situation is because my mom had in her head that going to church overrode everything else—and my friend's parents were dangerous solely because they didn't go to church."
- Another reader wrote, "I was told not to be 'unequally yoked,' meaning that I had to date a Christian, but no one ever told me to look for someone who was equally yoked when it came to the day-in and day-out of relationships, like whether they were lazy or not."

Lots of people know the Bible but don't know Jesus. Lots of people fit in with Christian culture but don't display the fruit of the Spirit (Gal. 5:22–23). Many people don't have pristine pasts but are "new creations" in Christ (2 Cor. 5:17). We need to go back to the same measures that Jesus gave us: "By this everyone will know that you are my disciples, if you love one another" (John 13:35).

But how are our daughters supposed to learn to discern good character when they are simultaneously being told that boys are simply not as morally capable as girls?

## She Should Know: Boys Should Be Held to the Same Standards as Girls

Picture this: Your daughter is ecstatic as she starts dating a Christian guy she's had a crush on for months. One day they're hanging out with friends at the beach and she lightheartedly teases him about a cowlick he got when his hair dried. His eyes go dark, and he glares at her for the rest of the visit. She feels a pit in the bottom of her stomach. After all their friends have left, he drives her home, berating her the whole way. She is sobbing and apologizing and spends the next week trying to make it up to him.

Is that the kind of boy you want your daughter to hang out with? Be friends with? Date? Marry?

I hope that most of us can recognize that if anyone jumps straight to anger at any perceived slight, they are likely an unsafe, potentially even abusive person. But what if we told you that anger is only *one* of the red flags girls are taught to overlook in order to honor Christian masculinity? Here are some that we found scattered throughout multiple Christian resources for teen girls:

- If you dress the wrong way, boys *will* lust after you, and it will be because of what you did to *them* (more on this in chapter 9).

- You can't expect a boy not to push you sexually because that's just how boys are—"even the Christian ones"[12] (more on this in chapter 8).
- If you misspeak, he will become angry, *and it's your fault* (more on that in a minute).

Girls are told that many things that are signs of poor character are actually God-given masculine traits. When we tell girls repeatedly, "This is just how boys are," we're putting the burden of boys' emotional immaturity on girls' shoulders instead of simply asking the boys to grow up. It is not your daughter's job to rescue a man-child from himself. It is God's job to redeem and restore that person's heart so that he can walk in the Spirit.

Let's explore in more depth how disastrous this can be by first focusing on the idea that boys' anger is girls' fault. Take this quote from Shaunti Feldhahn and Lisa Rice's book *For Young Women Only*:

> Many guys have a tough time expressing their feelings, and so they can't always explain why they are upset. But thankfully, there is a way to know when we've crossed the disrespect line: Watch for anger. . . . Rest assured, if he's angry at something you've said or done and you don't know why, there is a good chance that he is feeling the pain or humiliation of your disrespect.[13]

Let that sink in: if a boy is "really angry" at her (in Feldhahn's words), it's not a sign that he is a danger to *her* but a sign that she has been a danger to *him* by disrespecting him.[14] What happens to the girl with the angry crush? She reads a book like *For Young Women Only*, or talks to a youth leader who buys into this message, or hears a sermon about women's duty to respect men, and she thinks, "I may want him to be different, but this is just how boys are—*I am the problem.*"

Teachings like these prime girls to remain in toxic relationships far longer than they might have otherwise if they were taught that boys do not have an excuse to rage at them. Certainly we should teach both young women and young men that to purposely provoke someone to anger in order to get a rise out of them is cruel, and that if you hurt someone's feelings, they may naturally become angry. But to frame it this way—that if a boy is angry, it's probably because you disrespected him and therefore it's your fault—is dangerous because it convinces girls that their mistreatment is a sign not of abuse but of personal—even *spiritual*—failure. In fact, this is confirmed by research: although the number of abusive men does not seem to be higher in Christian circles, "abuse victims in religious communities are less likely to leave the abusive relationship, more likely to believe the abuser's promise to change his violent ways, more reluctant to seek community-based resources or shelters, and more commonly express guilt that they have failed their families and God in not being able to make the marriage work or stop the abuse."[15] What we teach our girls to expect in terms of treatment from others matters.

Another example of how girls are taught that they cannot expect boys to be honorable is found in some strange advice from Focus on the Family's *Brio* magazine. Girls are given the lowdown on how boys are, with the author writing, "The fact is, guys are not only visually stimulated and physical, but they really are the

---

### DARVO and Anger

**Deny**—"Men were made to need respect, so obviously they're going to get angry if they feel disrespected."

**Attack**—"You're being disrespectful, and you're not treating the boys in your life like God wants you to."

**Reverse Victim and Offender**—"He is so hurt by your disrespect that you caused him to become enraged at you."

sexual aggressor in any relationship. And you know why? God made them that way. That's right. God wired guys to be sexually aggressive, just as He made you to be the caring, nurturing one in the relationship."[16]

Yikes. So what does the author suggest girls do when faced with sexually aggressive young men? "Group dating is the safest way to go. It has so many positives because it takes all the pressure off! You don't feel as though you're on display or being taken for a test drive all the time. . . . But the best thing is, you're not alone with a guy in a car or somewhere you feel unsafe or uncomfortable."[17] We're not knocking group dates, but it's bizarre to us that the solution

---

### What Scripture Says about Angry People

Rather than telling girls that they should expect anger if they misbehave, let's help our daughters recognize that mishandled anger is a red flag that a relationship isn't safe. Instead of saying, "It's how God made boys," let's look at what God actually has to say about anger:

"Whoever is slow to anger has great understanding, but one who has a hasty temper exalts folly" (Prov. 14:29 NRSV).

"Those who are hot-tempered stir up strife, but those who are slow to anger calm contention" (Prov. 15:18 NRSV).

"Make no friends with those given to anger, and do not associate with hotheads" (Prov. 22:24 NRSV).

"Put away from you all bitterness and wrath and anger and wrangling and slander, together with all malice" (Eph. 4:31 NRSV).

Empower your daughter to get out of toxic friendships or relationships with the knowledge that "outbursts of anger" flow from the sinful nature (Gal. 5:20 NLT), whereas gentleness is a fruit of the Spirit (Gal. 5:23).

---

to dating a guy who makes you feel "unsafe or uncomfortable" isn't to dump him but to simply make sure you only date the sexually aggressive boy in groups.

God does not hold girls to a higher standard than he does boys. The Holy Spirit is not less alive in men than in women. Teach your daughter to see through this lie that boys are naturally angry and sexually forceful. Nowhere does Scripture hold men to a lower standard than women, and neither should we.

How can you foster a healthy environment for your daughter? How can you empower her to recognize red flags and not miss the warning signs? Work through these exercises with her to help her develop discernment to identify safe and unsafe people.

## MOTHER-DAUGHTER
### SECTION

We'd love to be able to tell you that everyone around you is a safe person. But we know that's not true, even in church, unfortunately. There are different kinds of dangerous people, and we want to give you and your mom a chance to discuss how to spot and avoid people who might hurt you, whether they are toxic frenemies or potential predators.

### What Would You Do?

Let's look at two different scenarios of relationships that aren't safe and talk about what you should do.

## The Mean Friend

Melanie and Yasmine spent tons of time together. Yasmine was a new Christian and Melanie had been a believer all her life, so Yasmine was thrilled to have a friend with such a strong faith. However, Yasmine started realizing that when she left Melanie's house, she always felt bad about herself. When Melanie wanted to do something Yasmine didn't find fun, Melanie would ridicule her ideas until Yasmine decided to just go along with Melanie's. If Melanie was gossiping about someone in a way that made Yasmine uncomfortable, Melanie would get angry at Yasmine if she mentioned it and punish her with the silent treatment. But at the same time, Melanie knew so many more Bible verses than she did and was so plugged in at church.

- What should Yasmine do?
- Why does Yasmine want to spend time with Melanie in the first place?
- Does Melanie's behavior show Christ?
- In church situations, there will always be Melanies. Do you know any?

### DAUGHTERS
Do any of your mom's friends strike you as a Melanie?

### MOMS
Do any of your daughter's friends strike you as a Melanie?

## The Angry Boyfriend

You make a stupid joke around your boyfriend that hurts his feelings. He blows up at you, face turning red, and warns you never to disrespect him like that again. You're terrified at his outburst of rage, and you apologize profusely. He glowers at you the rest of the date and gives you only one-word responses for the next few days.

DAUGHTERS

Does your insensitive joke excuse how he reacted?

MOMS

Have you ever been in a relationship with someone who blew up at you with almost no provocation? Who was it? What happened?

DAUGHTERS

Do you know someone who flies off in a rage? Talk to your mom about how she'd like you to handle it.

## Spot the Tricky Teaching

Unsafe people will sometimes use tricky teachings to engage in *grooming*. Grooming happens when your resolve or boundaries are slowly chipped away over time, whether by making you question your own sanity, training you to follow leadership unquestioningly, or causing you to take blame for other people's actions. When someone's been groomed, they might do something they otherwise never would have done.

Put your detective hat back on as you read through these tricky teachings that can be used to groom people. For each one, ask: What's the truth in this? What's the missing piece in this that makes it unsafe?

- You need to obey authority.
- You can trust me; I'm a Christian.
- "If he's angry at something you've said or done and you don't know why, there is a good chance that he is feeling the pain or humiliation of your disrespect."[18]
- No one else understands me like you do / no one else gets you like I do.

DISCUSS TOGETHER

Is there a situation in which any of these would be appropriate, depending on the person who says it?

 **What You Need to Know**

When Ellie had just turned fourteen, she caught the eye of a much older boy at her youth group. He'd single her out when in groups, and he'd call her to talk for four or five hours at a time at night. Ellie said,

> I felt *so special*. There was this older boy, and he liked *me*, and I was so flattered! I remember very vividly he and I talked on the phone until around 2 a.m. one morning. When I told my parents, they sat me down and told me it was not normal for an almost-eighteen-year-old boy to behave like that with a barely fourteen-year-old girl. I thought I was just mature, special, or different from other girls, but my parents' conversation with me really focused on how this kind of relationship wasn't healthy or normal.

Ellie's parents stepped in and got the boy's parents and their pastor involved, because some of what he was telling this young girl was very inappropriate. Although it was embarrassing at the time, Ellie told us, "Today, I'm so grateful I was in such a healthy church and family who all worked together to keep me safe. Looking back on it now, I can see that it was going in a really bad direction, and I was just too young to understand."

We're so glad Ellie's parents caught on to what was happening. But parents noticing fishy behavior is only half the picture. The other half is girls being able to identify dangerous people and running the other way, even if it means standing up to someone in charge.

Here are some signs things might be getting fishy that you can look out for on your own behalf but also for your friends:

- Someone older starts texting you late in the evening or multiple times a day.

- An adult starts hugging or tickling you or often has their arm around you.
- Someone sends pictures of themselves and asks you to send some back. These may start out harmless but get more invasive, personal, or pornographic.
- Someone older starts confiding in you about adult problems, such as their marriage.
- An older person often manages to end up alone with you (e.g., volunteering to give you rides, arranging to always be on the same volunteer shift with you when no one else is on the schedule, hiring you to babysit and coming home early).
- An older person sends links to videos that aren't outright pornographic but are inappropriate.
- Someone gives you gifts, opportunities, or money in a way that shows you favoritism and more attention than your peers are getting.

MOMS

Have you ever been in a situation in which one or more of these things was used to break down your boundaries? Share it with your daughter. What do you want your daughter to know about these things? What should she do if she's ever uncomfortable?

Now let's see how this may play out in real life.

You're looking at pictures on your friend's phone when she receives a text from an adult youth volunteer. It's really sexually suggestive and has some strange emojis. You click through and see that it's part of a huge conversation in which he's telling her about his marriage. You tell her that this isn't good, but she grabs the phone away, says you're over-reacting, and refuses to talk about it.

MOMS

What would you want your daughter to do if she saw this? What do you think the youth volunteer is after? How can your daughter be a real friend in this situation?

DISCUSS TOGETHER

What grooming steps may have been used to get the friend to the point where she is sexting the married youth volunteer? If your daughter ever sees someone doing any of these grooming steps, whom can she talk to about it?

# 7

## She Deserves to Know about Her Body

*Why Sex Ed Isn't the Bogeyman You've Been Told It Is*

King Henry VIII was famous for having six wives, the fourth being the very sheltered Anne of Cleves. On their wedding night, the king found himself unable to perform in bed. He blamed it on her large breasts, but it seems much more likely to have been caused by erectile dysfunction brought on by his myriad health problems. He kissed her good night, and the happy Anne informed her ladies in waiting that she might be with child. They were flummoxed. She and the king ended up with a very amicable divorce in which she received land and a castle in England and was thereafter given the title of the King's Sister—a much better life than the wives who lost their heads.[1]

Anne's lack of sexual knowledge may be understandable given the times, but tragically, that lack of knowledge has not similarly gone the way of the codpiece. When we conducted our survey for this book, we found that many of us who were raised in Christian homes didn't grow up with much more knowledge than poor Anne of Cleves!

We looked at ten sex education vocabulary terms to measure which ones our respondents knew in high school. On average, the Christian women taking our survey reported graduating from high school knowing only four of the ten terms. More than 10% of women graduated from high school without knowing *any* of the vocabulary terms (see figures 7.1 and 7.2).

In addition, girls were more likely to know male anatomical terms than female ones. More young women walked across the stage at graduation knowing the term "scrotum" than "vulva." We were also alarmed that 41.4% of Christian women raised in the church did not know about female orgasms until adulthood (see figure 7.3). This is doubly concerning considering our findings

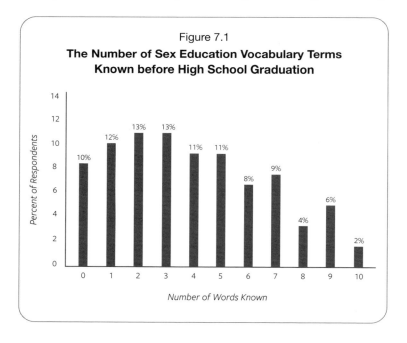

Figure 7.1
**The Number of Sex Education Vocabulary Terms Known before High School Graduation**

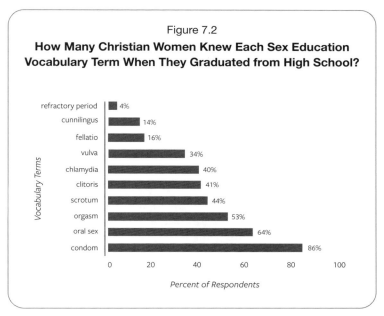

Figure 7.2

**How Many Christian Women Knew Each Sex Education Vocabulary Term When They Graduated from High School?**

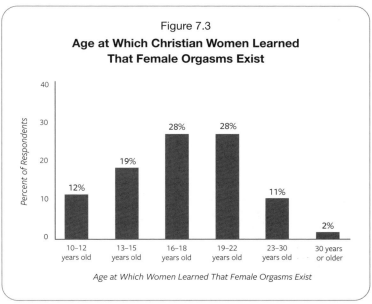

Figure 7.3

**Age at Which Christian Women Learned That Female Orgasms Exist**

that learning what a female orgasm is before turning eighteen is associated with higher sexual satisfaction later in life (see figure 7.4).[2] One respondent described her experience: "I grew up in a very conservative, sheltered family with only sisters. My mother taught me the very bottom-line, mechanical basics about sex when I was about ten or twelve years old. After that, there was almost zero conversation about sex for the rest of my growing up years.

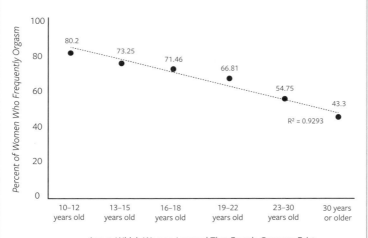

Figure 7.4

### How Likely Is a Woman to Frequently Orgasm Based on How Old She Was When She First Learned That Female Orgasms Exist?

To interpret these numbers, use this template: [Percent] of Christian women who first learned about female orgasms at [age] frequently orgasm in their later marriages.

*Age at Which Women Learned That Female Orgasms Exist*

**Key finding: Failing to provide teenage girls with adequate education about female pleasure is associated with less satisfying sex lives later.**

When my husband and I were engaged, I had to google basic male anatomy and 'what is an orgasm?'"

Rebecca and Joanna also didn't receive perfect sex education. In middle school, all Rebecca understood about penises was that it was like having another finger "down there." She could not understand why men would use their hand to scratch their testicles if they could . . . *you know* . . . use *that* finger instead. Thankfully, she got it all straightened out within a year or two. (Art history was quite the illuminating experience.)

Joanna wasn't so lucky. While she had a basic sex ed talk with her mom when she was in third grade, the pieces of how sex actually worked didn't click until she was twenty, nearly engaged, and staring at the female reproductive system in a medical textbook. Not knowing the difference between her vulva and her vagina despite earning academic accolades is one of the biggest reasons she so desperately wants to go back in time and give her younger self a big hug. Our bodies are intrinsic to who we are; we need the words to speak about them and to understand how they work, because what we can't name causes shame.

And as if shame weren't bad enough, lack of sexual knowledge is also correlated with higher rates of believing rape culture myths (i.e., beliefs that women who are raped somehow deserved it or even wanted it) and a higher likelihood of experiencing intimate partner violence.[3] Ignorance does not protect our daughters from abusers; if anything, it makes them more vulnerable.

We cannot expect that our daughters will make good choices around sex if we don't give them the language they need to talk about those good choices. Unfortunately, the evangelical world that you likely grew up in worked directly against teaching you important information and instead chose to scare you into compliance. That didn't work out well with your generation, and it isn't going to work with our daughters either. We need to do better, and that starts with recognizing how things got off the rails in the first place.

## She Should Know More about Sex than "Don't Do It"

When I (Rebecca) was twelve, I read a *Brio* article that terrified me. It was written in the form of a letter from a woman to her younger teenage sister about how she had contracted herpes without actually having sex. The older sister cries out, "He gives me a disease he got while sleeping around, while I, still technically a virgin, suffer like crazy. It's not even close to being fair!" It ended with this:

> Well, I've done what I set out to do: cry out a warning to the dearest person in the world to me. I'm so ashamed I could crawl into a hole, but there's no way I can let my shame and embarrassment stop me from begging you to commit to true sexual purity. This doesn't simply mean virginity, but a pure lifestyle. Avoid skin-to-skin or oral sexual conduct like the plague, Jessie, because that's exactly what it adds up to—a plague.[4]

From that moment, I was convinced that letting a boy kiss me or perhaps even just touch my stomach may lead to an incurable case of genital herpes.

*Brio* magazine did what we so often do in the church: it substituted spiritual language or euphemisms for actual words and definitions. Throw into the mix that the magazine had spent months teaching me that any touching counted as sexual activity—yes, even holding hands—and is it any wonder that I was so confused?

Sex ed has become a minefield in Christian circles because we've tried to avoid giving education around sex in favor of giving warnings not to do it. While many of us did not understand basic information about how sex works, we all knew one thing, loud and clear: never, ever do it until you're married. When Rebecca was ten and close to puberty, I (Sheila) took her away on a weekend to work through FamilyLife's *Passport to Purity* curriculum. Mixed with the sex talk and the teaching about body changes and puberty were exercises moms were to do with their daughters to tell them that sex would bond them to someone else. They were then to ask their daughters to make a pledge to remain pure.

I balked at that, and we ended up working through only about two of the exercises. The idea of sex grossed her out. I could have manipulated her into vowing never to touch a boy if I had tried! But asking her to take a purity pledge at ten was entirely inappropriate. She needed information; she didn't need it overshadowed by apocalyptic threats. In fact, a decade later, when Rebecca and her sister Katie and I put together an online course for moms to teach their daughters about sex and puberty, we left out the "don't do

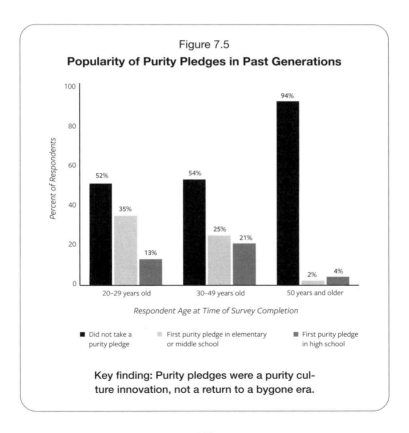

Figure 7.5
**Popularity of Purity Pledges in Past Generations**

Key finding: Purity pledges were a purity culture innovation, not a return to a bygone era.

it" messages from the younger version of the course, introducing it only when we talked to young teenagers, not to girls needing a training bra.

But the "don't do it" message was everywhere. Instead of opting for teaching kids about healthy sex, the evangelical church largely pressured millennial girls to make purity pledges (see figure 7.5).

Why do we focus so much on "don't do it" rather than on information? Perhaps it's because "don't do it" gives us a quick way to shut down an uncomfortable conversation. Explaining to an eleven-year-old who only recently put away her dolls what the word *masturbation* means can make us feel as if we're ruining her innocence. We know she needs the information, but it's awkward.

When Katie, my youngest, was fourteen, she arrived home from summer teen camp with much to tell me—including how stupid the sex ed talk was. "Ugh, Mom, can you just give the sex talk next year? They don't even understand that it's not just about sex—so many of my friends are having oral sex and they think it's no big deal because it's not actual sex!" I had no idea Katie even knew what oral sex was, let alone that she would have an opinion on how best to talk about it with fourteen-year-olds. (Now, with the research we've done today, I would suggest making sure your children know all this stuff well before age fourteen, and in retrospect, I'm glad she did know these things, but at the time we hadn't discussed it!) Yet she believed I would be cool with talking about it—and so I was determined to stay cool and keep my face neutral while inside I was freaking out about my little baby.

We often have a very hard time remaining matter-of-fact when it comes to talking about sex because we associate *knowledge about sex* with *having adult sexuality*. But this can inadvertently end up unfairly sexualizing our children. In *And the Bride Wore White*, Dannah Gresh warns girls against a cavalier attitude toward their bodies. Don't ever talk about your period, or period symptoms like cramps, in front of a boy. "Talking about your body in front of guys may be normal, but it also normalizes sexual familiarity and that's a risk to your purity!"[5] When Rebecca was working as a lifeguard, she didn't feel "sexually familiar" with her male coworkers simply because they knew where the tampons were in the staff office.

Body parts and functions aren't sexual until you make them sexual. Imagine you're at a gynecology appointment, and your male doctor refuses to use the word *vagina* and instead says "your special

---

### Period Embarrassment

One thing we didn't anticipate when we wrote the survey for this book was the profound effect teenage embarrassment about periods would have on women's later well-being. We were unsurprised to find that there was a strong correlation between embarrassment with menstruation and high school self-esteem (five times less likely to have above-average self-esteem), but we were saddened by how that self-esteem dampening persists even through adulthood. Additionally, girls who were extremely embarrassed by their periods throughout their teenage years were 55% more likely to have poor marital satisfaction and 74% more likely to have below-average sexual satisfaction if they married. But it gets worse: these girls were also *70% more likely* to be in an abusive marriage than girls who did not find their periods embarrassing.

Period embarrassment, then, especially if it's extreme, is bad for girls. How do we fix that? We treat periods as part of normal facts of life that every woman experiences. It's not a hush-hush secret. And what best protects girls from this embarrassment? Sex education. Increased knowledge of sex ed terms is strongly correlated with decreased embarrassment about periods. But the strongest effect is education from mom about what to expect. When your daughter can talk to you and turn to you with her questions, and you can model that this is a normal part of growing up that isn't embarrassing or shameful for you, not only will she feel less embarrassment now, but she'll also be set up for greater success long term.

---

place" or "your secret treasure" and is clearly uncomfortable about your state of undress. Now imagine your gynecologist pops into the office, dons some gloves, and announces, "Okay, says here you want to talk about vaginal odor. What would you like to know?" Who would you feel was sexualizing you? The one who used euphemisms and looked uncomfortable? Or the one who treated your body in an upfront, no-nonsense way?

Ironically, this idea that we must talk about sexuality and our genitalia in a completely different way than we talk about anything else does not impart an air of sacredness to sex but instead a sense of shame. As one respondent told us, "My parents even fast-forwarded kissing scenes in movies when I was a teen! I thought that sex was weird and dirty because it was totally taboo. . . . It didn't exist except for the purposes of having children."

## She Should Know Facts, Not Fear Tactics

In a now famous scene from the movie *Mean Girls*, the burly gym teacher, raising his pointer finger, warns the onlooking students: "Don't have sex, 'cause you will get pregnant, and die."[6] His dire warning is the source of many jokes, but his language doesn't sound a whole lot different from many of our evangelical resources:

- "Please know that your entire future, including your ability to have a successful marriage and your own children someday, is made up of one decision after another. . . . Because of their poor sense of direction, many of your peers are making decisions that lead them not toward an abundant, joy-filled life, but toward destruction and even death" (Josh McDowell, foreword for *Every Young Woman's Battle*).[7]
- "No babies. Ever" (Dannah Gresh, *And the Bride Wore White*).[8] This theme is repeated throughout the book, as this anecdote, one hundred pages later, shows: "Ashley

talked about being the most popular girl with the guys in high school and college. Then, she talked about having cervical cancer at the age of twenty-six. She knew it was because she'd had so many sexual partners and had acquired HPV. She had to have a full hysterectomy and would never have babies."[9]

- "Satan knows that one of the most beautiful things in our world is the sexual union between a husband and a wife when they wait to enjoy it after their wedding. He wants to rob you of that, so he lies to you. . . . He told my Christian friend Jennifer that she would lose her boyfriend if she did not provide for some of his sexual needs—though she told him she would not have sex with him. He raped her" (Gresh, *And the Bride Wore White*).[10] (We're not entirely sure what the moral of this story was meant to be. If you have a boyfriend, you will get raped?)

- "Do you want to live to walk down the aisle at your wedding someday? to hold your own babies in your arms after giving birth? to see your children grow up and make you a grandma? to grow old with your husband? If so, please pay close attention as we examine the possible consequences of losing the physical battle for sexual purity" (Shannon Ethridge, *Every Young Woman's Battle*).[11]

Quite frankly, the evangelical church has been lying to our teens for decades. *Sex* does not cause most unwanted pregnancies or sexually transmitted diseases; *unprotected sex* causes most of these things. But our resources stress that condoms don't work. Dannah Gresh explains that there are thirteen steps to using a condom, and they fail almost half the time[12] (we totally can't figure out what those steps are supposed to be). *Every Young Woman's Battle* also warns against the ineffectiveness of condoms. But condoms are actually very effective against unwanted pregnancies as well as sexually transmitted infections (STIs), including gonor-rhea, chlamydia, and HIV.[13] No, they are not as effective as abstinence, but they do provide broad protection. The National Health Service in the UK has found condoms to be 98% effective in preventing pregnancy when used properly, and still 82% effective with imperfect use.[14] In the vast majority of cases, condoms actually work.

When we rely on scare tactics to stop kids from having sex, we will fail. Our girls will inevitably know friends or family members who are having extramarital sex and who are not pregnant, heartbroken, riddled with STIs, rendered infertile, or dead. When our daughters realize our warnings mean nothing, they'll feel manipulated and may even abandon our ethics altogether.

Teaching someone to abstain from a behavior due to fear of repercussions pretty much works—until it doesn't. Why? Because the first time that you test the boundary and don't get the punishment, all the impetus to avoid the behavior vanishes. Imagine a dog who was trained to stay off the couch by its owner using a shock collar (we don't recommend this!). Fido may quickly learn to avoid the couch for fear of a shock. But then when Fido's owner isn't home to administer the punishment, he tries hopping up on the couch and—no shock. Just a cozy couch. What's going to happen? *That dog is going to go on the couch every single time its owner steps out the door.* Avoidance-based learning is not an appropriate long-term behavioral modification strategy.

We find this whole avoidance-based approach to sex education so strange because it's actually quite easy to just be honest with your children about the reasons you want them to wait until marriage to have sex. Here are some that we often hear from readers:

- In the case that birth control does fail, any children will be born in a stable environment.
- If everyone abstained from sex unless they were married, there would not be sexually transmitted infections.

- Sex is complicated and intimate, and saving it for a covenantal relationship means that we put the other person's well-being before our own physical urges.
- Abstaining from sex builds self-control and gives your partner assurance that later in your marriage, if sex is off the table for a period of time, they don't need to worry about infidelity.
- Keeping sex off the table while dating can help a couple grow their emotional connection without being clouded by a great physical connection that may cover up some deeper problems with the relationship.

We wait for sex out of wisdom and protection for ourselves and others, not because if you have sex you'll get pregnant and die.

Why has the church chosen this *"No babies. Ever."* message instead of a more nuanced discussion on emotional health and sex? It may be because the evangelical church hasn't understood sex as the deep "knowing" that it's portrayed to be in Genesis 4:1 (NRSV) but instead has mostly framed it as a physical thing, or even as a male need. Our book *The Great Sex Rescue* delves into the toxic messaging around sex in marriage that has messed up women's ability to feel pleasure and experience desire. If we better understood the purposes of sex to be intimate, mutual, and pleasurable for both, it would be easier to tell our daughters about the benefits of waiting without having to trick them or manipulate them.

Or, come to think of it, we could instill values without having to bribe our daughters, which is the next tactic that's often been used.

- "I truly believe that when we keep that covenant by saving ourselves to love someone with all the intensity of our heart and body, [God] is able to bless us immeasurably beyond what we could have imagined within our sex lives" (Dannah Gresh, *And the Bride Wore White*).[15]

- "The prize is the health, happiness, peace, and contentment that come from saving yourself for marriage, choosing a good mate, and bringing beautiful children into the world" (Josh McDowell, *Every Young Woman's Battle*).[16]

### Comparing Threatening and Hopeful Messaging about Sexuality

We measured two different beliefs about saving sex for marriage: one that promised kids incredible sex if they waited (see figure 7.6), and one that threatened destruction if they didn't (see figure 7.7). And even though both messages had the same underlying desire (get kids to wait until the wedding night), believing these messages produced opposite results (with the exception of vaginismus).

### Figure 7.6
**What Are the Effects When Women Believe in High School That "If You Wait to Have Sex until You Are Married, You Will Have the Best Sex Life Possible"?**

To interpret these numbers, use this template: Women who believed "if you wait to have sex until you are married, you will have the best sex life possible" are [percent] more likely to report [outcome variable].

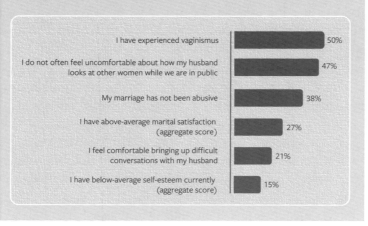

| | |
|---|---|
| I have experienced vaginismus | 50% |
| I do not often feel uncomfortable about how my husband looks at other women while we are in public | 47% |
| My marriage has not been abusive | 38% |
| I have above-average marital satisfaction (aggregate score) | 27% |
| I feel comfortable bringing up difficult conversations with my husband | 21% |
| I have below-average self-esteem currently (aggregate score) | 15% |

Figure 7.7

**What Are the Effects When Women Believe in High School That "If You Have Sex before You Are Married, You Will Have Ruined Your Chances of Having a Good Sex Life in Marriage"?**

To interpret these numbers, use this template: Women who believed "if you have sex before you are married, you will have ruined your chances of having a good sex life in marriage" are [percent] more likely to report [outcome variable].

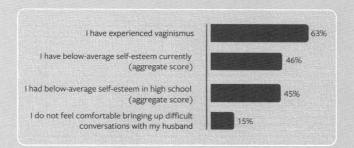

| | |
|---|---|
| I have experienced vaginismus | 63% |
| I have below-average self-esteem currently (aggregate score) | 46% |
| I had below-average self-esteem in high school (aggregate score) | 45% |
| I do not feel comfortable bringing up difficult conversations with my husband | 15% |

So what does this mean? It means that seeing sex as a sacred part of the marriage relationship protects them from the harms of hookup culture. But using a fear-based all-or-nothing approach is counterproductive. Now, we don't believe that bribing children with lies is necessary or ethical, because we believe there is a third option: honest sex education without bribes *or* threats. Let's set our girls up to make wise choices, mitigate risks, but also avoid shaming or fear-based messages that easily backfire.

So many women reported to us feeling cheated when they got married and sex wasn't amazing. They weren't given the tools to understand that sex can take a while to figure out, and instead they felt hopeless and alone. Bribing kids is lying to kids. We must do better.

## But What about Sex Ed and LGBTQ+ Issues?

We frequently are asked, "What should I do? My daughter's friend came out as gay." You may be reading this book because you want to protect your kids from the "LGBTQ+ agenda." Maybe you're angry about inclusive sex ed courses at your child's school, or you're worried about what will happen if your child starts questioning their own sexuality.

Your daughter will likely have many friends and acquaintances over her lifetime who are part of the LGBTQ+ community. Your daughter may even not be straight herself. But here's what we do know:

- A comprehensive review of over thirty years of research found that when LGBTQ+ youth are not given comprehensive sex education, they suffer. They are more likely to be victims of harassment or bullying, their mental health is more likely to decline, and they engage more frequently in risky sexual behaviors (unprotected sex, using substances before sex, having more sexual partners).[17]
- When LGBTQ+ youth grow up in homes with anti-homosexual religious beliefs, their suicide risk increases.[18]

Now, this is not a theological book—and there are many out there that you can read. But no matter what you believe about sexuality, more dead kids is never good fruit.

Marginalized people flocked to Jesus. They loved him, and he loved them. We need to take a big step back as a church and ask how we can be more like Jesus.

If your child or your child's friends are part of the LGBTQ+ community, how can you show them Jesus' love? Look at the evidence, and do what helps, not what harms.

### She Should Know: You Don't "Accidentally" Have Sex

In the 1990s, as teen pregnancy rates were rising, the purity culture backlash decided to make kissing a sin too (and books like *Boy*

*Meets Girl* threw in hugs and holding hands for good measure). In fact, we found that girls who grew up in purity culture were 2.8 times less likely to kiss before marriage than women who came of age earlier.[19]

Why this trend away from kissing? Likely because of teachings like these:

- Elisabeth Elliot pondered about how to convince girls that kissing was wrong: "How shall I speak of a few careless kisses as sin to a generation nurtured on the assumption that nearly everybody goes to bed with everybody?"[20]

- "Hey, but I'm not having intercourse. . . . I'm just really involved with my guy, you may be thinking. Read it again. God said sexual immorality. That includes prolonged or deep kissing and petting or physical contact. Why? Because the above leads to more!" (Focus on the Family's *Brio* magazine).[21]

- "So why am I getting so much mail from you saying 'I can make out with my boyfriend, I can drink, I can use bad language . . . and I'm still a Christian.' Gimme a break! You're being deceived" (Focus on the Family's *Brio* magazine).[22]

Combine fear with legalism and you end up with a toxic mess. But here's an easier way to talk about sexual temptation with teenagers: affection and showing love are good; deliberately arousing someone is unwise. We shouldn't "awaken love until the time is right" (Song of Sol. 8:4 NLT), but that doesn't mean kissing is a sin, even prolonged kissing! Instead of making this a conversation about morality or "what is a sin and what is not," having an open and honest conversation about goal-oriented decision-making may help your daughter make wise decisions without legalistic fear tactics. If you don't want to have sex, touching erogenous zones is unwise. So is taking off clothing. And so is making out for seven hours straight. But we can have these conversations in a way that encourages girls to be empowered in their decisions rather than afraid of sexual bogeymen.

## She Should Know: Sex Doesn't Leave Pieces of Yourself Behind

I (Joanna) was a middle schooler when my church took us to the Silver Ring Thing. Hundreds of youth from my hometown of

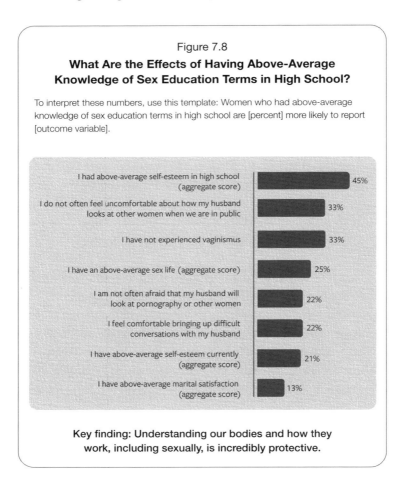

Figure 7.8

**What Are the Effects of Having Above-Average Knowledge of Sex Education Terms in High School?**

To interpret these numbers, use this template: Women who had above-average knowledge of sex education terms in high school are [percent] more likely to report [outcome variable].

| Outcome | Percent |
|---|---|
| I had above-average self-esteem in high school (aggregate score) | 45% |
| I do not often feel uncomfortable about how my husband looks at other women when we are in public | 33% |
| I have not experienced vaginismus | 33% |
| I have an above-average sex life (aggregate score) | 25% |
| I am not often afraid that my husband will look at pornography or other women | 22% |
| I feel comfortable bringing up difficult conversations with my husband | 22% |
| I have above-average self-esteem currently (aggregate score) | 21% |
| I have above-average marital satisfaction (aggregate score) | 13% |

**Key finding: Understanding our bodies and how they work, including sexually, is incredibly protective.**

Pittsburgh gathered in a church auditorium, which smelled of far too much Axe body spray. I remember the production value and the music—I think there were even smoke machines. And, of course, I was given a silver ring with a Bible verse inscribed as a symbol of my "purity." But what I remember most was the young man on the stage who took two colored pieces of paper, glued them together,

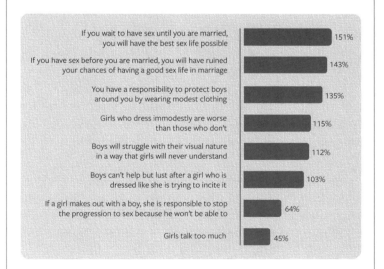

Figure 7.9

**How Is Believing Problematic Teachings Related to Having Below-Average Sex Education in High School?**

To interpret these numbers, use this template: Women who had below-average knowledge of sex education terms in high school were [percent] more likely to believe [teaching] in high school.

| Teaching | Percent |
| --- | --- |
| If you wait to have sex until you are married, you will have the best sex life possible | 151% |
| If you have sex before you are married, you will have ruined your chances of having a good sex life in marriage | 143% |
| You have a responsibility to protect boys around you by wearing modest clothing | 135% |
| Girls who dress immodestly are worse than those who don't | 115% |
| Boys will struggle with their visual nature in a way that girls will never understand | 112% |
| Boys can't help but lust after a girl who is dressed like she is trying to incite it | 103% |
| If a girl makes out with a boy, she is responsible to stop the progression to sex because he won't be able to | 64% |
| Girls talk too much | 45% |

Key finding: Girls who grew up in environments where evangelical teachings about marriage and sex were being internalized were less likely to have an adequate sex education.

and then ripped them apart. Bits of one sheet stuck to the other. "This is what happens when you have sex with someone," he explained. "A part of you is lost, and you gain a part of them forever."

Another event I attended as a teen, Acquire the Fire, featured a panel with two adults who shared that they'd had sex with each other before they were married. Even though they were happy that they'd married each other, they still reported that their sex life had fizzled a few years into their marriage, something they blamed entirely on their premarital sexual activity.

Our study, though, found no correlation between whether an engaged couple slept together before they got married and their future sexual satisfaction when we controlled for confounders.[23] Any correlation between premarital sexual activity and future sexual satisfaction was explained by marital satisfaction—which, incidentally, is something a couple can work to improve without the use of a time machine.[24] But because we've made premarital sex into a bugaboo, when couples who had sex before the wedding night end up unhappy in their marriage, they may be less likely to work on their marriage if they believe they're simply living out God's punishment. What could have been an easily fixed communication problem becomes years of unnecessary frustration.

"Soul tie" theology holds that any sex, even casual sex or, horrifically, even sexual abuse, causes a soul tie in which a bond is formed in the spiritual realm. When you break up with that person, that bond is still there at the soul level. Then when you have sex with someone else, your bond with them won't be as strong because part of you is still tied to someone else. The soul tie must then be broken in the spiritual realm through prayer, repentance, and/or deliverance. But this entire concept is extrabiblical—you're not going to find it anywhere in the Bible. In fact, it sounds more like the horcruxes in *Harry Potter* than it does anything in the Epistles or the Gospels. You have a soul, but it was redeemed by Christ on the cross—and no one can snatch you from the Father's hand (John 10:28).

But wait—isn't sex supposed to be bonding? Absolutely! In fact, there's a hormonal reason for that. When we have sex, we release a hormone called oxytocin, commonly called "the bonding hormone." It makes us feel close to the person we're with and produces feelings of affection and belonging. Women also produce that hormone when we breastfeed, when we kiss or hug our kids, etc. Of course we can become emotionally attached to people, and sex can intensify that attachment, so that when we break up, it can cause heartache.

But the soul tie theology says more than that. It claims the reason you can't get over heartache is because of spiritual oppression and *permanent* neurological rewiring. And it says that even if you don't feel sad, you'll never experience the fullness of a great sex life with your spouse without a big exorcism or prayer of deliverance. Interestingly, Jesus didn't seem to get this memo since he didn't perform an exorcism on the Samaritan woman who had had five husbands (see John 4). We're not saying that people can't undergo spiritual oppression because of relationships; we're merely saying that claiming that you can never be truly free or experience God's best for you because of past sins does not match with the gospel of the God who came to give us life, and give it abundantly.

And this soul tie theology has real-world consequences. We hear from many women who married their husbands simply because they'd already done the deed and felt their fate was sealed: "I married my husband because we had had sex! I believed that I literally could not marry anyone else because we were married in the sight of God, and to not stay together would mean stealing from whomever I would later marry. And in God's eyes, I would never truly be married except to the guy I slept with!"

The God who says that "anyone who belongs to Christ has become a new person" and that "the old life is gone; a new life has begun" (2 Cor. 5:17 NLT) does not tell us that we are connected to someone for life if we had sex with them. Jesus brings us freedom;

becoming a Christian should not make someone feel more tied to the past than they were already.

## She Should Know: Virginity and Purity Are Not Synonyms

When we asked women how they felt about the purity message that they were given as teens, by far the most common response was that their purity, or the state of their Christian walk, was defined by their virginity.

This can have heartbreaking consequences, as this commenter told us:

> When I was seventeen, I went with a group from our church to "Serve." This was when kids from different youth groups would go to a church, stay there, and serve the local community doing projects for free. Every morning and night we had a chapel time and we would have small groups. I remember one night was "Purity Night."
>
> I remember the youth pastor specifically told the girls, "You control how far you go with a guy because he's going to have a harder time stopping."
>
> At one point during his talk about how our purity gave us value, a girl from my small group walked out the back quickly with her two friends following behind her. I remember thinking that she must feel convicted about her sexual sins.
>
> At the end of the talk they held an altar call, but instead of people responding to the gospel, we were called to the front if we wanted to pledge our purity. At the front we would get a purity ring. Afterwards we met in our small group, and the girl who had run out the back came and asked to talk to me. She told me through sobs that she had been raped.
>
> I felt sick to my stomach, and I still think about it to this day. This girl had been told that without her purity she wasn't valuable. She had been told that she is responsible for how far a guy goes with her.

If our resources define purity as virginity, then sexual assault survivors can never be seen as pure. Yet it's virginity that our resources have proudly stressed:

- Elisabeth Elliot says, "A woman knew that she possessed a priceless treasure, her virginity. She guarded it jealously for the man who would pay a price for it—commitment."[25]
- Dannah Gresh echoes her, saying, "I never dreamed of having a ministry to encourage young girls to treasure their purity."[26] And she says, "God asks us to prize our virginity and hold it up as our only blood covenant to Him."[27]

Our girls should not be told that their relationship with Jesus is measured by decisions they might have made in the past rather than how they are living for him now—let alone imply that they are "less than" if someone has assaulted them.

But this emphasis on virginity doesn't affect just girls' self-worth; it can also affect how they see potential marriage partners. What happens to the girl who has saved her virginity but falls in love with an amazing young man who isn't a virgin? Will she be able to embrace her marriage wholeheartedly, or will she always feel cheated out of something?

Many resources, such as Elisabeth Elliot's *Passion and Purity*, put this unhealthy emphasis on both genders: "I knew the kind of man I wanted. He would have to be a man who prized virginity—his own as well as mine—as much as I did."[28] However, most of our evangelical resources have stressed girls' virginity far more than they have boys' virginity, even though biblically there is absolutely nothing asked of girls that is not also asked of boys. Shaunti Feldhahn, in her survey for her book *For Young Women Only*, asked boys if they would prefer to marry a virgin (the vast majority did). However, she did not ask girls the same question for her book to teen boys.[29] Often, virginity is talked about as a gift that girls give boys rather than the other way around:

- "She had made the mistake of giving him her most precious gift—her virginity—but now he was distant and cold toward her" (Eric and Leslie Ludy, *When God Writes Your Love Story*).[30] But in the story they tell, he was also a virgin before they had sex, yet he had not given up his most precious gift, apparently.

- "[I] gave away the gift that God meant me to give to my husband on my wedding night" (Nancy DeMoss Wolgemuth and Dannah Gresh, *Lies Young Women Believe*).[31]

Our girls should feel neither this kind of pressure nor this kind of guilt. We should always remind them that their purity is based on what Jesus did with his body, not what they do with theirs. Don't ever let your daughter feel like her worth in Jesus' eyes is based on what she's done sexually—or what's been done to her—rather than Jesus' love for her.

### She Should Know: The Goal Is Not Virginity but Following Christ

Conservative Christian teens are at a higher risk for unplanned pregnancy than less conservative Christian teenagers.[32] Why? It's certainly partly because they haven't been taught about contraception, but researchers believe there's more to it than that. Conservative Christian teens are more likely to engage in risky sexual behaviors because of all-or-nothing thinking, mixed with a lack of education about consent. If you and a boy make out when that's strictly against the rules because you've been told that makes you lose your purity, according to this mindset, you may as well go all the way because you're already "damaged goods."

But when you see virginity as a line, and you're either on one side or the other based on something that you did or that was done to you—then your agency is taken away from you today. According to this outlook, there's no point in choosing wisely, because you've already lost. This is how an emphasis on virginity erases the idea of ongoing consent and autonomy—the idea that you can change your mind at any moment, no matter what you've done up to this point. We heard this echoed among many of our focus group interviewees:

- "I had sex once, and then even if I didn't want to sleep with future boyfriends, I didn't feel I had a right to say no. I wasn't a virgin, so I had to say yes."
- "As a teenager, I was sexually assaulted by a boyfriend and then went down a path of believing I was 'damaged goods' so therefore it didn't matter what I did. I have carried a lot of guilt and shame from that season of life. I also became pregnant before my husband and I were married, which brought more shame. Over the years, though, I have started trying to work through that and overcome it. I have found the beauty in the redemption of Christ and his forgiveness and how we can be made new again, which has led to me having a much more fulfilling sex life with my husband."
- "I had one relationship before marriage, which essentially was what I now know to be a date rape in high school. Because of my strong faith, I stayed there for a long time, even continuing sex because I was already ruined and knew no one else would ever want me. I finally got out."

Think about that last statement she made: "Because of my strong faith, I stayed there for a long time." Because she was told that her purity was already gone, she felt like she was worthless. Do not let this be your daughter's understanding of "faith"! So many girls felt they no longer had a reason to say no because they had never been taught the value of protecting themselves; they had only been taught to protect their virginity.

Instead of protecting purity, let's teach our daughters to protect themselves. That will involve strong sexual ethics, yes, but such

169

ethics are ideally formed out of a deep sense of our daughters' inherent worth to be treated well, and a conviction that they are more than their sexual status. That's real sex education, and that's what girls deserve to know.

# MOTHER-DAUGHTER
## SECTION

It's time to talk about sex. We know it's awkward, but this is such an important conversation to have with your mom! Work through these questions and activities to give you a chance to check in and make sure you have the information you need and to spot some tricky teachings along the way.

 **Q&A**

MOMS

When you were growing up, were you embarrassed about your period? Do you feel embarrassed today?

DAUGHTERS

What about you? Is there something about your period that you're concerned about or confused about?

MOMS

How did your parents handle the sex and puberty talk? Was there something that you didn't understand until much later?

**What You Need to Know**

Go to figure 7.2 on page 147.

MOMS

How many words related to sex education do you think you would have known at your daughter's age?

DAUGHTERS

Are there any you don't know? (If you're embarrassed, you can just write them down.)

Something else we have to talk about is the idea of *sexual purity*. Typically, you may be told this means "just don't have sex." But that's not the whole picture! We want you to understand the difference between "virginity" and "chastity."

*Virginity* simply means you haven't had sexual intercourse before. *Chastity*, or to be chaste, means to live a lifestyle in which you submit sex to God. That means the way we express our sexuality should honor, respect, and dignify ourselves and the people around us. It isn't just about whether you've done the deed but is more about living to honor God with your body. And when you're married? Chastity means having sex with only your spouse in a way that honors your spouse and your relationship. The idea that purity = virginity just doesn't work when you're married. But the concept of chastity does, because it adds *context* to sexual activity.

So what does that mean for teenagers now? Living a chaste lifestyle by submitting your body to God isn't about running away from scary things. It means that even though, frankly, you likely wouldn't have long-term repercussions if you *did* have sex and used protection, you still choose not to out of reverence for God and out of respect for the image of God in others and yourself. It's not about being afraid of causing irreparable, permanent damage to your purity; it's about choosing to live differently simply because it's the right (and the wise!) thing to do.

## Spot the Tricky Teaching

Let's take a look at some tricky teachings that teenagers hear in the church about why to wait for marriage:

- If you have sex with someone, a part of you is with them forever even if you break up. You can never take that back.
- If you have sex before you're married, you'll never be able to bond as well with your future spouse.
- Stay pure until you're married.

### DAUGHTERS

How do you think these teachings would affect someone who had been sexually assaulted? Do you think these teachings adequately address other kinds of sexual situations (e.g., sexting, pushing boundaries, using pornography)?

### MOMS

Did you hear any of these growing up?

### DISCUSS TOGETHER

How would you change these so that they are more balanced?

 ## Quiz

Okay, girls, a lot of information is out there about sex. Some of it is true, but a lot of it's just plain wrong. We're going to give you some statements about sex, and we want you to guess if they're true or false (and don't worry, we'll give you the answers):

1. Most teenagers are having sex.
2. You can get pregnant only when you're fertile, which is about five to seven days a month.
3. Condoms fail about 50% of the time.

4. Condoms effectively prevent the spread of most STIs.

5. As long as you don't have intercourse, you're still a virgin, so oral sex or other kinds of sexual activity aren't as big a deal.

6. Once you've had sex, you're no longer a virgin, so there's no point in trying to wait anymore.

7. Most STIs will not render you infertile.

8. If you kiss a boy, you'll get so worked up that you'll likely end up having sex.

9. If you have sex before you're married, your sex life will never be as good once you are married as it could have been otherwise.

10. Pregnancy is preventable, even if you're having sex.

**Answer Key:** (1) False! Only around 40% of teenagers will have had sex by the time they graduate from high school.[33] (2) True, but unless you're tracking really carefully, you won't know when those five to seven days are. (3) False. Condoms have over a 98% effectiveness rate at preventing pregnancy. (4) True. (5) False. Even though non-penetrative sex doesn't typically lead to pregnancy, that doesn't mean it's "no big deal." All sexual activity has risks and should not be taken lightly. (6) False. It's about chastity, not virginity! You're not "damaged goods." (7) True, provided the person seeks medical attention. (8) It's complicated! While prolonged kissing can be exciting, which can lead to people wanting to do more, kissing does not need to go any further. (9) False. Most people who have sex before they're married go on to have marriages and sex lives that are about as healthy as those of people who abstained. (10) True. Many forms of contraception are very effective, but the condom is the safest one because it is the only one that also protects against STIs.

# 8

## She Deserves to Understand Consent

*"Boys Will Be Boys" and Other Lies*
*the Church Tells about Assault*

When Vera was sixteen years old, she suffered a severe concussion that resulted in horrible migraines for months. Her boyfriend, Colton, would take her back home when the pain got so bad that she couldn't handle being at school anymore.

After a few weeks of dating, during a particularly bad migraine episode when she could barely keep her eyes open, Colton raped her.

"I was confused about what had happened," Vera explained to me, "so I went to a Christian youth leader who worked at my school and told him that I had had sex, I didn't know how I felt about it, and I alluded to the force he used even though I didn't outright say he forced me. The youth leader just looked at me and said, 'Well, it takes two to tango.' And this was actually helpful because for the first time I realized, 'No, it doesn't actually always take two because this was not a tango! I was not tangoing!'"

Vera still wasn't able to call what had happened to her "rape," but she knew it wasn't right and the Christian youth leader at her school wasn't going to help her. So she turned to her youth pastor and his wife. "I told them what had happened and how I was confused, but my youth pastor just asked, 'What do you expect when you date a nonbeliever?'"

His wife then fetched a piece of blue and a piece of pink construction paper, glued them together, and when they dried ripped them apart. Pieces of pink stuck to the blue page, and a smattering of blue marred the pink paper. "When you have sex," she said to Vera, "parts of you are left on him and parts of him are a part of you now forever."

Vera was crushed. "I felt I forever had to carry him and that horrible experience with me. Now this person was forever a part of my body and my soul and he forever had ownership of a part of me I never wanted him to have."

Vera did not leave that conversation feeling heard or believing there was hope. Rather, she left with a deep sense of dread. "My youth pastor and his wife made it very clear: I had given away the best part of myself. I felt so empty and worthless, and I carried that for a long time until I realized years later that it was rape."

Vera received a typical sex education from her church. And unfortunately, it left her unable to identify that she had been assaulted—even though she felt something was wrong. She's not alone. Our survey found that 44% of our survey respondents could not identify date rape when they graduated from high school, and only 11.8% strongly agreed they could spot it. Other research has also found that abstinence-only sex education frequently omits the concept of consent from its discussions,[1] which may leave teens less able to adequately identify when they have been assaulted.[2] Although there is fear that teaching children about consent may accidentally give them permission to start fooling around, we actually found the opposite. In our sample, being able to identify date rape was associated with having *fewer* sexual partners and *higher* odds of waiting until marriage to have sex. There isn't a downside to teaching your daughter about consent (see figure 8.1).

Thankfully, the conversation to teenage girls in the evangelical sphere does tend to include assurances that forcible rape is

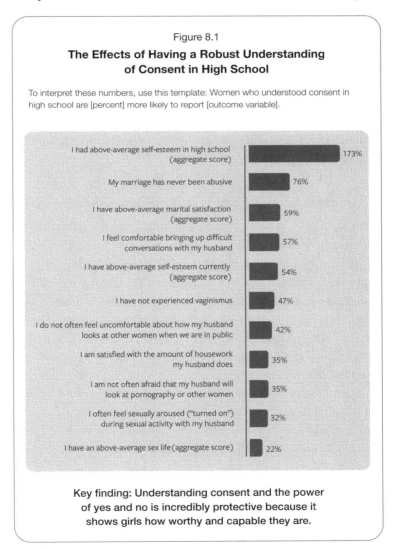

Figure 8.1

**The Effects of Having a Robust Understanding
of Consent in High School**

To interpret these numbers, use this template: Women who understood consent in high school are [percent] more likely to report [outcome variable].

| Outcome variable | Percent |
| --- | --- |
| I had above-average self-esteem in high school (aggregate score) | 173% |
| My marriage has never been abusive | 76% |
| I have above-average marital satisfaction (aggregate score) | 59% |
| I feel comfortable bringing up difficult conversations with my husband | 57% |
| I have above-average self-esteem currently (aggregate score) | 54% |
| I have not experienced vaginismus | 47% |
| I do not often feel uncomfortable about how my husband looks at other women when we are in public | 42% |
| I am satisfied with the amount of housework my husband does | 35% |
| I am not often afraid that my husband will look at pornography or other women | 35% |
| I often feel sexually aroused ("turned on") during sexual activity with my husband | 32% |
| I have an above-average sex life (aggregate score) | 22% |

Key finding: Understanding consent and the power
of yes and no is incredibly protective because it
shows girls how worthy and capable they are.

not their fault. But often that's as far as it goes. However, forcible rape is not the only kind of coercion, and it is not even the most common kind, so this talk leaves a gaping hole in girls' ability to recognize assault. Only 25.9% of our respondents were confident that they had a robust understanding of consent upon finishing high school. *Only one in four.*

We can never guarantee that our girls won't fall victim to predators, but we can make it more likely that they know the red flags so they can be more likely to avoid dangerous people, and more likely that if they ever experience assault, they will realize it was not their fault. So let's look at what your daughter *should* know and the tricky teachings that can undermine her understanding of consent.

## She Should Know: Feeling Safe Takes Precedence over Being Nice

I (Rebecca) had a friend named Taylor who was attractive, bubbly, and magnetic—especially to creepy men.

We often joked about the unwanted attention, but it stopped being funny when one man followed us for a block serenading Taylor on his guitar. What kind of men do that? *Men who don't respect boundaries.* Men who are hoping to make you so uncomfortable that you agree to a date or a kiss because you don't want to be rude. Men who, frankly, are taking advantage of someone's niceness for their own gain.

Although Taylor laughed it off, she was visibly uncomfortable. She'd banter with the men, laugh at their inappropriate jokes, and say, "I'm flattered," all in an attempt to make these men go away. But do you know what she never actually said? "You are being inappropriate and making me uncomfortable. Please leave us alone to finish our meal." When I asked her why she didn't tell the men to leave, she looked at me, confused, and explained, "I don't want to be rude." I asked her if she liked the attention they were giving her, and she snorted and said, "Gosh no." So then I pressed further:

178

"Why is it okay for those men to be rude but it's not okay for you to be firm and not encourage it?" She didn't have an answer.

I was in university when the news broke about a mass killing spree in Toronto. A young man had rammed his van into pedestrians in retribution for being forced into "involuntary celibacy."[3] Women didn't want him, women didn't like him, and so he killed them to get revenge. My university classes (I was a psychology major) talked about him from an anti-bullying perspective. Several male professors pontificated: "Well, if some girls had just been nice to him in high school, maybe he could have turned out differently."

I piped up rather angrily: "What if the reason girls weren't nice to him in high school wasn't because the girls were mean but rather because they could tell he was the kind of guy who would end up ramming a van into girls who didn't want to have sex with him?"

Yes, children should grow up in a world where they are not unnecessarily ostracized, bullied, picked on, or ridiculed simply because they are different. But that needs to be balanced with a careful conversation about how your daughter does not owe flattery and an ego boost to dangerous people, or people who don't respect boundaries.

When I (Joanna) was in junior high, I attended a small Christian school. Almost all of us were at least a little weird, but several boys crossed the line into true social ineptitude. They were often excluded from group activities, and so I tried to include them when I could. Unfortunately, at the first sign of friendliness, several would cross boundaries. I'd receive repeated invasive declarations of love. I stopped feeling safe because they never respected my no. Luckily I had a wonderful teacher whom I went to for help. She deftly put a stop to the whole ordeal. What could have been a long-term problem ended up just a crummy afternoon.

We must teach our daughters how to be kind while recognizing that some people are more dangerous than others. No matter how nerdy, sweet, or innocent someone may seem, if they repeatedly

179

disregard your daughter when she tries to draw boundaries, she needs to know that they are not a safe person and she is not mean, un-Christian, or a snob if she says no and blocks them on social media. It is not your daughter's job to teach anyone—girl or boy, adult or child—to respect her boundaries. Her only job when faced with someone who acts inappropriately toward her is to take steps to ensure her emotional and physical safety. It is not to make sure she's polite.

Studies have found that predators and abusers look for very specific traits when choosing a victim: submissive posture, signs of low self-esteem or naivete, and any signs that a girl or a woman may be deferential or shy.[4] In other words, they look for Taylor—someone who isn't going to make waves, someone who isn't going to speak up when she's uncomfortable, someone who's going to go along with it rather than make a scene.

But there are also behavioral markers that make a girl *less* likely to be targeted: assertive behavior, making direct eye contact instead of hurriedly looking away, being loud and boisterous, pretty much anything that communicates, "I'm not going to put up with your crap."[5]

Now obviously, this is going to come more naturally to some personality types than others. Some girls have naturally had a "don't mess with me" energy since they were nine months old. Your shy, people-pleasing daughter doesn't need to become someone she's not! But every girl needs to know how to deliver a firm, simple no.

Unfortunately, too many messages given to Christian teen girls emphasize their politeness over their safety. In *Every Young Woman's Battle*, girls are told to envision a make-out situation in which a boy tries to go further than she wants to. The advice? "Practice in your mind how you will politely refuse to go there."[6] Dannah Gresh, in *And the Bride Wore White*, gives similar advice, asking girls to come up with ten possible ways to politely stop the make-out progression, perhaps with humor. She gives examples like these: "Isn't it cool that God is watching us every minute?" Or, "Hey, have

I told you that my father dusts me for fingerprints when I get home from a date?"[7] A firm, simple no is not one of the ten suggestions.

Thankfully, *Every Young Woman's Battle* does eventually address a situation in which a boy keeps pushing: "You don't have to be offensive, just invite him to support your boundaries. If he

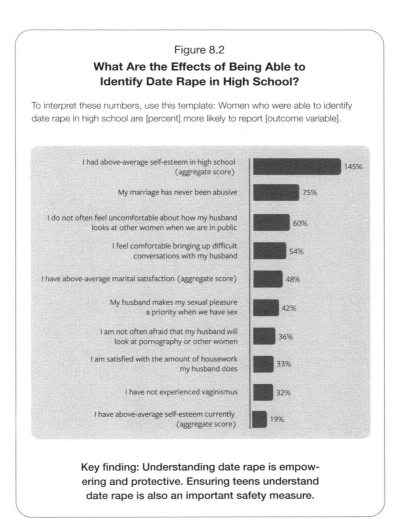

Figure 8.2

**What Are the Effects of Being Able to Identify Date Rape in High School?**

To interpret these numbers, use this template: Women who were able to identify date rape in high school are [percent] more likely to report [outcome variable].

| | |
|---|---|
| I had above-average self-esteem in high school (aggregate score) | 145% |
| My marriage has never been abusive | 75% |
| I do not often feel uncomfortable about how my husband looks at other women when we are in public | 60% |
| I feel comfortable bringing up difficult conversations with my husband | 54% |
| I have above-average marital satisfaction (aggregate score) | 48% |
| My husband makes my sexual pleasure a priority when we have sex | 42% |
| I am not often afraid that my husband will look at pornography or other women | 36% |
| I am satisfied with the amount of housework my husband does | 33% |
| I have not experienced vaginismus | 32% |
| I have above-average self-esteem currently (aggregate score) | 19% |

Key finding: Understanding date rape is empowering and protective. Ensuring teens understand date rape is also an important safety measure.

continues to push your boundaries, trying to get you to do things you don't feel comfortable doing, get offensive if necessary. Let him know that if he can't respect you, he can't spend time with you. Remember, no one else can guard your body and your sexual purity. That's your job."[8] It's wonderful that the authors give girls permission to be offensive—but note that it's still the last resort, not the first. We don't tell girls to give a firm no until they feel very threatened but instead tell them to be polite to the boy who

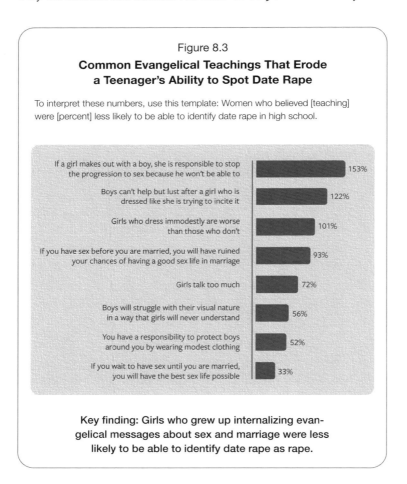

Figure 8.3
**Common Evangelical Teachings That Erode
a Teenager's Ability to Spot Date Rape**

To interpret these numbers, use this template: Women who believed [teaching] were [percent] less likely to be able to identify date rape in high school.

| Teaching | Percent |
| --- | --- |
| If a girl makes out with a boy, she is responsible to stop the progression to sex because he won't be able to | 153% |
| Boys can't help but lust after a girl who is dressed like she is trying to incite it | 122% |
| Girls who dress immodestly are worse than those who don't | 101% |
| If you have sex before you are married, you will have ruined your chances of having a good sex life in marriage | 93% |
| Girls talk too much | 72% |
| Boys will struggle with their visual nature in a way that girls will never understand | 56% |
| You have a responsibility to protect boys around you by wearing modest clothing | 52% |
| If you wait to have sex until you are married, you will have the best sex life possible | 33% |

Key finding: Girls who grew up internalizing evangelical messages about sex and marriage were less likely to be able to identify date rape as rape.

is actively making them uncomfortable right up until it seems he's about to rape them. Our girls need to know they are allowed to say no at *any* time, even if it makes a boy huffy.

That leads us to the next lesson your daughter should know: that boys *can* stop themselves.

## She Should Know: Boys Are Not Sex Fiends

Our propensity to excuse and accept bad behavior from boys can be traced backward to a five-year-old in a ponytail on the playground. From as young as kindergarten, girls are taught that boys are to be held to a lower standard. If a boy pulls a girl's hair, hits her, or throws something at her, it's because he likes her. The behaviors graduate in middle school to calling names, snapping bra straps, and making inappropriate jokes: that's just how boys express themselves when they admire or like a girl.

We are taught to excuse poor behavior from boys simply because we cannot expect them to behave better because of their Y chromosome. Even during puberty, how many of us as girls were told to give our male counterparts patience and grace because girls develop and mature ahead of boys? Contrast that with how few times we heard boys at the same age being told to look to girls for leadership and guidance because of their maturity.

This may lead to innocent consequences like getting pelted with crayons by the boy who has a crush on you in third grade, but the thinking that we need to cater to immaturity and inappropriate behavior from boys simply because they are male can lead to uncomfortable, and even dangerous, situations later in life.

Unfortunately, the church has allowed the idea that boys are incapable of self-control to excuse and even rationalize sexually predatory behavior. Many of our survey respondents reported that they internalized the message that "boys will try to push girls' sexual boundaries," and our research found that married women who had believed this as teenagers are less happy in their marriages and have worse sex lives today (see figure 8.4). Our survey of high school experiences also found that girls who believed this kind of teaching were more likely to experience low self-esteem. This makes sense: if a girl grows up believing that it's her job to make sure boys don't do bad things, then any time a boy hurts her, it's doubly painful because not only has she been mistreated but that mistreatment is also her fault. She takes on guilt she was never meant to have.

This idea that boys are overwhelmed by sexual urges is every-where. Dannah Gresh explains, "They are made to physically yearn for our bodies. That's not to say that you might not experience some of the same yearning for their bodies, but it is usually far more consuming for men."[9] In Shaunti Feldhahn and Lisa Rice's book *For Young Women Only*, the authors dedicate an entire chap-ter to the results of one of the survey questions they asked teenage boys: "Whether or not you are currently involved with a girlfriend, if you were to be in a make-out situation with a willing partner who does not signal a desire to stop, how would you feel about your ability to stop the sexual progression?" Boys could choose one of four possible answers:

- Why would I want to stop the sexual progression? (30%)
- Almost no ability. When the door is opened, it's just too tough to stop the fun. (18%)
- Some ability, but it would require a massive effort, and I might go further than intended. (34%)
- I find it easy to stop the sexual progression. (18%)

Presenting those answers, the authors warn girls that 82% of boys have "little ability" and feel "little responsibility" to stop a sexual progression.[10] (We have plenty of reservations about the wording of the question, the possible answers, and the grouping of 82%, and we don't believe that their conclusions here are accurate, especially since they portray a consensual situation but then make warnings based on nonconsensual ones).[11] In their conclusion of this reported research, the authors quote a teen respondent from their survey: "With a guy, if you want to be able to stop it, it's safest to not even start."[12] But they stop short of interpreting this quote for their readers—is this a warning for teen girls that guys really lack all ability to stop? Or is this a case study of how young men delude themselves into thinking they're not responsible? Readers are not directly told (and the ambiguous effect is amplified as this line is fashioned into a featured pull quote).

Later in the chapter, they do give a caveat for forcible rape. But after spending pages describing to girls just how incapable a boy is of stopping once a girl "allows" him to go past a certain point, a girl may be left feeling that *she* forced *him* to have sex with her by letting him go too far (in fact, we heard this very testimony from multiple women in our focus groups). How is a date rape victim supposed to be able to tease apart those intricacies when Feldhahn and Rice have just spent a chapter giving voice to guys who are repeating rape culture myths? Telling girls that 82% of boys cannot or will not stop in a make-out situation puts the responsibility for stopping on their shoulders. And if the boy doesn't stop? The reader has been told, "For a guy *even more than a girl*, making out often starts a physical drive toward sex that requires a *major* effort to override" (emphasis ours).[13] We believe wholeheartedly that Feldhahn and Rice were simply trying to protect girls from harm by telling them "how guys think."[14] However, we are concerned that this message—that it's harder for boys than for girls to stop the progression—leaves rape victims feeling that they should have done more.

What's especially puzzling is that apparently boys' sexual proclivities are so strong that even Jesus makes no difference. In his introduction to *Every Young Woman's Battle*, Steve Arterburn explains: "Years ago when I was dating, young men used young women like you for their own pleasure. . . . Why am I telling you this? Because I want you to know what guys are like—even Christian guys."[15] He further elaborates: "Believe me—more men than ever are looking at women as objects to be used for their own pleasure. For *every man* it's a battle just to view women in the proper light" (emphasis ours).[16] Actually, no. Not *all* guys want to just use girls for their own pleasure. This is not every man's battle, nor every young's man battle.[17] Christian boys do not sin "naturally, simply by being male."[18]

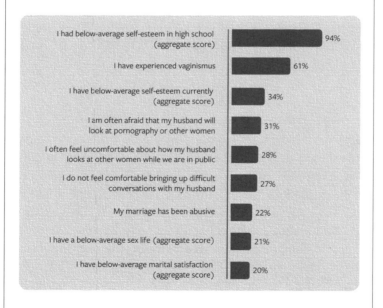

Figure 8.4

**How Does Being the Sexual Gatekeeper Affect Girls Down the Line?**

To interpret these numbers, use this template: Women who believed "if a girl makes out with a boy, she is responsible to stop the progression to sex because he won't be able to" were [percent] more likely to report [outcome variable].

| Outcome | Percent |
|---|---|
| I had below-average self-esteem in high school (aggregate score) | 94% |
| I have experienced vaginismus | 61% |
| I have below-average self-esteem currently (aggregate score) | 34% |
| I am often afraid that my husband will look at pornography or other women | 31% |
| I often feel uncomfortable about how my husband looks at other women while we are in public | 28% |
| I do not feel comfortable bringing up difficult conversations with my husband | 27% |
| My marriage has been abusive | 22% |
| I have a below-average sex life (aggregate score) | 21% |
| I have below-average marital satisfaction (aggregate score) | 20% |

**Key finding:** Not only is being a sexual gatekeeper in high school associated with poor self-esteem in high school, it also inhibits women's later sexual function and marital happiness.

Boys are not made less in the image of God than girls. They do not have less of the Holy Spirit than girls, and frankly, this messaging is denying the cross of Christ. Rather than telling girls that all men and boys will push their boundaries and won't be able to stop themselves, why don't we teach girls that these behaviors are red flags that the guy is dangerous and should be avoided?[19]

Here's another example of this type of messaging, this time from a young man writing to teen girls for *Brio* magazine. Telling the story of being on safari and coming upon a pride of lions, he explains how male sexuality is like a lion's instinct to hunt. Christian girls may just want to get out of the jeep and hug the lions because they're so cute (just like they want an affectionate relationship with Christian boys), but when they dress immodestly, it's like hanging fresh raw steaks around their necks and then approaching the lions. "It doesn't take a rocket scientist to say that you would've ended up on their breakfast menu!"

He concludes the lion analogy with this:

> That's not to say we don't have a responsibility to live self-controlled, pure lives. But a lion is a lion, and a guy is a guy; I don't care who he is. So, help us out. I was the most "godly" young man a parent could ask for. I was truly head-over-heels in love with my Lord and Savior. I prayed at least an hour every day, read and studied my Bible, and felt I was being used by God in my school and community. But I was still a lousy example of what God wanted me to be in my dating life. Give me an inch, and I'd see it as an invitation to go a mile.[20]

Let that last line sink in for a minute. He says, "Give me an inch, and I'd see it as an invitation to go a mile." And whose fault is this? *Girls*, for putting steaks around their necks and forgetting that boys are lions.

At the end of that article, the author announces proudly that he managed to make it to the altar, at age twenty-eight, as a virgin. But given what he's admitted about himself, does he have reason to boast? Personally, we would much rather that our daughters one day marry men who had had enthusiastic consensual sex with willing partners than that they marry someone who had taken a mile from a girl who had wanted to give only an inch. We'd rather they marry someone who wasn't a virgin than someone who technically was—but who also was a predator.

Our daughters need to know that a boy cannot say both, "I was the most 'godly' young man a parent could ask for," and, "I will take more sexually than what you willingly give." Do you know what it's called when a person takes more sexually than someone consented to give? *Assault*. Of course one can be a strong Christian and still struggle with sexual temptation, lust, or porn. But violating consent should not be normalized as succumbing to temptation.

A guy saying, "I am trying to save sex for marriage, so please don't try to push to the edge of my boundaries, because if you want to go all the way, I probably will too. Can we talk about how we can slow things down?" is totally different than him saying, "If you give an inch, I'll see it as an invitation to go a mile." The latter needs to be seen as assault, not as simply a lion nature. Acknowledging an area of weakness and excusing predation are two different things. Yet our evangelical culture has conflated them.

Is it any wonder that so many of our survey respondents reported feeling responsible for boys assaulting them?

- "As a young teen, I was blamed for my brother's friend getting aroused and literally touching me on the leg with his penis. The one time I actually reported a case of someone abusing me, it was turned on me and I was accused of being inappropriately dressed because I had on shorts."
- "I was raped by a high school teacher in a private Christian school and subsequently married him because I believed I had to, that I was damaged goods because I allowed or caused or participated or was complicit in the rape. I wasn't the first or last student he violated."

Your daughter does not need to be told, "Boys can't help themselves." What she needs to know is that she deserves a partner who displays the fruit of the Spirit, which includes self-control. She needs to know that her no is more powerful than any boy's sex drive—and if he continues past her no, it's a sign that he is a predator, not just that he is male.

## She Should Know What Sexual Coercion Looks Like

Not all force is physical—when someone is coerced into sex, that means they are made to do things they wouldn't otherwise do because they were manipulated or pressured until they gave in. Here are some examples of coercive sexual assaults:

1. **Flattery can be a form of coercion.**

   When Vanessa was just thirteen years old, the "it boy" at their local high school took an interest in her at a party. "We chatted for five minutes or so, he paid me lots of attention and asked me if I wanted to go hang out. As soon as we were alone, he started having sex with me. Our clothes weren't even fully off, that's how quickly it started. I didn't even understand how sex worked yet so I was totally unprepared. So was it a violent rape? No. Was I taken advantage of, as a young kid by an older boy? Absolutely. It took me five to ten years to call that what it was. I thought it just meant he liked me."

2. **Using a power imbalance is coercion.**

   When Jules Woodson was seventeen years old, Andy Savage, her twenty-two-year-old youth pastor, offered to drive her home one night after a church event. What happened next has been widely reported in mainstream news.[21] Instead of going straight to her house, Jules says he took her to the woods and told her to perform oral sex on him. She did. The next day, distraught, she reported it to another pastor, who quietly fired Andy while giving him a going away party. Because pastors are in authority and are widely revered in their social circles, they have an ability to manipulate people to do things they otherwise wouldn't.

3. **Gradually wearing a girl down is coercion.**

When Kay was sixteen, she was making out with a boy on a date. "The making out was consensual," Kay explained, "but he started to go past that. I'd ask him to stop, and he'd stop for a bit but then go back to pushing me. He was trying to wear down my resolve. I told him, 'This is the line, and I don't cross it,' and he took it as a challenge. He didn't physically force me to do anything, but he just kept pushing. Eventually, after he repeatedly ignored my nos, I thought to myself, 'I guess if I'm not going to win this, then get it over with.' I realize now he never should have gone past that first no."

A slow erosion of a girl's comfort level is wrong and coercive. And giving up saying no because she realizes her no means nothing is not the same as saying yes.

4. **Overt threats are coercion.**

It is all too common to hear stories of teenagers having sex with their partners under threat that if they don't, their partners will commit suicide, release incriminating photos of them, or spread horrific rumors. Those teens may be "choosing" to have sex rather than face the consequences, but that is still coercive and qualifies as assault.

## She Should Know: Compliance Does Not Equal Consent

When our goal for teens is reduced merely to abstinence, it can cause us to jump to warnings and condemnation rather than gentle questioning when we hear that a teenager has had sex. Unfortunately, this trigger-happy "having sex means you've sinned" mentality can lead to tragic interactions like this one:

A girl wrote in to Focus on the Family's *Brio* magazine for advice. "I'm 15 years old, and I recently lost the most valuable thing in my life—my virginity. I didn't want to do it, but my boyfriend did, so I gave in. . . . I'm totally depressed and I just want to die. Please help.—Ashamed, LaGrangeville, NY." And what was Ashamed from LaGrangeville told?

- "Part of the reason you feel guilty is that you've created a bond that was never supposed to be broken."
- "If you've repented (and repenting with a remorseful heart is pledging not to do this again), God has forgiven you."
- "When [sex is] shared outside of marriage, it invites emotional scars, physical risks (STDs, pregnancy, AIDS), and betrayal."[22]

There is nothing asking if she is okay. There is no suggestion of a suicide hotline. But most of all, there is no acknowledgment that *she may not have actually consented*. Many date rape survivors would describe their encounter using exactly these words. She kept saying no; her no didn't work; so eventually she gave up. That is not consent. Yet *Brio* never even entertains this as a possibility.

In an even more horrifying example, in *When God Writes Your Love Story*, Eric and Leslie Ludy open their chapter "Too Late? A Glimmer of Hope in a World of Lost Virginity" with this story:

One night [sixteen-year-old] Jason invited [twelve-year-old] Rebecca over to his house while his parents were out of town. Rebecca entered Jason's home as an innocent child of twelve, but hours later she left as a used and defiled sex toy. Overnight, Rebecca was forced from childhood into womanhood—but in the most unnatural and heart-wrenching way imaginable. She had lost her virginity before she had even fully developed physically or emotionally. . . . God's heart was breaking for Rebecca *and Jason*. (Emphasis ours)[23]

Instead of using the word *rape*, the authors mourn that her virginity is gone.

When the only message given is "don't have sex," it leaves girls like this twelve-year-old, like Vera (whose story was told at the beginning of this chapter), or like *Brio's* fifteen-year-old letter writer without adequate language to describe what happened to them. Rebecca's husband, Connor, was taught in his secular high school that "anything other than an enthusiastic yes is a no." Rebecca and Joanna never heard that in their youth groups.

Imagine you're volunteering for a youth group event, and a fifteen-year-old girl asks to talk to you privately. She confesses to you that she had sex with her boyfriend last week, and she feels horrible about it. "I didn't want to have sex," she says, "but he just kept touching me and grabbing at me every chance he had. I froze like a deer in headlights; I didn't know what to do. I really wanted him to stop forcing himself on me, but then I got turned on, and suddenly everything got carried away." Would you take the approach of *Brio* magazine and give her a lecture on soul ties? Would you do what Vera's youth leader did and tell her it takes two to tango? Or would you envelop her in a hug and tell her that this was not her fault, that compliance is not the same thing as consent, and that this was her assaulter's crime, not her sin?

We hope, after reading this chapter, that you would do the latter because you recognize the red flags in that story of coercion. We hope you would jump into action to support this girl in getting proper trauma counseling and criminal justice, if she chooses to pursue it.

Unfortunately, that story wasn't made up. One popular book for Christian teen girls tells this story from the author's own life when she was fifteen: "His desires were ones I could not identify with as he groped and grabbed at me every chance he had. I was like a deer in oncoming headlights. I did not know how to respond. I wanted him to stop forcing his desires upon me, yet they had awakened other desires within me."

In her books, she paints this experience as one of the defining moments of her life. She describes it as a "lonely, imprisoning act of sin." She had recurrent nightmares afterward. She resigned from teaching Sunday school and her job as a summer missionary because she didn't feel worthy. She didn't tell anyone about her "sin." Then over a decade after she had "given away the gift that God meant to be [her] husband's," and five years after she had wed, she reported, "I sat for three hours in a dark bedroom with my husband until a tearstained confession could make its way out of my lips." She now uses this story as a precautionary one in her talks, telling girls not to give up their purity the way that she did as a teen.

There's just one big problem. When we read her story, we don't see a girl who went too far and lost her purity. It is important to state that we do not know anything about the author's story beyond what she has written herself, but from a purely outside perspective and from reading the facts presented, we do not read this as a consensual encounter. Rather, this narrative appears to be telling the story of a sexual assault.

Let's examine how the story unfolds:

1. She "could not identify with" his desires (she didn't want this).
2. He "groped and grabbed" at her (sexual assault, since she did not want it and did not say yes).
3. He was "*forcing* his desires" on her (emphasis ours).
4. She felt "like a deer in oncoming headlights" (this is a classic description of the "freeze" part of the "fight, flight, freeze, or fawn" trauma reaction, typical of sexual assaults).
5. Her body had desires "awakened" (arousal).

From a clinical perspective, the first four elements paint a picture of a nonconsensual encounter: she didn't want it, he groped and grabbed anyway, he was forcing himself on her, she froze. So why did the author portray this as *her* sexual sin? Likely because of the fifth element—*her body became aroused*. But does arousal determine whether assault occurred?

## She Should Know about Arousal Non-Concordance

Arousal has two components: the mental component, when your mind says, "Let's have sex!" and the physical component, when your body shows signs of arousal, like lubrication or sensitivity in the erogenous zones. It's wonderful when these two things work in tandem, but quite often they do not. And in the case of sexual assault, it's very common for the body to experience arousal when the mind doesn't want it.[24] In fact, some studies even suggest that the arousal response is especially sensitive to fear,[25] because your brain goes into "fight, flight, freeze, or fawn" mode, in which the body's physiological responses are heightened since you're registering danger.

Because we don't commonly understand this about arousal, we may assume that if a girl became aroused, she must have wanted it. Those who have binge-watched twenty-odd seasons of *Law & Order: Special Victims Unit* may know that's not true, but those in the height of purity culture likely had no idea what "arousal non-concordance" is, with terribly sad results.

Because they were aroused, or because they froze and didn't push the boys off, many young girls assumed that they had consented when in actuality they had been assaulted. Compliance does not equal consent, even if your body responds. Afterward, these same girls then often stopped even trying to say no because they figured they had already "given in and said yes." They figured they had lost their purity. So what was the point of saying no anymore?

Let's use an illustration to clarify this. Picture two people who decide to take a train ride to Albuquerque to spend the weekend. They both buy tickets, pack bags, meet at the train station, walk onto the train, and ride together. That's consent!

Now imagine that he wants to go to Albuquerque, but she doesn't. He tries to convince her; she says no. He begs and cajoles; she still says no. But he asks her to help him pack his bag, and she figures that if she does that maybe he'll be satisfied and back off. He asks her to come to the train station to see him off, and she complies, again hoping that's the end of it. But while there, he handcuffs her to the train seat and forces her to come to Albuquerque with him.

Even if in the middle of that trip she looks out those train windows and says to herself, "Huh, train rides are kind of fun"; even if she gets off the train in Albuquerque of her own accord and allows him to show her the city; even if the next time he asks her to go to Albuquerque she goes without the handcuffs, figuring, "Well, I've already been once, I may as well go again"—*none of that negates the fact that she got to Albuquerque to begin with only because she was kidnapped.* Had he not kidnapped her, she never would have gone in the first place and thus wouldn't have returned on subsequent weekends.

Again, we do not know what happened with the author beyond what she herself wrote. Perhaps this was a fully consensual relationship. But the words she uses in her book describe a nonconsensual date rape situation—the very definition of sexual assault. They appear to tell the story of a sexually traumatized girl who

---

### DARVO and Consent

**Deny**—"If you had really wanted to not have sex, you would have stopped him."

**Attack**—"What were you expecting dating a non-Christian? It takes two to tango."

**Reverse Victim and Offender**—"Once boys get started, they can't stop without help. 'If you want to be able to stop, it's safest to not even start.'[26] You put him in an impossible position, and you should have known better."

didn't know how to handle the trauma and so became revictimized. Even if that does not accurately reflect her experience, what is the effect on readers like Vera or Kay that this encounter is framed as a sin instead of as an assault?

Your daughter needs to know about arousal non-concordance. We need to allow girls to properly name what happened to them, because when we don't, then all too often they go back and punish themselves over and over again.

In books like *For Young Women Only*, girls read messages from guys like, "If you want to be able to stop it, it's safest to not even start."[27] Vera's youth pastor says, "What do you expect? You were dating a non-Christian." Steve Arterburn says that even Christian guys want to use girls for their own pleasure.[28]

Rather than teaching girls a holistic understanding of consent, evangelical teachers have typically framed assault as a natural con-

### But I Could Have Prevented It

Most victims of sexual assault can think back to things they could have done differently that might have led to a different outcome. Not going to that party, not being alone with that boy, not getting in the car.

We frequently hear women say things like, "Even though I know it was assault, I still feel so guilty because I never should have started making out with him in the first place."

Just because you theoretically could have prevented the assault doesn't mean that you caused it in any way, shape, or form. No matter how many what-ifs you can think of, there was always one decision that could have been made that makes all the pontificating pointless: He could have chosen not to assault you.

A victim of sexual assault is in no way responsible for the offence against them. No matter what the scenario, there's only one defining decision that turned it from an encounter to an assault: the perpetrator decided to assault.

sequence of girls "letting" boys go too far. It's like we're so afraid that our girls will have consensual sex that we scare them into thinking that every boy is going to rape them. And then, when a boy actually does, the implication is that it's their fault and they should have known better.

Our girls deserve better than this.

They deserve to know about consent, red flags, and boundaries. Yes, we want our girls to set healthy boundaries for themselves. But they also need to know that those who try to cross them are dangerous.

## MOTHER-DAUGHTER
### SECTION

This is an important chapter. It's also a really heavy one, so often we as moms don't want to talk about this kind of stuff with you, our daughters. It's hard to acknowledge sexual assault as moms since we want to be able to pretend that our daughters are living in a world where this isn't a threat. But you know what that often leads to? You, the teenagers, not having the information you need to identify coercion, define consent, or recognize assault if it's happening to you or a friend.

You matter, and it is not rude, mean, or selfish to stand up for yourself, even if it makes someone else really uncomfortable. You do not matter less than anyone else—and if someone is putting you in danger or even just making you feel unsafe, they deserve to reap the consequences of that.

If someone is unwilling to take responsibility for their own sexual actions and put the brakes on, this is a red flag. If someone is not able to hear your no without having a hissy fit, this is a red flag. If someone is happy to shuttle the blame for crossing boundaries onto your side of the relationship, this is a red flag. All these things are signs that this person has unhealthy views about sexual entitlement and probably doesn't fully understand consent. You can date someone better! So let's talk about consent.

 **What You Need to Know**

### What Is Consent?

Consent isn't often talked about in church because many are worried that if we teach kids what consent means, they're going to start having sex. But consent is important to understand so that you can identify sexual coercion and make sure you never coerce someone yourself. Here's a handy short form: consent isn't just not saying no; it's an enthusiastic yes. Anything else isn't good enough. In other words, "I guess" isn't a yes. Make sure to read through the section on pages 189–90 under the heading "She Should Know What Sexual Coercion Looks Like" to learn about different ways coercion can erode your ability to say no.

### What Is Arousal Non-Concordance?

Sometimes people believe that if they physically felt good while having sex (got turned on, had an orgasm), that means they consented and it wasn't assault. However, that's not actually true—what happens physically and what happens mentally are not always connected. That's called *arousal non-concordance*. Arousal non-concordance can also happen with pornography—you see violent sexual acts or strange sexual behaviors that you are disgusted by, but your body still responds. This does not mean that you're actually attracted to what's on the screen or that you're a porn addict. This kind of material is designed to arouse people, and you're not strange if your body responds.

**Quiz**

From the list below, can you tell which ones are examples of coercion and which ones are not?

1. Your boyfriend wants to have sex with you.
2. Your boyfriend says if you don't have sex with him, he'll break up with you.
3. You're making out and your boyfriend gets an erection.
4. You're making out and your boyfriend puts his hand under your shirt. You say no, he stops, but then five minutes later he tries again. This happens several times.
5. You're dating a guy who also wants to save sex for marriage, but you really enjoy feeling powerful when you get him turned on. He's told you that he doesn't want you to touch him like that, but you sneak it in while you're kissing just to see the effect it has on him.
6. A year ago, you sent a picture you now regret to a boy you liked. He says he'll show it to others unless you send him another one.
7. You've been secretly dating your twenty-four-year-old gymnastics coach for the last year, and you're sure you're going to marry him when you're old enough. He invites you to his apartment, and you're so excited that your first time is going to be with him.
8. You and your boyfriend were making out and you went a little further than planned, but you both were able to stop when you realized "holy crap, what are we doing?"
9. You were making out for a while, and your boyfriend started getting really physical really fast. You froze, but he kept going even though you tried to squirm away. You were panicking, but at some point your body started enjoying what was happening

even as you knew you didn't want to be doing this. You ended up having sex, and you feel incredibly guilty.

**Answer Key:** (1) Not coercion unless he tries to force or pressure you. You're allowed to have different desires as long as you don't infringe on each other's boundaries. (2) Coercion, and a sign you should break up. (3) Not coercion; bodies are gonna do what bodies do! (4) Coercion. Sometimes we can go further than intended, but if someone is repeatedly violating your clear boundaries, that's a problem. (5) Coercion. You are not honoring his boundaries. (6) Co-ercion, and this is a bigger situation than you can handle on your own. Please tell an adult, even if it's embarrassing. (7) Coercion. Adults do not date children, and especially not in secret. (8) Not coercion, and you can brainstorm together some ways to make it easier to stick by your convictions together. (9) Coercion. If you say no, it means no. If you don't say yes, it also means no. Sometimes when we are trauma-tized, our bodies freeze up, and sometimes they even respond sexually when we are frightened. This does not mean you consented.

## 🔍 *Spot the Tricky Teaching*

This time you're going to try to find some tricky teachings from a real-world scenario. Reread Vera's story that opened this chapter.

### DAUGHTERS

What tricky teachings did Vera hear from church leaders? How did those affect her?

### MOMS

If you were Vera's mom, what would you have said to her? What would you want her to know?

One of the biggest roadblocks many girls have to understanding consent is the tricky teaching that "boys will be boys." Here are some ways you may hear this:

- If you want a guy to stop, it's safer to not even start.[29]
- Boys reach a point of no return where they can't stop themselves.
- All boys will want to push your sexual boundaries.
- Boys only want one thing.
- If you give him an inch, he'll see it as an invitation to take a mile.

### DISCUSS TOGETHER

What is tricky about each of these teachings? Is there any truth to any of these teachings? How could these teachings lead to a scenario in which a boy is let off the hook for assaulting someone?

### DAUGHTERS

Have you heard any of these? Who did you hear them from?

### MOMS

How do these statements make you feel? What do you want your daughter to know about them?

## What Would You Do?

At some point, you're likely going to have to say no in some uncomfortable situations. Let's work through some potential scenarios.

### Scenario 1

You're sitting on a bus and a man is leering at you and trying to chat you up. He's making you very uncomfortable, and you're in a public place. What do you do?

201

### Scenario 2

You're at a coffee shop studying for a test and an older man sits down at your table and tells you you're really cute. He asks for your number, and everything about this is feeling really creepy. What do you do?

### Scenario 3

You keep getting texts from a classmate that are very sexual in nature. You find his hidden blog online where he has written erotic poetry about you. You feel he has massively crossed a line. What do you do?

### Scenario 4

You want to go on a youth overnight trip, but you know that Grant, a boy who raped your friend at a party last month, will be going. You're not comfortable being somewhere overnight with him, but the leaders aren't taking it seriously that this boy is a threat to girls. They defend him going by saying, "He needs to know Jesus." You know that there are other girls going on this trip. What do you do?

# 9

## She Deserves to Exist as a Person, Not as a Threat

*Your Daughter Is Not a Stumbling Block*

In my (Rebecca's) preteen years, my family spent six weeks every spring practicing for our homeschool group's track and field competition. The parents took turns starting us off with warm-up stretches. One particular mom began with a warning to the girls about appropriate attire, insisting that shirts shouldn't be more than two inches below the collarbone and demonstrating how to measure with our hands. All of us were encouraged to verify right then and there that we weren't offending anyone.

That was the first time my mom (Sheila) had ever heard specific modesty rules suggested, but I had already been hearing them for years through reading *Brio*.

Modesty rules were the hot topic during Joanna's and my formative years in the church. Secret Keeper Girl, Dannah Gresh's curriculum for mothers and daughters that taught girls about "their worth in God," was in its heyday during those middle school years, focusing extensively on making sure girls stayed covered up. It was difficult to find an edition of *Brio* from when we were growing up that didn't include at least one mention of modesty or tips for how to be fashionable without showing "too much." Our favorite Christian girl bands wrote articles on how they created fashionable looks for their concerts that kept them covered up. The phrase "modest is hottest" appeared on T-shirts, and churches hosted modesty fashion shows. The popular *Rebelution* website even conducted its own survey in which guys of all ages could tell girls exactly what got them going, including when girls walked with too much bounce in their step. See, it made their chest bounce,

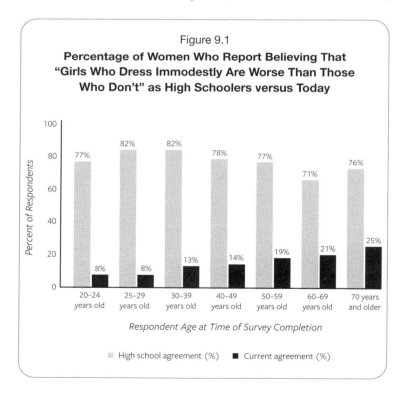

Figure 9.1

**Percentage of Women Who Report Believing That "Girls Who Dress Immodestly Are Worse Than Those Who Don't" as High Schoolers versus Today**

*Respondent Age at Time of Survey Completion*

High school agreement (%)  ■ Current agreement (%)

causing 76% of guys to call walking with too much pep immodest.[1] I remember other advice from the Rebelution survey, such as avoiding going outside with wet hair lest it remind a boy that you may have showered and so may have been naked recently.[2]

But today, modest is no longer hottest. Or at least *saying* "modest is hottest" can get you into hot water.

In June 2021, singer and songwriter Matthew West debuted his song "Modest Is Hottest," in which he played an overprotective dad crooning to his daughters. Though he claimed it was only satire, it doubled down on modesty messages—that girls should cover up, that boys are only interested in one thing, and that girls who show more are worth less. The internet pushback was immense and swift.[3] Women and men alike spoke up in droves, angered that this mentality was being passed on to the next generation. West soon took the song down.

We doubt that pushback would have happened even five years prior, but the cultural conversation is shifting. We're starting to realize the dangers of an overemphasis on girls' modesty, and many of us have rejected those modesty teachings altogether (see figure 9.1).

### The Effects of the Modesty Message

Many of you likely grew up with strict modesty rules: teachers having you kneel and measuring hemlines from the floor, rules about covering your shoulders, church memos warning against two-piece bathing suits at the youth retreat. This is not a fringe concept, nor one exclusive to evangelical Christianity. News headlines about girls being sent home for dress code violations proliferate, and researchers are concerned that dress codes end up sexualizing the very teenagers they are designed to protect. One study found that dress codes end up being enforced more often for bigger busted girls than for girls with smaller busts, even when the same amount of skin is showing or the same items of clothing are being worn.[4] What does this tell girls? It tells them it's not actually about the clothes—it's about their bodies. It says, "You are sexual in a way your peers are not, and your body is inherently dangerous."

Perhaps that's why the backlash to West's culturally tone-deaf song was so strong—so many had heard the modesty message, internalized it, and suffered for it, and now they were seeing it repeated to the next generation. And yet, too often when people like West are called out for promoting harmful teachings, they seem eager to paint themselves as the victim of yet another abuse victim's triggered outrage. As Christian commentator Allie Beth Stuckey said on Matthew West's podcast, where the two discussed the "modest is hottest" debacle, "When there are people who elevate *their* truth above *the* truth then everything is personal. Lived experience trumps any kind of objectivity."[5] They framed the pushback not as legitimate correction but rather as an emotional overreaction due to people's prior abuse.

Here's what West and Stuckey don't seem to understand: it wasn't that women were projecting their hurt from past traumas onto the modesty message; *it's that modesty messages themselves cause trauma.* We measured three different iterations of the modesty message:

1. Girls who dress immodestly are worse than those who don't. (In our survey, we did not define "worse" but let respondents define this in their own minds.)
2. Boys can't help but lust after a girl who is dressed like she is trying to incite it.
3. You have a responsibility to protect boys around you by wearing modest clothing.

Our survey found that if girls believed any of these three messages in high school, their self-esteem took a hit. That hit continued even into adulthood, even if they don't believe the messages today. These modesty teachings lead to bad fruit.

Obviously no one was setting out to harm people by spreading the modesty message. But your daughter may still be exposed to some harmful messages by unwitting teachers. Here's how you, as a mom, can teach her where her worth really lies.

### She Should Know: The Clothes Do Not Make the Girl

Sheila here—when Rebecca was twelve and her sister was ten, I went to the local Christian bookstore to find a mother-daughter study that I could use with them. There, on a large display, were bright blue *Secret Keeper Girl* manuals. Because of its inviting cover filled with pictures of grinning young girls, I plopped down my credit card and exited the store.

I had thought I was buying a Bible study. And though the book advertises itself as a curriculum that teaches girls how to discover their worth in Christ, the back cover (which, in retrospect, I should have read more carefully) says it answers questions like: "Just what is real physical beauty? What's the source of beauty? How can I feel it? Why do I have to dress modestly? So, how do I know if I'm dressed modestly? Who is most likely to influence my sense of style . . . for good or for bad? Am I enhancing or distracting from my beauty with what's inside?" The bestselling Christian material for preteen girls was almost entirely about . . . *how they look*. Even their character ("what's inside") is judged based on how it detracts or adds to their outer beauty.

In the very first of eight mother-daughter dates, *Secret Keeper Girl* asks girls to label themselves as disposable or indispensable based on how they dress. Dannah Gresh instructs the girls: "Decide in each category whether you are a Styrofoam cup, a ceramic mug, or a price-less teacup."[6] Then moms are prompted to ask their daughters, "Do you ever see girls presenting themselves as trashable in any of these ways? (The ways that we dress, talk, act, or the places we're willing to go.)"[7] *Literally one of the first things girls are asked to do is think about which of their friends is the trashiest.* When I originally saw the instructions to moms to prepare for this first date, I was excited because it needed china teacups, and I have fifty family heirlooms from my grandmother. But then I saw what the Styrofoam cup was supposed to represent. We got halfway through the first study and I tossed it aside, telling Rebecca and Katie it wasn't for us. I didn't want them to start thinking about the girl down the street who wore Spice Girl crop tops and just desperately needed love like she was "trashable." (Note: this exercise remains in Gresh's 2021 book, *8 Great Dates for Moms and Daughters,* a rebranded version of *Secret Keeper Girl.*[8])

Now, we seriously doubt that *Secret Keeper Girl,* and now the rebranded version, intended to teach girls that their worth is based on how they dress. But it's not difficult to follow the logic: If wearing a shirt that shows my belly means I am disposable, and that's not how a girl who follows God would act, then that girl over there in a crop top is not a good Christian. She is more disposable than I am because my belly is covered up. All the caveats in the world that our worth is unchanging mean nothing when paired with repeated warnings that how we dress can quickly morph us from china cups to Styrofoam garbage.

Our young girls were told that they have inherent value and worth, but it was often with an asterisk: *your inner worth is revealed by what you do with your outer body.* By the continuous pairing of the Christian life of a young girl with the policing of what she wears, teenagers learned that an immodest neckline overshadows a girl's wisdom, courage, or insight. They were taught that clothing shows character.

Secret Keeper Girl wasn't just a curriculum though. It was also a huge event where hundreds of moms and girls would crowd into a gym or church for a fashion show, a chance to bond, and instructions on how to be modest. Gresh's modesty teachings shaped a generation of evangelical girls—those girls who are today's Sunday school teachers and youth group leaders. We asked on our Facebook page if anyone had been to a Secret Keeper Girl event and, if they had, what stood out most to them. Many women told us that they loved hearing they were God's princesses, and those messages made them feel special and cherished. Nevertheless, there was a great big *but* coming: these women also reported overwhelmingly that they came away from the events with new attitudes toward their peers. "It made me much more judgmental of other girls," one told us. Another said, "I would look down on girls who I felt dressed inappropriately. It made me start judging all of the other girls at youth group."

In recent years Gresh has admitted that there were some problems with her original Secret Keeper Girl curriculum, especially the emphasis on the word *modesty* and keeping secrets. Replying to a Facebook commenter, Gresh explained her new approach: "We have grown and use the word modesty less and less. And words like appropriate and dignity more and more."[9]

We are thrilled to see an author grappling with the damaging message they inadvertently spread, and we applaud Gresh's bravery in doing so. But what if the modesty versus dignity change is a distinction without a difference? Today, teachers and influencers simply work the Christianese so that their messages don't *sound* legalistic—even though they may be even more strict than messages were fifteen or twenty years ago.

- Bethany Beal and Kristen Clark from Girl Defined say, "We can dress in a way that reflects virtue, honor, and dignity. We can dress in a way that reflects respect for ourselves, for our King, and for those around us."[10] They also advocate for wearing boys' basketball shorts instead of girls' shorts, and making sure your shoulders are covered.
- Allie Beth Stuckey says that talking about modesty is important, "because the same God also says that we should clothe ourselves in the new self, put on righteousness."[11] This sounds lovely, but there is no "righteousness" aisle in the clothing section at Target.
- The updated version of Gresh's *Secret Keeper Girl* book (*8 Great Dates for Moms and Daughters*) admonishes their eight-to-twelve-year-old audience: "God created you and

me incredibly beautifully. Women are alluring, interesting, intoxicating, attractive, and a lot of other powerful things. We can use those powers to bring attention to ourselves, or we can dress with dignity so nothing distracts from our primary purpose to bring attention to God."[12]

Is this new way of talking about modesty better? Certainly we want to be dignified and respect ourselves. But what does it mean to "clothe ourselves in the new self"? To dress in a way that brings attention to God? What does it mean for clothing to be, as Girl Defined says, "a representation of Christ shedding his blood to save us?"[13] *And what if legalistic rules about hemlines weren't the main problem?* At least when the homeschooling mom told girls to make sure their necklines did not dip more than two fingers lower than their clavicles, there was an objective measure. Now it's entirely subjective. *"Everleigh, you can wear that if you want, we're not legalistic after all, but I encourage you to ask yourself: Does that outfit say 'gospel' to you?"*

We believe there's a fundamental misunderstanding of how and why the modesty message harmed girls. It wasn't just that girls felt shamed by specific rules; it was that a girl's faith was reduced to her clothing choices. It was the fact that modesty discussions taught young girls that being a woman of valor was less about being brave or wise or insightful and more about choosing the right neckline. And unfortunately, that message hasn't changed. It has simply been cloaked in more spiritual-sounding words. (And don't worry, we'll help you have these conversations with your daughter in a minute.) Now let's look at why people reacted badly to telling teenage girls that dressing in turtlenecks is best.

### She Should Know: She Is Not a Walking Temptation to Be Used by Satan

A 2007 *Brio* article taught how to alter 60s-style mod dresses to make them modest. The article concludes with a warning about wearing these over leggings: "These short dresses make a guy want to see more of a girl's body, so Satan can use you as a walking temptation to make guys sin. As Christian girls, our goal should be to prevent sin, not encourage it!"[14] *Walking temptation to make guys sin.* Wow.

But this attitude from *Brio* that girls can "make" guys sin simply by donning a too-short skirt persists. Shaunti Feldhahn, in a 2019 article titled "A Letter to Our Teenage Daughters about How They Dress," says this to young girls:

> Instantly, even the most honorable guy is instinctively tempted to want to visually take in, linger on and fantasize about all the details of this great body he's seeing. . . . So if you dress in a barely-there outfit, not only your date but every other guy in the room (and not to freak you out, but EVEN the dads who are there at the picture party) sees you, notices how little you're wearing and has the same temptation.[15]

Feldhahn then drives the "even the adults" rhetoric home:

> Also, keep in mind that this is not just your date or your boyfriend. This is any guy—all your guy friends from school, your friend's brother, his father, and the total strangers at the restaurant while you're eating dinner before the dance. One told us, "When we see a hot girl, the first 10 seconds of a guy's thoughts are pretty raw. We go straight into fantasy mode. And we have to really work to pull things back."[16]

Although Feldhahn adds a caveat in her post that she is not blaming girls for boys' poor behavior, her caveat is invalidated when a takeaway from the article is that girls need to help grown men not have predatory thoughts about their developing, peri-pubescent bodies. The rest of the article, other than that small caveat, tells girls that their sexual objectification by men is a "biological" reaction, that at the sight of an immodestly dressed girl, "a part of his brain called the *nucleus accumbens* is automatically stimulated," and that even if a man *wants* to honor a girl by not thinking of her sexually, he is biologically unable to do so, unless "you're not calling overt attention to your body." Yes, Feldhahn says she's not blaming girls, but "if the dress is a bit longer, the top less revealing, or you're wearing something that covers more of the leggings, that center in his brain isn't biologically triggered, and that temptation doesn't arise in the same way."[17] So a young girl reading this might hear that it's not her fault *but also that she alone can prevent it.* That it's totally his choice, *but it's a biological response to seeing her body that he has no control over because this is how God made him.* That it's not his fault because he can't help it; it's hers because she could have prevented it. *But no one's blaming her.* See how confusing it is?

This rhetoric, that men cannot help but be sexually ravenous at the sight of a girl showing some skin, is particularly nefarious when you consider its effects on girls who have been sexually assaulted. We heard from many different women in our surveys and focus groups who, after their rape, thought *they* had harmed the *boy* by *forcing him* to assault her by wearing too immodest clothing!

- "I would tell him I didn't like it [when he forced me to give him a hand job] and I asked him to stop and he would tell me that he couldn't help it and I was hurting *him* by wearing revealing clothes, so he was taken over. He said he needed my help to stop assaulting me, and if I kept dressing like that I knew what I was doing." (She was thirteen at the time, and was wearing a T-shirt and sweatpants.)

- "I kept telling him I didn't want to go further, but he kept pushing. Eventually I felt I had to give in because hadn't I made this happen? I knew this skirt was too short, if I had simply worn a different skirt maybe he would have been able to stop."

- "I was harassed and assaulted by several boys in my childhood and teen years. . . . It finally occurred to me that maybe all this nonsense about boys being unable to control themselves was actually true, maybe the assaults were my fault for being too friendly or flirty or provocative or opinionated, *maybe my own body was the problem.* . . . In college, I developed crippling social anxiety and PTSD, *changed my wardrobe*, and agonized over every decision (Is this the right, godly choice? Can I trust my own instincts?)" (emphasis ours).

I hope that we can all agree that blaming a girl for her own assault, regardless of clothing, is evil and abhorrent. So how did we get to the point, as a church, where girls are internalizing that if they are raped, they may have *forced* the boys to do so simply by having a female body in their presence?

### She Should Know: The Difference between Girls' and Boys' "Visual Natures" Has Been Overblown

We've taught both boys and girls this simple axiom: boys are visual in a way girls aren't. Sure, some women are visually stimulated, but it's nothing compared to what men go through on a daily basis. In fact, this is such a widespread message that over 85.8% of our survey respondents believed this in high school.

What is the basis for this belief? Much of the rhetoric, including from Shaunti Feldhahn herself,[18] comes from the work of neuroscientist Louann Brizendine, a pop-psychology author who has written books on the differences between male and female brains. At the time of publication fifteen years ago, they were scoffed at by the scientific community (a simple Google search will show you this; go ahead and search "Louann Brizendine scientific review" and scan the results from scientists). As the prestigious journal *Nature* says about her book *The Female Brain*, Brizendine "disappointingly fails to meet even the most basic standards of scientific accuracy and balance."[19] This is the "overwhelming research" on which evangelicalism has built its theology of male libido: a neuroscientist who was laughed out of the scientific community over a decade ago.[20]

In contrast, here's what today's scientific consensus actually says: Men's and women's brains are far more similar than they are different.[21] Much of the way that we react to visual stimuli is dependent on culture and the meaning that we give to it, meaning it's not a biological imperative designed by God. Women react visually to sexual stimuli as well—they're just less likely to report subjectively feeling aroused, even if arousal begins in their body.[22] Modern neuroscience meta-analyses have found that the difference within genders is far larger than the difference between genders. In other words, women are more different from each other individually than women as a whole are different from men as a whole.[23] Yet we have no problem believing that we can understand our fellow womenfolk.

By insisting that boys are visual and boys are tempted to lust in a way that girls never can be, we don't just cause girls to feel shame for boys' sin. We also leave girls who find boys' bodies alluring feeling like they're some kind of sex-crazed freaks. The idea that visual lust is merely a male battle is becoming obsolete in our increasingly sexualized culture. And yet, how many Sunday school teachers and youth leaders still have the mentality that girls don't struggle with sexual sin?

But if the science behind this evangelical belief is bunk, what about the theological arguments? Let's take a look.

### She Needs to Know: She Has the Right to Exist in a Female Body

The prevailing theological argument for modesty hinges on the idea that girls can "make boys sin." Even as recently as January 2022, when we posted that we should not tolerate grown men lusting after fourteen-year-olds, commenters turned the tables:

- "Perhaps we should look at both sides of it! The man could certainly be a problem, but many men see ladies dressed immodestly and have bad thoughts without meaning to. As women we need to protect both our heart and the hearts of good men by covering our body in a way that is pleasing to God."
- "How about we teach girls and women to have self-respect so that they don't feel the need to show their cleavage, tight pants, etc., etc.? Can we at least address BOTH sides of this issue?"

Why is it that girls dressing immodestly is considered "equally important" as the men in churches sexually objectifying children and women? Because according to this mindset, both are sinning equally. The men are lusting, sure; but by dressing immodestly, women and children can be *stumbling blocks* to men and boys by enticing that lust. After all, they say, Paul himself warns, "Be careful, however, that the exercise of your rights does not become a stumbling block to the weak" (1 Cor. 8:9). If men can't help but, in the words of Feldhahn, "visually take in, linger on and fantasize about all the details of this great body he's seeing,"[24] then the logic flows that the fourteen-year-old girl has sinned against the forty-two-year-old man who lusted after her.

But is that really what the Bible passages about stumbling are all about? What if chastising girls for causing lust actually becomes a stumbling block for *girls*? One woman shared:

When I was sixteen, I was told to put a sweater on at Christian school because my figure was causing a male teacher to stumble. I was dressed within our dress code and nothing inappropriate was showing. I matured early and there was no hiding it, nor should I have had to. My parents tried to find a solution with that staff member and his solution was for me to get to school early so that we could "pray for my soul" together before classes started. Luckily my parents had discernment and pulled me out of that school, but I was ashamed of my body and have struggled since with body image, allowing true intimacy in my marriage, etc. as a result of that experience.

In this scenario, who is putting up a stumbling block to someone's faith? The sixteen-year-old girl just trying to get through puberty, or the adult male teacher who is in a position of authority over this child he is lusting after?

How many teen girls have been shamed at church or Christian schools for causing pastors, elders, or teachers to lust? If we want

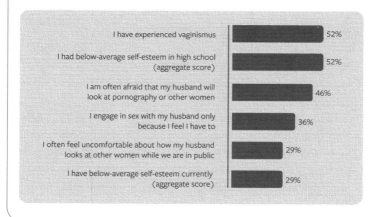

Figure 9.2
**The Effects of Various Iterations of the Modesty Message**

To interpret these numbers, use this template: Women who believed [message] in high school were [percent] more likely to report [outcome variable].

**The Effects of the Message: "Boys Can't Help but Lust after a Girl Who Is Dressed Like She Is Trying to Incite It"**

| Outcome | Percent |
| --- | --- |
| I have experienced vaginismus | 52% |
| I had below-average self-esteem in high school (aggregate score) | 52% |
| I am often afraid that my husband will look at pornography or other women | 46% |
| I engage in sex with my husband only because I feel I have to | 36% |
| I often feel uncomfortable about how my husband looks at other women while we are in public | 29% |
| I have below-average self-esteem currently (aggregate score) | 29% |

### The Effects of the Message: "Girls Who Dress Immodestly Are Worse Than Those Who Don't"

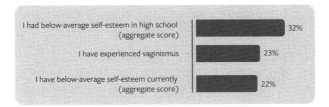

| | |
|---|---|
| I had below-average self-esteem in high school (aggregate score) | 32% |
| I have experienced vaginismus | 23% |
| I have below-average self-esteem currently (aggregate score) | 22% |

### The Effects of the Message: "You Have a Responsibility to Protect Boys around You by Wearing Modest Clothing"

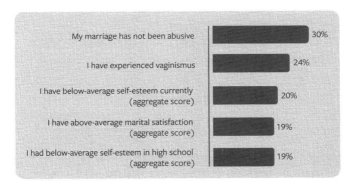

| | |
|---|---|
| My marriage has not been abusive | 30% |
| I have experienced vaginismus | 24% |
| I have below-average self-esteem currently (aggregate score) | 20% |
| I have above-average marital satisfaction (aggregate score) | 19% |
| I had below-average self-esteem in high school (aggregate score) | 19% |

### The Effects of the Message: "Boys Will Struggle with Their Visual Nature in a Way Girls Will Never Understand"

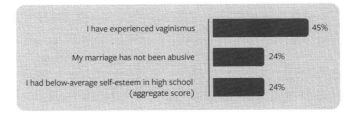

| | |
|---|---|
| I have experienced vaginismus | 45% |
| My marriage has not been abusive | 24% |
| I had below-average self-esteem in high school (aggregate score) | 24% |

Key finding: Even if there were some protective elements, every iteration of the modesty message that we measured resulted in overwhelmingly negative long-term effects for high school girls.

to use the "don't cause a weaker brother to stumble" passages to address modesty dress codes, we must be intellectually honest and recognize that when we tell children they have "caused" grown men to lust, we have actually caused *girls'* faith to weaken by saying there is something inherently evil about their bodies.

In fact, our survey results found that believing modesty messages led to some pretty rotten fruit. If a girl believed in high school that she was at least partially responsible for stopping male sin, she was:

- 1.68 times more likely to end up in a sexually abusive marriage,
- 1.57 times more likely to end up in a verbally abusive marriage,
- 1.52 times more likely to end up experiencing vaginismus.

The fruit is bad for our girls. But let's take it one step further and look at another passage about stumbling. Matthew 18:6–9 tells us that for those who cause a little one to stumble, it would be better for them to "have a large millstone hung around their neck and to be drowned in the depths of the sea." Let's say that one morning Monica gets dressed wearing an outfit that she feels pretty in. It fits her figure nicely, and the color makes her eyes pop. She feels confident as she heads off on the school bus.

Now imagine that Jordan sees Monica and notices how the sweater hugs her breasts. He starts imagining what's under the fabric and finds himself daydreaming during English class about sexual encounters with her. Monica was not intentionally causing Jordan to lust; Monica didn't even get dressed with the intention of attracting Jordan; Monica just wanted to feel pretty. But if we believe the "stumbling block" mentality around modesty, then what we're really saying is this: *Some people, even if they love God with their heart, soul, mind, and strength, will cause people to sin simply by existing in their vicinity.* And what does Jesus say about stumbling blocks like that? *It would be better for them to have a millstone tied around their neck and be thrown into the sea.* Do we really believe that a girl, whose only fault is existing in her own body, would be better off if she were thrown into the sea because of the effect she has on the boys around her?

We would hope not! Yet, logically, that is where this argument goes. The modesty message says that men's right to exist without women's bodies near them is greater than women's right to exist in a woman's body. Is it any wonder the stumbling block message wreaks such havoc on self-esteem?

Interestingly, the words of Jesus put the responsibility on Jordan, not Monica. Matthew 18:9 says, "If your eye causes you to stumble, gouge it out." Jesus never lays the responsibility for sin at someone else's feet. And we need to stop laying the blame for boys' or men's lust at the feet of our daughters.

One Christian Reddit thread blew up last year when a sixteen-year-old girl wrote in turmoil about having to delete her Instagram when her father wanted to become a deacon at their church. Members of the board of elders saw her feed and felt it was inappropriate. What was it that offended them? She explains:

> Some of the photos were a few years old too, and the photos they mentioned were from me in gymnastics and on family vacations and how my bathing suit at the beach was "inappropriate" when I'm not even allowed to wear a two-piece. . . . In regards to the specific gymnastics photos they pointed out, they weren't even photos that I took. They were from one of my meets where they hired a photographer, and I only posted some of them because my team did well. They said it was inappropriate because "it's easy for others to take things out of context."[25]

Apparently, she ended up deleting her Instagram and her Facebook accounts because she was creeped out by adult men scouring

219

them, looking at her then-thirteen-year-old body in a sexual way. But then she was asked to have a meeting with the women of the church and the elders because she deleted "with the wrong mindset."

So she is not allowed to enjoy memories of her family vacation. She is robbed of the ability to feel proud of the hard work she put into gymnastics, and instead she is shamed for sharing her memories of success. Why? Because adult men on a board of elders might

### What If a Woman Tells You You're a Stumbling Block?

If this modesty message that tells girls their bodies are dangerous is so harmful to women, why do so many *women* still teach it? We ran the numbers and found that women who believe the modesty message today are four times more likely to believe other measures of internalized misogyny (more on that in chapter 10). They are also 55% more likely to report that their marriage has been abusive.[26] For some women, the modesty message may be a trauma response: "If we stay modest, maybe we can stay safe." They are trying to protect out of a place of hurt.

But there are other reasons too. Maybe the men in their lives really are unsafe and lustful people, and these women don't know that men can be different. Maybe these women are married to men whom they love but who struggle with lusting after young girls, and it's easier to blame the women and girls than it is to face a reality that their husbands may have a sexual sin problem. Maybe it's that these women, like so many others in the evangelical church, have been taught that noticing attractiveness is the same as experiencing lust (see *The Great Sex Rescue* for the research on that!).

There are countless reasons why women may be the primary teachers of this message to young girls, and all of them point to one conclusion: They don't have enough information or discernment to be good mentors for your daughter in this area. And your daughter needs your permission not to listen.

"take things out of context." It is not about her intentions; she is to blame for the fact that other people may have intentions she can't control, *and* she is to blame because she refuses to accept that blame. Who is it here who is causing others to stumble?

The way we discuss modesty doesn't echo the words of Jesus. Instead, it takes his daughters and tells them that God designed them as weapons against his sons.

### She Needs to Know: She's Not the Dangerous One

It is true that we give people first impressions by what we wear, which is why it's unwise to go to a job interview wearing a "That's what she said" T-shirt. But that's very different from saying that our clothing is responsible for how someone treats us. In *Every Young Woman's Battle*, we read, "Rose and Christi both discovered the hard way that you teach people how to treat you by what you wear."[27] They chose immodest attire, and so they were portrayed as being to blame when guys stuck ice cubes down their shirts, rubbed their hands over them, and wouldn't accept their no. But let's make this clear: there is not a single piece of clothing that can cause someone to sexually assault you against their will.

The Duggar family also has a method for dealing with women dressed immodestly: The girls stay on the lookout for women "showing skin" and yell "NIKE!" if any come into view. The boys then look at their shoes until "danger passes."[28] Let's break this down, bit by problematic bit. First, it turns girls into the threats and *ignores the fact that the boys are actually the threats.* Let's not forget that Josh Duggar molested his sisters (and at least one other girl) while he was a teenager and has now been convicted of serious charges regarding the possession of child sexual abuse material. But this hypervigilance makes girls doubly responsible for boys' sin. Not only must girls dress appropriately so as not to cause lust, but they also must protect their brothers from seeing other girls. This paints other girls and women as the enemy, while they literally

---

### DARVO and Modesty

**Deny**—"Boys are just visual; it's how God made them."
**Attack**—"You're dressing like someone trashable."
**Reverse Victim and Offender**—"You're a stumbling block; you are causing him to fall into sin."

---

become their brothers' keepers. It makes female bodies dangerous, so boys must be protected from female bodies.

That's the message Focus on the Family gave loud and clear to teen girls when they published a *Brio and Beyond* article that said, "If a guy sees a girl walking around in tight clothes, a miniskirt or short shorts, you might as well hang a noose around the neck of his spiritual life."[29] Think about that: if a guy so much as *sees* a girl in tight clothes, his spiritual life will be dead. He doesn't even have to seek girls out or intentionally look at girls—if one merely comes into view, he's toast. Girls' bodies are so dangerous they can kill boys' spiritual lives.

And yet, if a boy is lusting after a girl and feeling unable to control himself, who poses the true threat? And who is actually the one in danger?

### She Should Know: Adults Who Find Children "Intoxicating" Are Called Pedophiles

In September 2020, Netflix released its movie *Cuties*, a film critiquing the sexualization of young girls.

The problem? Many people, especially evangelicals, felt that the filmmakers were committing the very act they critiqued. Backlash was huge—thousands of Netflix accounts were canceled, and Twitter blew up in outrage. How dare Netflix sexualize such young girls in this way!

Figure 9.3

Figure 9.4

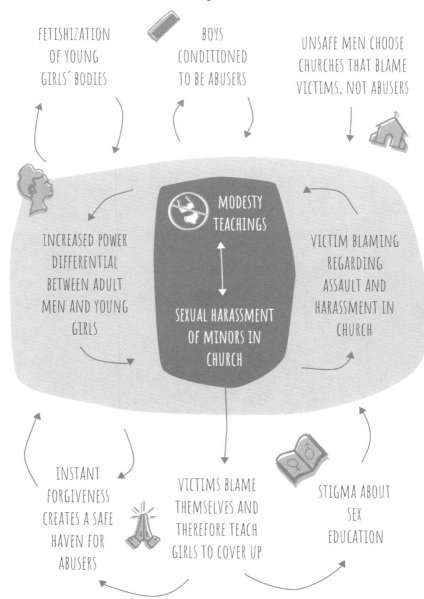

What is ironic is that many of these same people didn't recognize the sexualization of their own children occurring within the walls of their churches.

Before we go further, let us be very clear: the modesty message harms girls and women of all ages. It puts the burden of men's sins on the shoulders of their victims. It encourages competition, suspicion, and judgment between women. It causes victims of assault to question if they were really the ones in the wrong, leaving them feeling guilty about "forcing" their assailant to go too far by wearing the wrong clothes. It's unconscionable.

But there's one more aspect of the modesty message we have to grapple with: it told eight-year-olds their bodies were intoxicating to grown men.

Talking to postpubescent teens about covering up causes them harm. But, developmentally, the conversations seem logical: these girls' bodies look like adult bodies, and they likely have had some sexual feelings themselves. But *Secret Keeper Girl* and *8 Great Dates* are not for girls putting on eyeliner and lipstick for their driver's license photo—they are for girls ages eight to twelve.

*Eight to twelve.*

Eight years old means you aren't even two-whole-hands-old yet.

There's a picture in the Gregoire house of a young eight-year-old Rebecca on the monkey bars at our local playground. It's one of my (Sheila's) favorite photos of Rebecca at that age—she's smiling proudly as she swings hand-over-hand in her navy plaid skirt and matching headband, hair tousled in the wind.

She looks free, strong, and joyful. She is the picture of childhood innocence.

But she was old enough to have books like *Secret Keeper Girl* warn her that the bit of her belly that peeked out when she reached for the monkey bars was "intoxicating" to the dads at the playground around her. In her "Truth or Bare Fashion Tests" in *Secret Keeper Girl*, Gresh tells girls this: "Bellies are very intoxicating, and we need to save that for our husband!"[30] Directly to the right of this warning is a picture of a young child raising her arms to demonstrate what a modest T-shirt would be like. It's very unsettling to see the words "bellies are very intoxicating" next to a photo of a clearly prepubescent child posing to demonstrate how to hide an intoxicating midriff. And eight-year-olds today are old enough to be asked in the 2021 updated edition, "What can you do to avoid wearing clothes that invite people to finish the picture of your body?"[31] And although the horrifying "bellies are very intoxicating" quote is now gone, Gresh still summarizes in date number 8, "Your daughter has been learning that her body has the power to intoxicate guys."[32]

Let us be clear: There is no context, no nuance, no *anything* that makes it appropriate to tell an eight-year-old girl that her body is intoxicating. There is no context in which it is appropriate, as a grown man, to see a nine-year-old and "think only about [her] body," and yet this warning is given to prepubescent girls in the 2021 version of Gresh's curriculum.[33] If a man sees a ten-year-old's body and is "intoxicated," or can think of nothing else, there's a word for that: *pedophilia*. When we were reviewing materials for this chapter, this aspect of the modesty message was the most horrifying to us, that women were teaching our young children—*not even adolescents*—that their bodies were threats to the men around them.

Now, Gresh's stated reason for starting so young was to reduce shame by introducing the modesty message before girls had developed more womanly bodies, so that when they started developing breasts and hips, the modesty message wouldn't be a *reaction* to their new body shape. And that's a worthy goal—we genuinely believe that Gresh had girls' best interests in mind when writing her books. But what was the result? Rather than training girls to recognize "this will be important later," the book told literal children that their bodies were intoxicating *now*. The culture that embraced *Secret Keeper Girl* thus removed childhood innocence and normalized pedophilic obsession with prepubescent bodies.

Regardless of what you feel about modesty, we hope we can all agree that an eight-year-old's body is never a sexual thing. Ever. There is no context in which it is appropriate to teach children—yes, children—that they are sexual to the grown men around them and to warn girls that *they* may harm the *men* by wearing clothes that intoxicate them. In fact, if we are to teach our children anything about their bodies and attraction, it should only be that anyone who is intoxicated by them needs to be on an FBI watch list.

Picture an eight-year-old in your mind. She likely still plays with dollies and stuffies. She is likely struggling with her five times tables. She watches children's cartoons, she plays dress-up, she has pretend tea parties with her friends. She may still sleep with a blankie.

Now read this excerpt from *Secret Keeper Girl* that a generation of moms taught that young, playful child:

Mom: Do you remember what Dannah . . . said our beauty has the power to do to a man?

Daughter: (Some will remember the word *intoxicate*, and others may need help.)

Mom: That's right! Is a person in control when he is intoxicated?

Daughter: (Some will understand what this means, and some will need some help. Explain that it means to be out of control. If they've ever been anesthetized . . . you may use that to give them an idea of how a person might feel out of control. . . .)

Mom: Well, when a man views a woman's body . . . whether it's her curves or some of her skin . . . he is intoxicated. . . . But here's the difficult thing . . . a man doesn't necessarily mentally choose to become intoxicated. He is intoxicated by what he sees in the environment. Let me make sure that you understand this is a good thing. Who created our bodies to have that power?

Daughter: (God.)

Mom: Who created men's bodies to respond to that power by being intoxicated?

Daughter: (God.)[34]

They were eight years old.

Lord, have mercy.

# MOTHER-DAUGHTER
## SECTION

The Bible talks about many women as being beautiful—including Sarah, Rachel, and Esther. Being pretty is not a problem. But too often in churches when we talk about "modesty," the conversation turns to making sure girls do not become stumbling blocks to men. Let's look at what the Bible actually says about lust.

### What You Need to Know

Paul says that the one who is lusting should put lust to death (Col. 3:5). Jesus says that anyone who looks at a woman with lust should gouge their eyes out (Matt. 5:29). He doesn't say that the woman should cover up. According to Jesus, if someone is "distracted" by your body, that reaction to you is *their* reaction; it is not on you. And if anyone ever tells you that you are dressing in a way to cause them to sin, that is a red flag that that person is not safe to be around. It does not mean you have done anything wrong.

When it comes to modesty, the Bible isn't actually talking about not causing others to sin. The main verse people quote about modesty is: "I also want the women to dress modestly, with decency and propriety, adorning themselves, not with elaborate hairstyles or gold or pearls or expensive clothes, but with good deeds, appropriate for women who profess to worship God" (1 Tim. 2:9–10). Notice how in these verses, Paul is worried about three things:

- decency
- propriety (appropriateness)
- not flaunting wealth

When we talk about modesty, we often think it means "should you wear a bikini or not?" But in this passage, what Paul is really worried about is that people were coming to church and not feeling welcome because they weren't rich. And Paul was saying, "Don't be cliquey, and don't make people feel uncomfortable with what you're wearing, like they don't belong." Paul wants us to be approachable so that other people feel like they belong in the body of Christ just as they are, no frills necessary.

Now, some types of dress simply are inappropriate. How do we tell? It's all about *context* and *consent*. It is inappropriate to show up in an athletic one-piece bathing suit to church. But if you're going to swim team practice, it's the uniform! It's not appropriate to walk around topless at your local ice cream shop, but if a woman is breastfeeding her baby, it's necessary for her breast to be out! Wearing a cute, ruffled sundress is appropriate when you're going for ice cream on a very hot summer day; but if you're playing touch football or babysitting toddlers, it may be less appropriate, because people didn't consent to see your butt—which they will see as you end up falling on the ground.

I (Rebecca) am not bothered by being in a lady's changing room with women in various states of undress because I know to expect nakedness, and by entering the changing room I consent to see nakedness. But if that same woman who changed beside me approached me fully naked in the grocery store, I would be very uncomfortable and concerned about her mental well-being.

Good questions to ask when deciding what to wear include these:

- Is this appropriate for the activity that I will be doing?
- Am I showing any parts of my body that people do not expect to see?
- Is what I'm wearing in line with what other people my age would wear to similar events?

Listen, there are going to be different opinions (mainly from older folks) on what's appropriate to wear. Fashions change, so what really matters is that you're not being *shocking* or wearing something that's *culturally inappropriate*—not whether the sixty-three-year-old elder "gets" it.

Now, a big caveat to this: *what's popular on your Instagram feed and what's popular among the kids your age in your town may be different.* Twenty years ago, magazine covers were filled with influencers wearing crocheted bikini tops paired with low-rise jeans and walking around Los Angeles. However, no one was dressing that way in southeastern Ontario mini-malls.

So now that we've gotten that out of the way, let's look through some scenarios to figure out how to dress appropriately in a way that is considerate of others.

 ### What Would You Do?

Here are three stories that relate to what we wear, but in different ways. Let's talk through them.

### Flaunting Designer Labels

Olivia walks into her camp cabin, where Megan is her leader. Megan and everyone in her clique are wearing brand-name pajamas that Olivia knows cost more than $200. Olivia looks over at her friend Tracy, who comes from a family with very little money and who she knows is very self-conscious about it.

DAUGHTERS

Picture yourself as Tracy. How would you feel if you were the only one who didn't have super expensive clothes? If you're in a situation someday in which you feel singled out because you aren't brand-name enough, what does that tell you about that group?

MOMS

Have you ever felt left out like Tracy?

DAUGHTERS

Now picture yourself as Megan. Do you think Megan purposely wanted to leave out Tracy? Are there areas where you might be accidentally flaunting something you have in a way that makes others feel small?

DAUGHTERS

Now picture yourself as Olivia. What could Olivia do to help Tracy feel welcome? What would you say to Tracy if you were Olivia?

DISCUSS TOGETHER

What are some ways, other than clothes, that we can flaunt our "wealth" in a way that makes us unapproachable?

## Unkindly Seeking Attention

As Michelle is getting ready for youth group, she gets a text from Mitch saying, "Hey, are you coming tonight? Looking forward to seeing you!" Michelle knows Mitch is madly in love with her, and although she's not interested and doesn't want to date him, she loves the attention. She rummages through her closet for her cutest outfit—a pink sundress with off-the-shoulder sleeves. She knows Mitch won't be able to keep his eyes off her.

### DAUGHTERS

What could Michelle have done differently? Where do you think the line is drawn between enjoying looking attractive and playing with people's emotions?

### MOMS

Have you seen people use clothing to gain power like this? Have you ever done this yourself when you were younger?

The way we dress can actually be *unkind* if we are doing it in order to get attention for ourselves at the expense of others. Now there's nothing wrong with being pretty! But weaponizing other people's emotions and crushes in order to make ourselves feel better is not a kind thing to do. But that's not the only way we can dress in a way that's unkind. Think about these scenarios:

- Wearing clothing that is politically inflammatory in a way that can feel threatening to minorities (e.g., confederate flags).
- Wearing shocking or rude clothing specifically to offend people because you like the reaction.
- Upstaging the person who is supposed to be the center of attention (like wearing a nicer dress than your friend when it's her quinceañera!).

### DISCUSS TOGETHER

Have you ever experienced any of these situations? What (if any) do you think is the most common among the adults in your life? What about the teenagers?

## Becoming Self-Conscious

Ava just turned fourteen, and over the last year she's gone through three different bra sizes. Her mom has recently taken her shopping to find some clothes that flatter her new shape, and although she's still feeling a bit self-conscious about how quickly her body changed, she's feeling confident and pretty for the first time in a while. As she's hanging up her coat, one of the female youth leaders comes up to her and says, "Just so you know, what you're wearing could be very distracting to some of the boys, so maybe make sure to sit behind them so they don't, you know, have a hard time concentrating." Ava is flustered and runs to the bathroom. She's just wearing a cute top and jeans, and her newfound confidence evaporates.

DAUGHTERS

Have you ever been told something like this? How did it make you feel?

MOMS

Have you ever been in a situation in which you were made to feel ashamed because your body caused someone else to sin? Or did you see this happening to others around you? Talk to your daughter about this.

DISCUSS TOGETHER

Why do you think women often are the ones who make girls feel self-conscious about what they are wearing?

MOMS

Do you want your daughter to see herself how this woman saw Ava? What type of women do you want your daughter to go to for advice, and what are some signs that a woman is not someone she should turn to for counsel?

# 10

## She Deserves Permission to Be Big

*Girls Come Second to Christ Alone*

Rebecca and I (Joanna) grew up living and breathing Bible quizzing. Every year we'd memorize new books of the New Testament and then compete to see who knew the minutiae best. Quizzing is how I met my husband, Josiah—and how I met Rebecca and Sheila. Rebecca, her sister Katie, Josiah, and I were all very successful in quizzing—we all made the international team from our various districts across North America. My team won the international (USA and Canada) tournament twice, and I frequently placed in the top fifteen individuals. But when I was quizzing in my home district, I never came in first place. My friend Griffin did. I vividly remember one of the grown-ups congratulating my family on (yet another) second-place finish: "It's good for her to practice coming in second."

Funnily enough, that grown-up never seemed to remind the boys they needed to practice coming in second.

Now, this isn't entirely a church problem. The beliefs that lead churchgoers to tell teen girls to get ready to be second are also found in our culture. Girls are told that they can be anything because boys and girls are equal, but when you actually look at how this is playing out, the culture is really saying, "Girls, you can do boy things too." Boys, though, aren't encouraged to engage in traditionally "girl" activities. We tell girls to become engineers, but we don't tell boys to become daycare workers. At the splash pad in our neighborhood, little girls dart through the water in black and brown hand-me-down rash-guard shirts from their big brothers, and no one bats an eye. But when a little boy shows up in his big sister's pink rash-guard hand-me-down, everyone thinks his parents have an agenda.

Our society, although it would love to believe otherwise, prefers boys to girls. Girly things and traditionally feminine roles are seen as "less than" or "uncool." It's why so many girls take on the "I'm not like other girls" personality. It's quirky and cool to watch football and monster trucks—it's flighty and ditzy to like makeup and boy bands.

Your daughter is being raised in a world where femaleness is seen as inherently inferior to maleness. And while the church may give lip service to verses like Galatians 3:28 that proclaim there is no longer male nor female, for we are all one in Christ Jesus, our girls are still being raised in a church *and* a wider world that teach them that we aren't one at all but instead they naturally come second.

### She Should Know: Girls Don't Talk Too Much

Every Christmas new waves of families inexplicably decide it's a good idea to take their yearly Christmas card photo featuring Mom and daughters with duct tape over their mouths, while the dad and sons happily hold a chalkboard that reads, "Finally! Peace on Earth!"

It may seem like a silly joke, but the belief that girls talk too much isn't fringe. In fact, we found that 52.1% of women believed that girls talk too much while they were in high school, and 15.8% still believe it today (see figures 10.1 and 10.2). And what happens if a girl actually believes that girls talk too much? Our survey found that when a woman believed that girls talk too much while they were in high school, then as an adult:

- She's *more* likely to end up in a sexually abusive marriage.
- She's *less* likely to feel comfortable bringing up concerns with her husband.

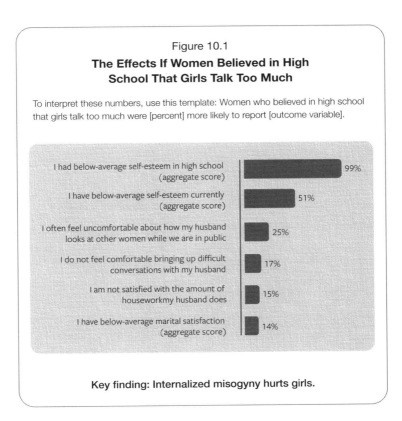

Figure 10.1
**The Effects If Women Believed in High School That Girls Talk Too Much**

To interpret these numbers, use this template: Women who believed in high school that girls talk too much were [percent] more likely to report [outcome variable].

I had below-average self-esteem in high school (aggregate score) — 99%

I have below-average self-esteem currently (aggregate score) — 51%

I often feel uncomfortable about how my husband looks at other women while we are in public — 25%

I do not feel comfortable bringing up difficult conversations with my husband — 17%

I am not satisfied with the amount of houseworkmy husband does — 15%

I have below-average marital satisfaction (aggregate score) — 14%

**Key finding: Internalized misogyny hurts girls.**

- She's *less* likely to have a satisfying sex life.
- She's *more* likely to feel uncomfortable with how her husband looks at other women when she and her husband are out in public.
- She's *less* likely to have a husband who does his fair share of the chores around the house.

Let's take a look at that last point about housework to tease out what's happening. We ran the numbers and found that among households in which both husbands and wives work outside the home, women who believed that girls talk too much are *almost twice as likely* to do the vast majority of the housework compared to their counterparts who never believed it. That means they are in marriages

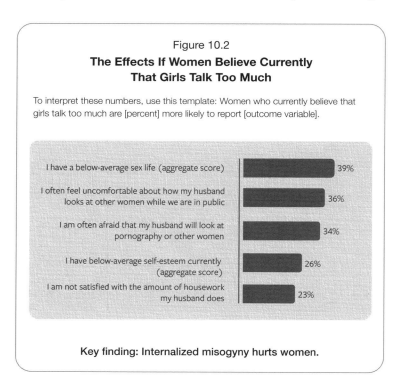

Figure 10.2
**The Effects If Women Believe Currently
That Girls Talk Too Much**

To interpret these numbers, use this template: Women who currently believe that girls talk too much are [percent] more likely to report [outcome variable].

| | |
|---|---|
| I have a below-average sex life (aggregate score) | 39% |
| I often feel uncomfortable about how my husband looks at other women while we are in public | 36% |
| I am often afraid that my husband will look at pornography or other women | 34% |
| I have below-average self-esteem currently (aggregate score) | 26% |
| I am not satisfied with the amount of housework my husband does | 23% |

Key finding: Internalized misogyny hurts women.

in which the wives are doing almost all the cleaning and childcare, even though both spouses work outside the home. Women who never believed this message, on the other hand, are twice as likely to divide up housework more evenly with their husbands.

And what about the women who used to believe in high school that girls talk too much but don't anymore? Although they are 30% more likely to have an even split in household tasks than women who still believe it today, they are also 16% less likely to have a spouse who does his fair share of the household chores than women who never believed at all that girls talk too much.

How does believing girls talk too much affect how much vacuuming you do twenty years later? Well, if a girl believes she talks too much, she has internalized a message that her opinions and needs are an inconvenience to those around her. She's been primed to refrain from speaking up—and it shows in the quality of her relationships (see figure 10.3). She may run herself ragged with housework while her husband plays video games, endure a disappointing sex life, or feel trapped in a marriage in which she doesn't feel free to bring up her opinions or concerns. She may not feel that she deserves better, and she's much more likely to marry a man who agrees.

When we were writing our survey, we scoured the academic literature for good measures of what researchers call "internalized misogyny"—when women themselves believe messages that women are less important, capable, or desirable than men. One misogynistic trope that researchers have uncovered is the belief that women dominate conversations and talk too much. Their silence is more valuable than their voices.

Our society certainly promotes this unspoken belief. We call a talkative person a "Chatty Kathy," not a "Talkative Tommy." Mark Gungor, highly popular pastor, marriage speaker, and comedian, quips, "Say what you will about women but I think being able to turn one sentence into a six hour argument takes talent."[1] James Dobson, founder of Focus on the Family, started the idea that

239

Figure 10.3

CAN LEAD TO GIRLS HAVING

BELIEF IN MALE SUPERIORITY & SELF GASLIGHTING TENDENCIES & A LACK OF AUTONOMY & LOW SELF-ESTEEM

WHICH IN TURN CAN LEAD TO THEM BEING

TAKEN IN BY A DANGEROUS MAN & UNABLE TO IDENTIFY AND/OR ACT UPON RED FLAGS

FINALLY LEADING THEM INTO

MARRYING AN ABUSIVE SPOUSE

women talk more than men by claiming in his 1983 book *Love for a Lifetime* that women say 50,000 words a day while men say only 25,000, and he frequently admonished women not to talk too much lest they wear out their husbands.[2] Yet he never provided citations for the source of this scientific claim. The idea caught on, but the numbers kept changing. Evangelical marriage author Gary Smalley claimed that women speak 25,000 to men's 12,000.[3] Neuropsychiatrist Louann Brizendine claimed on the original dust cover for her book *The Female Brain* that women say 20,000 words a day to men's 7,000, leading to ridicule from the scientific community.[4] Again, there is no actual evidence for any of this.

Many girls had this message that chattiness is a female blunder repeated to them by Christian sources. *Brio* magazine had a "Guy Talk" segment in which editors published boys' responses to questions submitted by young girls. These responses included warnings to girls that one of boys' pet peeves is when girls talk too much.[5]

Hold on—you may be wondering, "Isn't it possible that girls talking too much is simply an uncomfortable truth?" Well, actual research gives a very different picture: *men and women talk roughly the same amounts.* Despite what the church and wider culture teach us, any differences in the number of words men and women utter are negligible.[6] In fact, the problem is not that girls talk too much but that in many coed situations they don't talk *enough*—and boys don't listen when they do. Take the famous Mendelberg and Karpowitz experiments from Cambridge University.[7] They formed groups of five people with varying gender balances to see what it took for women to speak as much as men. Each group was given a task: decide which model of economic redistribution would work best in society at large. The experiment found that men were far more likely to interrupt than women and far more likely to be voted the most influential in their group. And when it came to talking time?

> Equality would suggest that each person in a group of five has the
> floor 20 percent of the time, but it took not just a female majority

but a supermajority (meaning four out of five) for women to finally speak their proportionate talking time. At best, outnumbered women in the study spoke three-quarters of the time a man spoke; on average, women spoke just two-thirds as much as a man. And missing voices means missing perspectives. . . .

A lone female spoke the least. A lone male? Nothing will hold him back, Karpowitz and Mendelberg found. "Men are willing and eager to jump into conversations, and they come with a level of confidence where they just expect themselves to be influential," says Karpowitz. "They go for it no matter what."[8]

### Is Modesty Another Measure of Internalized Misogyny?

**What happens to beliefs about modesty when women internalize the "girls talk too much" message?**

When women believe today that girls talk too much, their chance of agreeing with various modesty messages skyrockets. They are:

- 2.74 times more likely to agree that "boys will struggle with their visual nature in a way girls will never understand"
- 3.99 times more likely to agree that "girls who dress immodestly are worse than girls who don't"
- 4.28 times more likely to agree that "boys can't help but lust after a girl who is dressed like she is trying to incite it"
- 3.01 times more likely to believe that "you have a responsibility to protect boys around you by wearing modest clothing"

If "girls talk too much" is a well-established measure of internalized misogyny, and the modesty message corresponds with it so consistently, then perhaps the modesty message is also a sign of internalized misogyny. After all, the modesty message prioritizes men's comfort. It says men's needs to be free of temptation and discomfort are greater than women's needs to be free of shame, objectification, and harassment. Once again, men matter more than women.

Boys have been primed to take up more space than girls, and girls have been primed to let them. The problem is not that your daughter takes up too much space; it's that she doesn't take up *enough*. Your daughter needs your permission to be big.

But that's not what she's being told. Instead, girls are taught that their job is not just to make themselves small by being quiet but also to make sure they don't even *think* out of line.

### She Needs to Know: Disagreement Is Not Rebellion

The 2021 book *8 Great Dates* (Dannah Gresh's replacement for the original *Secret Keeper Girl* book) includes a "Submission Scale" quiz for eight-to-twelve-year-old girls. Despite the caveat that "submitting doesn't require you to mindlessly follow a bad example,"[9] many of the questions dock a girl "submission" points if she even *thinks* differently than those in authority, or if she has any emotion other than cheerfulness. Take question 2, for example:

When the teacher gives me homework, I usually

   a. refuse to do it
   b. do it, but the whole time I think it's dumb because I already know it all
   c. wish I didn't have to, but I don't want to disappoint my teacher
   d. do it without thinking too much; after all, she's the teacher![10]

Personally, we think only *a* is describing rebellion to authority. In all other cases, the homework is being done. However, if the girl selects *b* or *c*, even though she obeys her teacher and gets her work done, she can still use improvement. The only girl who is deemed a "submissive servant"[11]—the goal for all—is the one who will "do it without thinking too much."

Do we recognize how irresponsible and dangerous it is to raise daughters to specifically not think too much? It makes them an ideal victim for sexual predators. In another question, where the scenario is "I think someone has made a mistake," the girl taking the quiz falls short of perfection if she watches for a good time to bring it up quietly. The only way to get full points is to "wait for adults or others in authority to make things right."[12] How is any young girl supposed to feel empowered to use her voice when this implies that speaking up in any way, even in private, is not God's best for her?

We are very grateful that the biblical Esther, who stood up to the biggest authority in the land to rescue her people, risking her life in the process, did not take the Submission Scale quiz when she was twelve.

Your daughter may disagree with those in leadership at times. She will likely recognize hypocrisy or errors in judgment among those in authority over her. What will happen to your daughter if she's repeatedly told this is a sin, and doubly so because she's a girl?

While the Bible tells all believers to submit to one another (Eph. 5:21), girls especially are the recipient of this message in the church today. Now, we're not against submission; we just mimic Inigo Montoya in *The Princess Bride*, saying, "I don't think that word means what you think it means."[13] A submissive spirit is the mark of a Christian, motivating us to radically value the well-being of others. Submitting to one another as believers is about honoring the *imago Dei* in those around us and humbly working for their good; it's not about erasing our personhood. We fail to see in Scripture *any* verses that preclude a woman from having thoughts simply because she doesn't have a penis.

Let's take our cue from Jesus, who said that we shouldn't worry about power or authority or trying to lord over others like the world does but instead should serve one another (Matt. 20:25–28). Let's have the same mind that Jesus does; he didn't try to become great but instead humbled himself to become the servant of all (Phil. 2:1–11). These instructions are for everyone, not just for girls. Let's remember that Peter proclaimed, "We must obey God rather than men" (Acts 5:29 NASB 1995). Paul wrote that we have no mediator between God and ourselves except Christ Jesus (1 Tim. 2:5), and he praises the Bereans for testing and questioning all teachings against the Scriptures (Acts 17:11). No blind loyalty there. Yet instead of encouraging girls to "be wise as serpents and harmless as doves" (Matt. 10:16 NKJV), and encouraging them to follow their Savior's voice, no matter where it takes them (John 10:4), too often the church tells our daughters their role is to fall in line unquestioningly.

How does the church convince our bright, excited, unique girls to erase their opinions and cheerfully follow the leader? They tell them that they can't trust their opinions because girls are more easily deceived.

### She Needs to Know: She Isn't More Likely to Be Deceived

You may have heard that women are more easily deceived than men. This theology is based on a simplistic reading of 1 Timothy 2:14, which asserts that it was Eve who was deceived, not Adam. But many scholars have pointed out that the verse says nothing about women being *more* susceptible to deception than men, simply that Eve was deceived.[14] Nonetheless, this bias against women's intelligence remains. It's pervasive in church culture:

- Disgraced former megachurch pastor Mark Driscoll said of Paul's words in 1 Timothy 2, "Without blushing, Paul is simply stating that when it comes to leading in the church, women are unfit because they are more gullible and easier to deceive than men."[15]
- John Piper asserts that it "may be true" that women are "more gullible or deceivable than men and therefore less fit for the doctrinal oversight of the church."[16]
- Joseph Pipa, president of Greenville Presbyterian Theological Seminary for twenty years, said, "Paul is saying

that (a woman) is not to teach men or exercise authority because of her susceptibility to deception. . . . God has not made her to exercise the kind of hard, judgmental discernment that is necessary in theological and scriptural issues. By nature, a woman will more likely fall prey to the subtleties of mental and theological error."[17]

The propensity for women to be deceived is even the entire premise of the hit book *Lies Young Women Believe*. Nancy DeMoss Wolgemuth and Dannah Gresh claim that "Satan continues to target women of every age for deception," and that for reasons that we don't fully understand, Satan chose to deceive a woman, not a man.[18]

So let's ask once again: Is it empirically true that women are more susceptible to deception? Here's the evidence:

- From a religious standpoint, women throughout history have made up the majority of the church and are more likely to practice spiritual disciplines.[19] Women, then, are statistically more likely to follow God, who is the ultimate Truth.

- A study out of the University of Michigan found that women were 19% *less* likely to be duped by financial scams than men.[20]

- Researchers from the University of Pennsylvania and from Berkeley found that *because* people believed women were more easily deceived, people were more likely to lie to women and try to trick them during business practices.[21]

It's not that women are more likely to be deceived; it's that they're more likely to be *victimized*. And as the Berkeley study found, women's increased victimization is largely happening because men believe the same things that are preached by our evangelical resources—that girls and women are particularly prone to deception. And they attempt to exploit that perceived weakness.

So if it's not girls' role to have a voice in the church, to exercise discernment, or to have opinions because of their propensity toward deception, what *does* the church suggest is a girl's role?

Why, to make the boys feel big, of course.

### She Needs to Know: It's Not Her Job to Make Boys Feel Good about Themselves

There is a common theme among evangelical teachings to women about "how men are" that goes like this: *Ladies, a man's job is to take the responsibility of leadership on his shoulders. That's a big task! Wow! I can't imagine that kind of pressure. But that doesn't mean God hasn't got a job for us too. We have a profoundly important role found in God's design of women: it's our job to support and cheer our men on. Sisters, God has given you such amazing influence over the men in your life. He has given you so much power to cause such good things to happen—but if we try to usurp God's design for women to submit to men, if we try to take charge and control the men in our lives, that's not God's way. Our men are under a lot of stress because they feel this weight—they love us, they want to protect us, so our job is to let them! And let's make sure they know how much we appreciate them and that we see how hard they're trying.*

Many evangelical books even encourage teen girls to practice living in respectful deference to the boys around them *now* as practice for when they will have to submit to their husbands:

- "If you, as a young woman, learn how to treat guys with respect right now, these attitudes and habits will carry over into your marriage one day" (Shaunti Feldhahn and Lisa Rice, *For Young Women Only*; the authors also insist that this respect must be unconditional).[22]

- "If you intend to one day live within a marriage where the husband lovingly and sacrificially leads the wife, as God's Word instructs, then you have to begin now to be content and to let the guy do the leading!" (Wolgemuth and Gresh, *Lies Young Women Believe*)[23]

Girls are told that one of their jobs is to make sure boys' egos stay intact. In *For Young Women Only*, Feldhahn and Rice quote a teenage boy desperate for girls to understand that "the male ego is the most fragile thing on the planet."[24] We must handle boys with care, as the authors show in this example of a conflict between a boy and a girl over a group project:

One high schooler said that when his female class-project partner asked him, "Have you not started the PowerPoint presentation yet?" he found himself getting angry—even though she didn't ask it in an accusing tone. He said, "After all, I told her I would do it. The deadline was still days away, and I felt like she had no trust that I would find a way to get it done. She should know I'm not an idiot. She didn't need to act all suspicious and disappointed."[25]

Let's picture a real-life example of how this plays out. In any given senior year classroom, you're likely to find a Braydon and a Shantal. Braydon gets C minuses in school and spends most of his free time on his PlayStation or walking around the mall with his buds. He hasn't thought much about college but figures he'll take a gap year to make prank videos on TikTok. Shantal, on the other hand, is working on maintaining a GPA that will get her a full ride to the college of her choosing, she holds down a part-time job, and in the summers she volunteers to help pad her résumé for internship applications down the line.

If Shantal were assigned a class project with Braydon as a partner and was looking for advice on how to work with him, what would Rice and Feldhahn say?

Basically, remember that boys love hearing that they measure up, and so girls should help boys feel like they measure up. Girls are encouraged to "always assume the best" about the boys around them.[26] But what if the best isn't true? That option is left hanging. Instead, girls are told that every boy secretly wants to be seen as a superhero, so they have to be the Mary Jane to his Peter Parker. The authors ask girls like Shantal, "What message are you giving the guys you care about? Is it a selfish message of, 'You're not quite enough'? Or an encouraging message of, 'Go get 'em, tiger!'"[27]

But Shantal's full-ride scholarship is on the line; she has the right to be disappointed and upset if a team member isn't doing his best but rather is willing to just "find a way to get it done." Why should Shantal be charged with making Braydon feel like a superhero if he's unreliable with basic tasks? His actions affect *her*, and her future may be on the line. Painting her as the offender when his apathy is putting her at risk is classic DARVO once again, resulting in the girl who is worried about how a bad lab partner may affect her college applications being told she's victimizing him by asking him to pull his weight.

We recognize that boys like feeling like superheroes—we all do! And Braydon, for all the ways he's imperfect, is deeply loved by God and on his way in life. But why are we telling girls like Shantal to make themselves smaller so that boys like Braydon can feel bigger? Why don't we instead tell the boys like Braydon, "Sometimes others are going to be shinier than you. Instead of puffing up your ego, you'll be better off if you look to those around you who are doing well—including the girls—and imitate their example."

When the goal is that boys never feel "less than," strong girls become a threat to the natural order of things. In no universe is a Braydon equipped to lead a Shantal. But how can a man feel like he's able to fulfill his God-given duty to be in charge if there are women who are better suited for the role?

We actually find this type of teaching to be offensive not only to the girls it attempts to silence but also to our boys. As the mother of a son, I (Rebecca) am horrified that so many within the church think it is not only acceptable but also God-designed that my son is so fragile that he needs the women around him to convince him of his own grandiosity, even if he has not achieved it.

Remember Sarah's story, from chapter 6? Sarah ended up married to a larger-than-life abusive pastor because she felt that in God's order of things she must marry a man who was stronger, bigger, and shinier than she was. In her own words, Sarah experienced what she called "grooming" by the church's advice on marriage but also by the church's advice on gender roles. Sarah grew up with two conflicting beliefs: she believed she was meant to do big things for God, but she also believed she had to make sure she didn't outshine the men around her. When she landed at Bible college, this belief that she shouldn't be "too big" followed her. Though she was asked to lead an outreach project, the men on her team kept pushing back any time she brought up an idea. She explains what happened next:

> One of my guy friends in the group told me that the reason none of the guys would listen was because they were pastoral students and I was a woman. He suggested that I relay my plans to him ahead of time, and he'd present them as his own. With a man saying it, the pastoral students would likely agree, and it would all work out in the end.

Even though she felt sick about it, she believed the godly thing to do was to be willing to step aside for male leadership. She figured, "If I have to erase myself from the equation to get the job done, fine." Sarah read us a passage from a journal she kept during this time of her life:

> It is a constant battle to reconcile who I am and who I was with who I want to be versus who the people around me want me to be. [Leader] talked to me personally during worship telling me that he

sees I have incredible gifts in leadership that he wants to see developed, which is, of course, why he wants me to come to his school.

I DON'T WANT TO BE A LEADER.

I am afraid of leadership.

If I were a man, that would be different. But I am a woman. . . . I would much prefer to be like [woman] married to someone who is the face of it all, the visible leader, and she is doing her part beside him. But what if you're surrounded by weak men? Does that mean you have to make yourself weaker than them to maintain a role of biblical submission? How am I supposed to be anything God has called me to be when God has called me to be someone who is supposed to stay smaller, but I was created to be big?

## The Love Story She Almost Missed

From a reader:

> Even as a teen I had a confident personality and I wasn't afraid to speak my mind. I was not allowed to date until after my freshman year of college, but I was constantly told throughout my teen years that I would need a strong man to handle me. Fast-forward to my junior year of college, this sweet guy and I started talking. I really liked him and our personalities mixed really well. But after a couple issues came up where he didn't assert dominance, I broke up with him because I had faithfully swallowed the belief that the man I needed would behave in a domineering way.
>
> This story has a happy ending, though, because after three years of distant friendship, we started dating again and got married the next year. My husband is one of the best blessings in my life, and I love and appreciate his gentleness. (He doesn't have to beat his chest and shout "I am in charge." He wants to make decisions together. He thinks my perspective is valuable.) I am so thankful that I didn't find the bullying tyrant I was told I should be looking for.

Sarah's journal doesn't read like that of a woman bent on controlling men. Rather, like those of so many young girls on fire for Christ, Sarah's writings present the heart of someone in profound turmoil.

## She Needs Your Permission to Take Up Space

It's easy to understand how a naturally meek and submissive girl, with low self-esteem, from a dysfunctional family background, could become a target for a controlling, abusive man. We look at girls like her and think, "She needs confidence so she doesn't end up with a bad guy!" But often the church's teaching takes those girls and makes them even *more* submissive. The girls who are already at risk, the ones who in order to be safe should have been told, "You have a voice that matters," have been told instead, "God's design is that you erase yourself and defer to the man in charge."

What we miss, though, is that this theology that says women please God by putting themselves under men takes even the girls who no one expected would end up in these situations—girls like Sarah—and primes them to seek out narcissists, because they're the only ones who are bigger. It makes them doubt themselves. It makes them hide their gifts. It makes them anxious, depressed, and sad. And the more dedicated they are to Jesus and the more determined they are to follow him, the more this pressure to be small can impact them.

But why do we have this pressure in the first place? Are women's voices really so threatening? It certainly seems that way among some conservative denominations. The Southern Baptist Convention, for instance, has a history of barring churches from its fellowship if they ordain women or allow women pastors, but not if they have a pedophile in the pulpit.[28] It would seem that a woman who wants to preach the gospel is deemed a greater threat to the congregation than a man who has sexually abused children.

Why? The evangelical church is one of the last bastions of society where men get to be important *just because they are men*—and they don't even need to be impressive or competent or safe. One Tennessee pastor sexually assaulted a girl under his care and literally got a standing ovation when he confessed it.[29] And when men have power not because of their competence but solely because of their gender, then women's competence is a huge threat to their power.

Research has shown that competent, skilled women are seen as threats to men who are not as skilled. In fact, a 2015 study of men's attitudes while playing *Halo 3* showed that highly skilled female-voiced players were most likely to experience verbal abuse from unskilled male players. The men playing who were good at the game didn't care that the women were doing well too.[30] Who benefits from keeping women small? Men who have status only because there's no competition. The church is one of the few institutions in society that is still a stratified system based on gender rather than merit.

And thus the church is a very comfortable place for men, with few expectations placed on them. The Gospel Coalition recently posted an Instagram video talking about how wives can't expect their husbands to do "risky" things for God unless they first show their husbands respect. What were these things that were so risky they could not be done without a wife's support? Getting the children ready for church on Sunday, praying and reading the Scriptures, and thinking about life from a biblical perspective.[31] Golly, if that's risky, being a stay-at-home mom must be the equivalent of a trip to Jumanji. We could go on and on (we've literally written a book on it), but in too many pockets of evangelicalism, men are not expected to do even the bare minimum but are given ultimate power and authority over women anyway. That's a very cushy place to be. It's no wonder that the power structure in these churches wants to freeze this just as it is.

### She Should Know That Not All Churches Will Try to Keep Her Small

Many women believe, as Sarah McDugal did, that they need to choose: obey God and be content with being small, or leave Jesus entirely. But that's simply not true. Many denominations—including evangelical ones—also base their understanding of women's roles on Scripture but come to wildly different conclusions than denominations and churches that put women in boxes. And what did Jesus say we should do when we are judging between two different interpretations of Scripture? We should look at the fruit. Well, the fruit of teachings that tell your daughter to subjugate herself to boys and men is rotten.

We know that many of our readers may have theological differences with us on this topic. But can we simply ask: If there are two forces in this world, which is more likely to benefit from a theology that silences one-half of the population while encouraging passivity and laziness in the other? And what should that tell us?

In *The Making of Biblical Womanhood*, Beth Allison Barr argues that the idea that women should be under the authority of men due to gender roles is a modern Christian teaching, not a historical one. In ending her book, she asks the question, "What would happen if we all just stopped?"

One hundred and eighteen years before Barr asked that question, Lucy Maud Montgomery, author of *Anne of Green Gables*, actually answered it. Her short story "The Strike at Putney" is a masterful tale of a small rural church that functions only because the women of the town do a tremendous amount of work, while the men mostly just show up.[32] When the men refuse to let a visiting female missionary speak from the pulpit, since she's a woman, the women declare, "If women aren't good enough to speak in church they are not good enough to work for it either." After a week with dusty pews and wilting flowers, without organists or Sunday school teachers, plus no plans for bake sales to raise money for new carpets, the husbands and the pastor beg the women to come back—and everyone enjoys the talk from the visiting missionary.

What both Barr and Montgomery point to is that women, though unwittingly, have often supported the very structures that keep us small. Our work allows others to *seem* competent and big without having to *be* competent. But is this of Jesus? That's a big question that we need to answer about the church as a whole, and that's for other books to tackle.

But let's bring the question home, outside the church and seminary doors, and walk inside your front door instead. Let's go down the hall to your daughter's bedroom and peek in. Do you see her? She's full of promise. She's been gifted by God to tackle so many things. God planned good works for her to do before the very foundation of the world (Ephesians 2:10). She is precious. She is loved. *She deserves your permission and blessing to be who God called her to be.*

### Rebecca's Prayer for Her Daughter

Joanna and I (Rebecca) each have two kids. When we wrote *The Great Sex Rescue*, three of those children had been born, and we wrote each child a small reflection at the end of the book. We wrote this book throughout my pregnancy and postpartum period with my newest little one, Vivian Louise.

Giving birth to a daughter while analyzing the teachings evangelicalism often speaks over our girls is sobering. As I think of our results, and look into her eyes, I think of what her life will be like.

My daughter is growing up in a world that will judge her mercilessly in a way it will not judge her brother.

She will grow up with air-brushed models surrounding her in grocery store aisles. With people scrutinizing her body to make sure she's not "too big" or "too small." With pressure to have the ability to keep up a great job, parent her kids, and keep a perfect house all at the same time.

She will face pressure to have it all together. Pressure to be happy. Pressure to be beautiful. Pressure to be perfect.

I want God to be my daughter's safe place where she knows she can simply *be*.

But I look at the God presented in the teachings of far too many churches to young girls, and I don't see that safe place. Listen to their teachings, and God sounds like an angry schoolmarm, watching over you ruler in hand, just waiting for you to mess up. The God presented to me growing up in evangelicalism was one who saw me as the problem—my body was a stumbling block, my vivacity a threat, my giftings dangerous. My parents were able to shield me from the worst of it—but I don't want my daughter to need a shield from the church.

I don't want my daughter to feel like God sees her as a problem to neutralize with high necklines, forced positivity, and silence. God forbid my daughter feels that in order to serve God, she must become less of herself.

When I look at the church my daughter was born into, the primary problem is not even about sexuality. It goes deeper than that. The problem is that we present our children with a God who says, "You're not measuring up." We give caveats and we tell them God loves them, but our teachings are two-faced. And they leave our girls grappling with yet another way they're not good enough.

I don't want my daughter to grow up desperately trying to please a God who judges her—I want her to grow up rejoicing in the God who delights in her.

### In Search of "Biblical Women" in the Bible

Look closely at the women in Jesus' genealogy as found in the Gospel of Matthew. None of these women would meet the criteria given to Christian girls in our culture.

- Tamar—disguised herself and became a prostitute to pressure her father-in-law, Judah, to do right by her. And she was rewarded for it, because it was clear that it had been Judah who was in the wrong. She didn't just submit to mistreatment; she asserted her rights—even if the only way to do so was to be a prostitute.

- Rahab—had been an unbeliever and a prostitute, but she used her bravery to keep Israel safe and asserted her superior knowledge to save her own family rather than deferring to the men around her. It's a good thing she didn't "wait for others in authority to make things right," even if it means she wouldn't have gotten full submission points on the Submission Scale quiz.
- Ruth—according to the law, should not have been allowed in Israel, as Moabites were unclean to the tenth generation. Yet King David was only four generations removed from Ruth. And she was quite forward in getting Boaz to notice her and marry her—something Elisabeth Elliott would frown upon!
- Bathsheba—the victim of a sexual assault by King David, made the most of her situation and spoke up vehemently, insisting that David do right by their second son, Solomon.
- Mary—when asked to do an incredibly brave thing, even at the expense of her reputation and family, consented to carry the baby Jesus when presumably the men in her family would have abandoned her. But she sought God's kingdom first.

These women didn't focus on their role; they focused on what was right. God gave them permission to be big. And big they were.

## What If Mothering Didn't Have to Be So Hard?

Our job is not to raise obedient daughters who won't make waves. Our job is to raise daughters who will run after Jesus without worrying if they're faster or slower than the boys around them.

You can be an awesome mom and give your daughter all the right lessons and all the right encouragement. Your voice may even be louder than the voice that she might hear from a church that tells her she needs to be small, be quiet, and not think so much. But wouldn't it be nice if you didn't have to yell? Wouldn't it be nice if your voice and the church's voice were both saying the same thing rather than trying to drown each other out?

Being part of a church community protects girls and helps them—in general. But some Christian spaces fall short of Jesus' example. If you find yourself always apologizing for what the youth group or pastor said, always trying to explain how "our family sees it differently," always having to undo what she learned in small group—maybe it's time for a change.

In the first chapter of this book, we told you that religiosity is a positive thing for girls. Going to church is associated with great things!

But we also gave you a caveat. The teachings at some churches are so toxic that the benefits of religiosity disappear. In fact, outcomes look like this:

- Highest self-esteem: going to church and not believing toxic teachings
- Second highest self-esteem: not going to church or going to church and believing toxic teachings
- Worst self-esteem: not going to church and believing toxic teachings

Now we'd like to invite you to travel back in time to fourth or fifth grade when you studied averages. The average is what you get when you measure the outcomes of a whole bunch of different things—it's the middle.

So let's look at this differently. We know that:

- Religiosity, *on average*, is a positive force.
- Churches with toxic teachings *pull the average down*.

If churches with toxic teachings pull the average *down*—but the average is still *positive*—then there must be other churches pulling the average *up* to compensate.

We're not asking you to lose faith in church. We're asking you to find that which brings up the average—that which gives life rather than saps it. That which puts wings under our girls and lets them fly like eagles rather than causing them to fall under the weight of condemnation and shame.

We've spent this book showing you how to look out for bad fruit. And there's a lot of it in the conservative evangelical church today. It's hard to grapple with the fact that the tree we're eating from may be rotten.

But Jesus also promised that there would be good fruit. Don't stick around where there's rot and decay. Good trees are out there, and your daughter deserves to sit under their shade. So, go and find them.

## A Final Note to Moms

This chapter doesn't have an exercise to do with your daughter, because choosing a healthy Christian environment is not her responsibility while she's still a child. While sexism is rampant throughout society, some environments will *encourage* sexism while others will work *against* it. There are very few places outside Christian circles where your daughter will explicitly be told from those in authority that she is capable of less or designed for less simply because she is female. You cannot control every one of your daughter's environments, but you can minimize how many areas of her life will be steeped in sexist ideologies. You can decide if she's in a sexist church, homeschooling group, Christian school, or missions organization or even if she spends time with sexist family members.

No matter what environment your daughter is in, Christian or otherwise, she needs sex education. She needs to know how to handle predatory people. She needs to know how to draw boundaries. But she doesn't need to learn how to navigate a faith that seeks to restrict her simply because she's a girl—*unless you put her in that position.*

This is not her burden to carry. This is yours, as her parent. There are girls who grow up never being told, "God wants you to be smaller simply because of your sex."

Some of you may agree that "there is neither male nor female, for we are all one in Christ Jesus," but you're still at a church that restricts women's roles because the youth group is great or it has other amenities you don't want to give up. But we ask you to consider, is that truly the best option for your daughter long term? It may be working now while she's young, but if you stay in that kind of environment, what kind of man is she likely to meet when she wants to get married? Will it be someone who will treat her as a partner, or will it be someone who sees her as an appendage?

Others of you may be in a gender-hierarchy church, but you're not sure what you believe—you're struggling with big questions that are making you feel shaky in your faith. Lean into the questions. Jesus is big enough to handle them.

And some of you may in fact believe that women's role is to follow men, and you're uncomfortable with us, or even angry at us, for challenging what you consider biblical truth. If that's you, we simply ask that you don't close your eyes to the repercussions that may await your daughter if you raise her with that same interpretation.

We know the role of women in church and the home is a big and thorny topic for many people, and we tend to frame it in terms of theology. This book is asking you to put your daughter's face to your theological debates. This isn't just about an interpretation of the Bible; this is about the kind of man she may marry, what she may put up with in her marriage, and how she thinks that God sees her. This is big stuff. And she deserves better.

# Acknowledgments

This book took on a life of its own. We were not planning on doing a *Great Sex Rescue 2.0* survey, but as we began to plan what we wanted to say in *She Deserves Better*, the project got bigger and bigger and bigger. And we're so happy with the final result.

But we simply could not have done this without the support of our Bare Marriage patrons.[1] They gave us the financial breathing room we needed so we could do this very big project right, while also giving us a place online where we could truly be ourselves and share our disappointments and our hopes. We love the community we have with you, and we cannot say thank you enough. We also want to thank our larger online community on the *Bare Marriage* blog and Sheila's social media channels, who engage with us and learn alongside us. Our online chats in comments sections and on social media introduced us to people we talk to almost on a daily basis, whom we consider friends. We are so grateful.

Every book is a labor of love—but it seems as if *The Great Sex Rescue* and *She Deserves Better* have always been paired with actual labors. *The Great Sex Rescue* was written when Joanna's daughter Mari and Rebecca's son Alex were babies, and this one was written when Joanna's daughter Tali and Rebecca's daughter Vivian were babies. Looking into these baby girls' eyes as we were writing and running stats helped us to remember why we are doing this.

Because there are three of us, we each have so many people we could thank on a personal basis for encouraging us, FaceTiming with us, keeping us grounded, and more. To our family and friends who are always there for us—we so appreciate you, especially our three bearded husbands (may Desiring God understand).

We are so grateful for the team at Baker, who has been so professional and encouraging. Dwight Baker believed in us and supported us even when he had to take flak for doing so. Stephanie Duncan Smith is the best editor we've ever worked with. Stephanie, you really "got" this book, and you understood our heart and our passion but also our desire to do this with integrity. Thank you for pushing us in all those directions at once and for your persistence in making sure we got things right (and in on time!). Wendy Wetzel, we just love you. You're so funny and such a great cheerleader and you actually answer emails quickly! It's been wonderful to have marketing on our side. And to the whole team that was so patient with us when we kept wanting to make just one more tweak—thank you.

Chip MacGregor, we're so honored and blessed to have you as an agent. You have always believed in us, you're always available when we need to chat, you run interference for us constantly. We are so grateful we're in such good hands.

To the journalists and the hundreds of podcast hosts who have picked up stories about our research and our findings and have helped spread the message of freedom and hope, thank you.

To the Bare Marriage team, who helps us organize our lives and who keeps our schedules on track and gets the work done behind the scenes, thank you, especially to Connor and Tammy. One day we shall celebrate all in person again.

Writing *The Great Sex Rescue* and *She Deserves Better* made us all persona non grata to many in the evangelical establishment. But we have been embraced by individual pastors, counselors, podcast hosts, and, most importantly, readers, who have spread the word, sometimes in whispers, about these life-changing books. We couldn't do this without you.

We have found an online community that has embraced us even as the establishment has not, and that community has been so life-giving. To Beth Allison Barr, Kristin Du Mez, Rachael and Jacob Denhollander, Aimee Byrd, Sarah McDugal, Natalie Hoffman, Ngina Otiende, Gretchen Baskerville, Marg Mowczko, Patrick Weaver, Andrew Bauman, Kyle J. Howard, Jay Stringer, Johnna Harris, Julie Anne Smith, Amy Fritz, Melissa J. Hogan, Carl Thomas, Camden Morgante, Andrew Whitehead, Samuel Perry, Wendy Snyder, Michael John Cusick, Carson Weitnaer, Lori and Jason Adams-Brown (and to the many, many others who fill our Twitter feeds every day), you have been a city on a hill for us as we often find ourselves navigating areas of darkness.

Dr. Lora Mize, you have been a shining light for us, and your professional opinion and perspective have been such a gift. We hope this book helps physiotherapists everywhere engage in prevention of pain for those raised in religious circles, and we have been so grateful for your collaboration in this regard.

Finally, and most importantly, we want to thank the thousands of women who gave us at least half an hour of their lives to fill out our survey, and the dozens who participated in rather personal focus groups and interviews. We are so appreciative of the stories you trusted us with, and this book would not exist without you. Even if your own story didn't make it into the book, we hope you can see yourself in these pages. We will keep fighting for you until, we pray, one day when we won't have to.

# Notes

## Chapter 1 She Deserves to Be Set Up for Success

1. Girls who took a purity pledge in elementary or middle school were 1.50 times more likely to save sex for marriage (p < 0.001; 95% 1.32–1.71). *P* values are defined as the odds of a larger test-statistic result being obtained if the observation was repeated presuming that the null hypothesis is true. A confidence interval (CI) gives an interval around the point estimate such that if the observation was repeated one hundred times, 95% of 95% confidence intervals would contain the true parameter.

2. Girls who took a purity pledge in elementary or middle school were 1.34 times more likely to have below-average knowledge of sex education terms when they graduated from high school (p < 0.001; 95% CI 1.19–-2.03). They were also 1.22 times more likely to have below-average self-esteem in high school (p = 0.001; 95% CI 1.08–1.38) and are 1.22 times more likely to have below-average self-esteem today (p = 0.001; 95% CI 1.09–1.38).

3. Girls who took a purity pledge in elementary or middle school were 1.24 times more likely to develop vaginismus (p = 0.004; 95% CI 1.07–1.44).

4. John P. Bartkowski, Xiaohe Xu, and Stephen Bartkowski, "Mixed Blessing: The Beneficial and Detrimental Effects of Religion on Child Development among Third-Graders," *Religions* 10, no. 1 (2019): 37, https://doi.org/10.3390/rel10010037.

5. Ying Chen and Tyler J. VanderWeele, "Associations of Religious Upbringing with Subsequent Health and Well-Being from Adolescence to Young Adulthood: An Outcome-Wide Analysis," *American Journal of Epidemiology* 187, no. 11 (2018): 2355–64, https://doi.org/10.1093/aje/kwy142.

6. Because our surveys and our research are concerned with the evangelical church in North America, when we say words like "church" in this book, we are referring specifically to evangelical churches and the evangelical culture as a whole while recognizing that there are churches of other denominations or of subcultures within evangelicalism that do not teach these things.

7. More on why we used self-esteem as a measure in chapter 2. Self-esteem was evaluated using the Rosenberg Self-Esteem Score.

8. The 95% confidence intervals overlap for the means of all teachings when comparing those who attend church "a few times a year" and disagree with any given teaching with those who attend church services or activities more than once a week and agree with the teachings. When looking at those who attend church once a year or less and who disagree with the teaching, the 95% confidence intervals overlap for all teachings except those that are directly related to waiting until marriage to have sex ("if you wait to have sex until you are married, you will have the best sex life possible," and "if you have sex before you are married, you will have ruined your chances of having a good sex life in marriage").

9. We developed a sexual satisfaction score using the following equation: sexual satisfaction = frequency of sex (from 1 to 6) + closeness during sex (from 1 to 6) + frequency of arousal (from 1 to 6) + communication about sexual desire and preferences (from 1 to 6) + orgasm frequency (from 1 to 5, doubled) + priority on female sexual pleasure (from 1 to 6) - 7.

10. Leonardo de Sousa Fortes, Flávia Marcele Cipriani, Fernanda Dias Coelho, Santiago Tavares Paes, and Maria Elisa Caputo Ferreira, "Does Self-Esteem Affect Body Dissatisfaction Levels in Female Adolescents?," *Revista Paulista de Pediatria* 32, no. 3 (October 3, 2014): 236–40, https://doi.org/10.1590/0103-0582201432314.

11. Shiva Bigizadeh, Nader Sharifi, Shohreh Javadpour, Neda Poornowrooz, Fatmeh Honarmand Jahromy, and Safieh Jamali, "Attitude toward Violence and Its Relationship with Self-Esteem and Self-Efficacy among Iranian Women," *Journal of Psychosocial Nursing and Mental Health Services* 59, no. 4 (December 10, 2020): 31–37, https://doi.org/10.3928/02793695-20201203-06.

12. Georgia Kalemi, Ioannis Michopoulos, Vasiliki Efstathiou, Georgios Tzeferakos, Sevasti Gkioka, Rossetos Gournellis, and Athanassios Douzenis, "Self-Esteem and Aggression in Women: Differences between Female Prisoners and Women without Criminal Records," *Women & Health* 59, no. 10 (2019): 1199–211, https://doi.org/10.1080/03630242.2019.1593284.

## Chapter 2  She Deserves a Big Faith

1. Lisa Miller and Merav Gur, "Religiousness and Sexual Responsibility in Adolescent Girls," *Journal of Adolescent Health* 31, no. 5 (November 1, 2002): 401–6, https://doi.org/10.1016/s1054-139x(02)00403-2.

2. John Wesley, "The Letters of John Wesley," ed. Jerry James, The Wesley Center Online, accessed May 16, 2022, http://wesley.nnu.edu/john-wesley/the-letters-of-john-wesley/.

3. While Protestantism is five hundred years old, the evangelical movement as we know it now started in the 1700s.

4. Elisabeth Elliot, *Passion and Purity* (Grand Rapids: Revell, 2002).

5. Lucie Hemmen, *The Teen Girl's Survival Guide: Ten Tips for Making Friends, Avoiding Drama, and Coping with Social Stress* (Oakland, CA: Instant Help, 2015).

6. From an advertisement for the True Girl event on the Born to Be Brave website, accessed July 25, 2021, https://borntobebrave.com/.

7. This is similar to what John MacArthur said leading up to the 2020 election. For an example, see https://thefrontporch.org/2020/09/politics-and-the-christian-faith-thoughts-on-john-macarthurs-statement/, accessed May 16, 2022.

## Chapter 3 She Deserves to Be Heard

1. Natasha H. Bailen, Lauren M. Green, and Renee J. Thompson, "Understanding Emotion in Adolescents: A Review of Emotional Frequency, Intensity, Instability, and Clarity," *Emotion Review* 11, no. 1 (2018): 63–73, https://doi.org/10.1177/1754073918768878.

2. "Adolescence and Emerging Adulthood."

3. "Major Depression," National Institute of Mental Health, U.S. Department of Health and Human Services, January 2022, https://www.nimh.nih.gov/health/statistics/major-depression.

4. Bailen, Green, and Thompson, "Understanding Emotion in Adolescents."

5. Crystal Amiel Estrada, Marian Fe Lomboy, Ernesto R. Gregorio, Emmy Amalia, Cynthia R. Leynes, Romeo R. Quizon, and Jun Kobayashi, "Religious Education Can Contribute to Adolescent Mental Health in School Settings," *International Journal of Mental Health Systems* 13, no. 1 (2019), https://doi.org/10.1186/s13033-019-0286-7.

6. Michael Rusch, "Sugarless Haribo Gummy Bear Reviews on Amazon Are the Most Insane Thing You'll Read Today," *BuzzFeed News*, July 14, 2021, https://www.buzzfeednews.com/article/michaelrusch/haribo-gummy-bear-reviews-on-amazon-are-the-most-insane-thin.

7. Marc Alan Schelske, *The Wisdom of Your Heart* (Colorado Springs: David C. Cook, 2017), 52.

8. Nancy DeMoss Wolgemuth and Dannah Gresh, *Lies Young Women Believe: And the Truth that Sets Them Free*, updated ed. (Chicago: Moody, 2018), 151.

9. Bethany Beal and Kristen Clark, "5 Tips for Overcoming Crazy Girl Emotions," YouTube video, 7:18, accessed May 16, 2022, https://www.youtube.com/watch?v=Jxx1Ypbdwog. Interestingly, the video also quotes another book by DeMoss, *Lies Women Believe*.

10. Rob Reimer, *Soul Care* (Franklin, TN: Carpenter's Son Publishing, 2016), 162–64.

11. Wolgemuth and Gresh, *Lies Young Women Believe*, 90.

12. "Religiosity and Suicidality among LGBTQ Youth," The Trevor Project, September 30, 2021, https://www.thetrevorproject.org/research-briefs/religiosity-and-suicidality-among-lgbtq-youth/.

13. Megan C. Lytle, John R. Blosnich, Susan M. De Luca, and Chris Brownson, "Association of Religiosity with Sexual Minority Suicide Ideation and Attempt," *American Journal of Preventive Medicine* 54, no. 5 (March 14, 2018): 644–51, https://doi.org/10.1016/j.amepre.2018.01.019.

14. For example, see *Soul Care* by Rob Reimer, and Neil Anderson's books, including *Victory over the Darkness* and *Bondage Breaker*.

15. Reimer, *Soul Care*. "In some cases, people can be sexually assaulted by a demon. These spirits are called incubus or succubus spirits; they come in through rape or sexual molestation. These spirits victimize some people repeatedly. These people wake up in the night because it feels like someone is raping them, but no one is there. They feel all the physical sensations of sexual assault, but a demonic spirit perpetuates it. This is becoming increasingly common in our society because of sexual assault, abuse, and date rape. If I talk about this in a classroom of fifty people, I always have a handful of people come up to me afterward and, through tears, tell me their tale of horror" (162–63). Reimer also claims that demonic influences

were found in more than two-thirds of his doctoral students at Alliance Theological Seminary (166).

16. Bethany Beal and Kristen Clark (@girldefined), "To the sister who's really struggling tonight," Instagram, March 27, 2022, https://www.instagram.com/p/Cbnyo ULPM6l/?utm_source=ig_web_copy_link.

17. Beal and Clark (@girldefined), "There's so much uncertainty in the unknown," March 17, 2022, https://www.instagram.com/p/CbN2N6lOBGb/?utm _source=ig_web_copy_link.

18. Kendra Cherry, "What is Spiritual Bypassing?," VeryWellmind.com, December 6, 2020, https://www.verywellmind.com/what-is-spiritual-bypassing-5081640. John Welwood, a Buddhist, first coined this term, but it has been adapted for use by other religions, including Christianity, because it describes well the all-too-common religious propensity to bypass growth and distance ourselves from uncomfortable emotions using spiritual language and practices.

19. Elisabeth Elliot, *Passion and Purity* (Grand Rapids: Revell, 2002), 54.

20. Wolgemuth and Gresh, *Lies Young Women Believe*, 30.

21. "Major Depression," National Institute of Mental Health.

22. Marie-Helene Delval and Arno Delval, *Psalms for Young Children* (Grand Rapids: Eerdmans Books for Young Readers, 2003), 25.

23. Wolgemuth and Gresh, *Lies Young Women Believe*, 151.

## Chapter 4  She Deserves to Be Respected

1. George M. Hayward, "Religiosity and Premarital Sexual Behaviors among Adolescents: An Analysis of Functional Form," *Journal for the Scientific Study of Religion* 58, no. 2 (February 1, 2019): 439–58, https://doi.org/10.1111/jssr.12588.

2. Jason A. Ford and Terrence D. Hill, "Religiosity and Adolescent Substance Use: Evidence from the National Survey on Drug Use and Health," *Substance Use & Misuse* 47, no. 7 (March 2012): 787–98, https://doi.org/10.3109/10826084.2012 .667489.

3. Julia August, "The Grudge," *Brio*, 2002, https://web.archive.org/web/2005 0212032255/http://www.briomag.com/briomagazine/spiritualhealth/a0003038 .html.

4. Elisabeth Elliot, *Passion and Purity* (Grand Rapids: Revell, 2002), 137.

5. David French and Nancy French, "They Aren't Who You Think They Are," *The French Press*, *The Dispatch*, March 28, 2021, https://frenchpress.thedispatch .com/p/they-arent-who-you-think-they-are.

6. "Duggar Interview," *The Kelly File*, Fox News, June 3, 2015, https://www.you tube.com/watch?v=qudoA-yqwNs.

## Chapter 5  She Deserves the Whole Story about Dating

1. *I Survived I Kissed Dating Goodbye*, directed by Jessica Van Der Wyngaard (Nashville: Docs/ology, 2018). Many of the main proponents of purity culture have since recanted their stance. Josh Harris himself, who wrote the biggest treatise on it, has publicly disavowed his book (and his faith). In 2016, a representative for BarlowGirl reported that they no longer agree with their earlier stance against dating. But for those of us who were raised in a culture that treated teenage dating

as worldly lust, navigating these waters with our own daughters can feel even more daunting.

2. Compare data from Statistics Canada on teen pregnancy rates in the 1970s versus 1990s, for example. Surinder Wadhera and Wayne J. Millar, "Teenage Pregnancies 1974 to 1994," *Health Reports* 9, no. 3 (Winter 1997), Statistics Canada, https://www150.statcan.gc.ca/n1/en/pub/82-003-x/1997003/article/3452-eng.pdf?st=AeVMOCOg; "Teen Pregnancy by Pregnancy Outcomes, Females Aged 15 to 19," Statistics Canada, https://www150.statcan.gc.ca/t1/tbl1/en/tv.action?pid=13100 16601&pickMembers%5B0%5D=1.1&pickMembers%5B1%5D=2.1&pickMembers%5 B2%5D=4.2&cubeTimeFrame.startYear=1998&cubeTimeFrame.endYear=2000& referencePeriods=19980101%2C20000101; John Elflein, "Fertility Rate of Teenagers in Canada from 2014 to 2020," Statista, March 9, 2022, https://www.statista.com /statistics/937516/teenage-fertility-rate-canada/#:~:text=In%202020%2C%20there %20were%205.5,has%20decreased%20in%20recent%20years.

3. Self-esteem in high school, respectively 27.35, 26.79, 23.25, 20.76. These values were obtained using the Rosenberg Self-Esteem Scale.

4. Susie Shellenberger, "God said . . . I said," *Brio*, May 2000, 26–32.

5. Bethany Beal and Kristen Clark (@girldefined), "Have you ever had a crush on a guy," Instagram, June 14, 2021, https://www.instagram.com/p/CQH0Ubejl7L/.

6. Susie Shellenberger, "Dating + Love = Marriage . . . Then Sex," *Brio*, 1998, https://web.archive.org/web/20040617025131/http://www.briomag.com/brio magazine/relationships/a0005214.html.

7. Elisabeth Elliot, *Passion and Purity* (Grand Rapids: Revell, 2002), 61.

8. Elliot, *Passion and Purity*, 119.

9. Sarah Bessey, "The (Successful) Pursuit of God: Family, Work, Ministry, and the Ghost of A. W. Tozer," *Fathom*, October 23, 2019, https://www.fathommag.com /stories/the-successful-pursuit-of-god.

10. Bessey, "The (Successful) Pursuit of God."

## Chapter 6  She Deserves to Be Protected

1. Our survey found that 7.94% of respondents were exposed to an inappropriate relationship involving church leadership and were aware of it in high school; 7.62% were exposed but weren't aware until later.

2. ($p = 0.025$, 95% CI 1.02–1.53).

3. ($p < 0.001$, 95% CI 1.31–1.73).

4. ($p = 0.023$, 95% CI 1.02–1.35).

5. ($p = 0.011$, 95% CI 105–1.47).

6. Sheila Wray Gregoire, Rebecca Gregoire Lindenbach, and Joanna Sawatsky, *The Great Sex Rescue: The Lies You've Been Taught and How to Recover What God Intended* (Grand Rapids: Baker Books, 2021), 32.

7. Gregoire, Lindenbach, and Sawatsky, *Great Sex Rescue*, 32.

8. Nancy DeMoss Wolgemuth and Dannah Gresh, *Lies Young Women Believe: And the Truth that Sets Them Free*, updated ed. (Chicago: Moody, 2018), 92.

9. Shannon Ethridge and Stephen Arterburn, *Every Young Woman's Battle: Guarding Your Mind, Heart, and Body in a Sex-Saturated World* (Colorado Springs: Waterbrook, 2008), 85.

10. John MacArthur, "The Subordination and Equality of Women," Grace to You Library of Sermons, April 25, 1976, https://www.gty.org/library/sermons-library /1844/the-subordination-and-equality-of-women.

11. Laura MacKenzie, "What's Wrong with Missionary Dating?," *Brio*, December 2004, https://web.archive.org/web/20041206134722/http://briomag.com/brio magazine/relationships/a0005176.html.

12. Ethridge and Arterburn, *Every Young Woman's Battle*, 1–2.

13. Shaunti Feldhahn and Lisa A. Rice, *For Young Women Only: What You Need to Know about How Guys Think* (Colorado Springs: Waterbrook, 2009), 37.

14. Feldhahn and Rice, *For Young Women Only*, 20.

15. Michal Gilad, "In God's Shadow: Unveiling the Hidden World of Domestic Violence Victims in Religious Communities," *SSRN Electronic Journal* 11, no. 3 (January 2013), https://doi.org/10.2139/ssrn.2331015.

16. Richard A. Bergland, "The Inside Scoop on Guys," *Brio*, 2002, https://web .archive.org/web/20050320212947/http://www.briomag.com/briomagazine/rela tionships/a0004575.html.

17. Bergland, "Inside Scoop on Guys."

18. Feldhahn and Rice, *For Young Women Only*, 26.

## Chapter 7  She Deserves to Know about Her Body

1. Elinor Evans, "Anne of Cleves: Henry VIII's Most Successful Queen?," History Extra, May 5, 2022, https://www.historyextra.com/period/tudor/anne-of-cleves -henry-viii-successful-queen-fourth-wife-tracy-borman/.

2. Odds ratio (OR) 1.21, p = 0.001, 95% CI 1.08–1.35.

3. Eva S. Goldfarb and Lisa D. Lieberman, "Three Decades of Research: The Case for Comprehensive Sex Education," *Journal of Adolescent Health* 68, no. 1 (October 12, 2020): 13–27, https://doi.org/10.1016/j.jadohealth.2020.07.036.

4. Sandra Julian Barker, "Dear Jessica," *Brio*, 2001, https://web.archive.org /web/20080925024949/http://www.briomag.com/briomagazine/relationships /a0004415.html.

5. Dannah Gresh, *And the Bride Wore White: Seven Secrets to Sexual Purity* (Chicago: Moody, 2012), 114.

6. *Mean Girls*, directed by Mark Waters (Los Angeles: Paramount Pictures, 2004).

7. Shannon Ethridge and Stephen Arterburn, *Every Young Woman's Battle: Guarding Your Mind, Heart, and Body in a Sex-Saturated World* (Colorado Springs: Waterbrook, 2008), x.

8. Gresh, *And the Bride Wore White*, 26.

9. Gresh, *And the Bride Wore White*, 125.

10. Gresh, *And the Bride Wore White*, 24.

11. Ethridge and Arterburn, *Every Young Woman's Battle*, 164.

12. Gresh, *And the Bride Wore White*, 26.

13. King K. Holmes, Ruth Levine, and Marcia Weaver, "Effectiveness of Condoms in Preventing Sexually Transmitted Infections," *Bulletin of the World Health Organization* 82, no. 6 (2004): 454–61, https://www.ncbi.nlm.nih.gov/pmc/articles /PMC2622864/.

14. "How Effective Is Contraception at Preventing Pregnancy?," National Health Service, last reviewed April 17, 2020, https://www.nhs.uk/conditions/contracep tion/how-effective-contraception/; "Birth Control for Teens," Caring for Kids, April

2018, https://www.caringforkids.cps.ca/handouts/preteens-and-teens/birth-con
trol-for-teens. Condoms are more effective in preventing pregnancy among adults
because adults tend to use them more consistently, and adults are more likely to
use them correctly. So the answer isn't that condoms don't work as much as it is
a call for more information so that teens who choose to have sex know how to
protect themselves.

15. Gresh, *And the Bride Wore White*, 162.

16. Josh McDowell, in the foreword to Ethridge and Arterburn, *Every Young
Woman's Battle*, xi.

17. Goldfarb and Lieberman, "Three Decades of Research."

18. "Religiosity and Suicidality among LGBTQ Youth," The Trevor Project,
September 30, 2021, https://www.thetrevorproject.org/research-briefs/religiosity
-and-suicidality-among-lgbtq-youth/; Jeremy J. Gibbs, "Religious Conflict, Sexual
Identity, and Suicidal Behaviors among LGBT Young Adults," *Archives of Suicide
Research* 19, no. 4 (2015): 472–88, https://doi.org/10.1080/13811118.2015.1004476.

19. OR 2.77. First marriages only included. Growing up in purity culture was
determined (in 2021) as age between eighteen and thirty-nine.

20. Elisabeth Elliot, *Passion and Purity* (Grand Rapids: Revell, 2002), 131.

21. Richard A. Bergland, "The Inside Scoop on Guys," *Brio*, 2002, https://web
.archive.org/web/20050320212947/http://www.briomag.com/briomagazine/rela
tionships/a0004575.html.

22. Susie Shellenberger, "You Won't Like This," *Brio*, June 2002, 23–24.

23. Binary logistic regression was utilized using alpha = 0.05. Confounders
included parental marital quality, knowledge of sex ed terminology, high school
self-esteem, and high school church attendance. P = 0.08.

24. Binary logistic regression utilized with having above- or below-average sexual satisfaction as the outcome variable. Marital satisfaction, measured on a scale of
1 to 25, was statistically significant in the model (OR 1.24, p < 0.001, 95% CI 1.23–1.26).
Having one's sexual debut on the wedding night was not statistically significant
in the model (OR 1.06, p = 0.377, 95% CI 0.93–1.21). An alternative model was also
run using pairwise comparisons between saving sex for marriage and the number
of partners before marriage (fiancé vs. others). None of these comparisons were
statistically significant when marital satisfaction was included in the model. (I had
had consensual sex with my fiancé but with no one else [OR 0.97, p = 0.692, 95% CI
0.81–1.15]. I had had consensual sex with my fiancé and with other people [OR 0.96,
p = 0.657, 95% CI 0.82–1.13]. I had had consensual sex with other people but not
with my fiancé [OR 0.79, p = 0.104, 95% CI 0.60–1.05]).

25. Elliot, *Passion and Purity*, 17.

26. Gresh, *And the Bride Wore White*, 18.

27. Gresh, *And the Bride Wore White*, 152.

28. Elliot, *Passion and Purity*, 23.

29. You can compare the surveys from *For Young Women Only* and *For Young
Men Only* to see the differences for yourself. Both used to be available on shaunti
.com/research/; however, it seems that as of the time of this publication, she has
redirected the links for both books to the survey of girls. You can access that survey
on her site here: https://shaunti.com/wp-content/uploads/2022/05/FYMO-Survey
-corrected-2017_rev050122.pdf. Luckily, the survey of young men is still available
via the Wayback Machine, and you can access it here: https://web.archive.org/web

/20200422162254/https://shaunti.com/wp-content/uploads/2017/09/fywo-survey
-results-dec1013.pdf.

30. Eric and Leslie Ludy, *When God Writes Your Love Story* (Colorado Springs: Multnomah, 2004), 223.

31. Nancy DeMoss Wolgemuth and Dannah Gresh, *Lies Young Women Believe: And the Truth that Sets Them Free*, updated ed. (Chicago: Moody, 2018), 102.

32. Lisa Miller and Merav Gur, "Religiousness and Sexual Responsibility in Adolescent Girls," *Journal of Adolescent Health* 31, no. 5 (November 1, 2002): 401–6, https://doi.org/10.1016/s1054-139x(02)00403-2.

33. "YRBSS Data Summary & Trends," Centers for Disease Control and Prevention, February 8, 2021, https://www.cdc.gov/healthyyouth/data/yrbs/yrbs_data
_summary_and_trends.htm.

## Chapter 8  She Deserves to Understand Consent

1. Ashley Parent, "Sexual Consent in Middle School Sex Health Education: An Analysis of Health Education Standards in Minnesota" (master's thesis, Minnesota State University, Mankato, 2020), Cornerstone: A Collection of Scholarly and Creative Works for Minnesota State University, Mankato, https://cornerstone
.lib.mnsu.edu/etds/1062/.

2. This pattern continues into marriage. In our research for *The Great Sex Rescue*, we found that none of the thirteen evangelical sex and marriage books we reviewed included any explanations of sexual coercion, marital rape, or other factors that can erode one's ability to consent. In fact, none of them even used the word *consent*. The only book we found with clear pictures of what coercion looked like was the secular book we used as a control: *Seven Principles for Making Marriage Work* by John Gottman.

3. For information about the Toronto van attack, see https://en.wikipedia.org
/wiki/Toronto_van_attack.

4. Chuck Hustmyre and Jay Dixit, "Marked for Mayhem," *Psychology Today*, January 1, 2009, https://www.psychologytoday.com/intl/articles/200901/marked
-mayhem; Betty Grayson and Morris l. Stein, "Attracting Assault: Victims' Nonverbal Cues," *Journal of Communication* 31, no. 1 (1981): 68–75, https://doi.org/10
.1111/j.1460-2466.1981.tb01206.x.

5. Hustmyre and Dixit, "Marked for Mayhem"; Grayson and Stein, "Attracting Assault."

6. Shannon Ethridge and Stephen Arterburn, *Every Young Woman's Battle: Guarding Your Mind, Heart, and Body in a Sex-Saturated World* (Colorado Springs: Waterbrook, 2008), 110.

7. Dannah Gresh, *And the Bride Wore White: Seven Secrets to Sexual Purity* (Chicago: Moody, 2012), 117.

8. Ethridge and Arterburn, *Every Young Woman's Battle*, 193.

9. Gresh, *And the Bride Wore White*, 93.

10. Shaunti Feldhahn and Lisa A. Rice, *For Young Women Only: What You Need to Know about How Guys Think* (Colorado Springs: Waterbrook, 2009), 148.

11. For more on the methodological problems with this survey question, please see the blog post Connor Lindenbach, "Fixed It For You! We Fixed a Survey Question so It Doesn't Enable Date Rape," Bare Marriage, January 25, 2021,

https:/baremarriage.com/2021/01/fixed-it-for-you-we-fix-a-survey-question-so-it
-doesnt-enable-date-rape/.

12. Feldhahn and Rice, *For Young Women Only*, 149.

13. Feldhahn and Rice, *For Young Women Only*, 148.

14. Feldhahn and Rice, *For Young Women Only*, 148.

15. Ethridge and Arterburn, *Every Young Woman's Battle*, 1–2.

16. Ethridge and Arterburn, *Every Young Woman's Battle*, 3.

17. In all our research, the book that caused us the greatest concern was *Every Young Man's Battle*. The book uses language that we found to be objectifying of girls. We feel it does not treat date rape seriously enough and that it fails to adequately identify or condemn the assaults it describes, and we found its portrayal of pornography salacious and unnecessarily graphic. We believe this book to be harmful on this topic and would not recommend its use by youth groups.

18. Stephen Arterburn and Fred Stoeker, *Every Man's Battle* (Colorado Springs: Waterbrook, 2000), 61.

19. As authors, we find it very disturbing that Steve Arterburn repeatedly states in his books that all Christian men act in a sinful way. This is not biblical, wise, or accurate, and we believe it sheds serious doubt on whether we should be listening to Arterburn for moral advice.

20. Rory Partin, "Straight from a Guy," *Brio*, 2001, https://web.archive.org/web /20041028104723/http://briomag.com/briomagazine/relationships/a0004406.html.

21. "I Was Assaulted. He Was Applauded," *New York Times*, March 9, 2018. https://www.nytimes.com/2018/03/09/opinion/jules-woodson-andy-savage-assault.html.

22. Susie Shellenberger, "Dear Susie," *Brio* 10, no. 9 (Sept. 1999): 4.

23. Eric and Leslie Ludy, *When God Writes Your Love Story* (Colorado Springs: Multnomah, 2004), 222.

24. Roy J. Levin and Willy van Berlo, "Sexual Arousal and Orgasm in Subjects Who Experience Forced or Non-Consensual Sexual Stimulation—A Review," *Journal of Clinical Forensic Medicine* 11, no. 2 (2004): 82–88, https://doi.org/10.1016 /j.jcfm.2003.10.008.

25. See famous study: D. G. Dutton and A. P. Aron, "Some Evidence for Heightened Sexual Attraction under Conditions of High Anxiety," *Journal of Personality and Social Psychology* 30, no. 4 (1974): 510–17.

26. Feldhahn and Rice, quoting a survey respondent in *For Young Women Only*, 149.

27. Feldhahn and Rice, quoting a survey respondent in *For Young Women Only*, 149.

28. Ethridge and Arterburn, *Every Young Woman's Battle*, 1–2.

29. Feldhahn and Rice, quoting a survey respondent in *For Young Women Only*, 149.

## Chapter 9 She Deserves to Exist as a Person, Not as a Threat

1. Shaney Irene, "Why the Rebelution's Modesty Survey Was a Bad Idea," HomeschoolersAnonymous, April 10, 2013, https://homeschoolersanonymous.net/2013 /04/10/why-the-rebelutions-modesty-survey-was-a-bad-idea-shaney-irenes-story /; Rick Beckman, "Modesty Survey," February 15, 2007, https://www.rickbeckman .org/log/modesty-survey/.

2. The survey results have been taken offline.

3. Bob Smietana, "Christian Musician Matthew West Deletes 'Modest Is Hottest' YouTube video after Pushback," Religion News Service, June 25, 2021, https://

religionnews.com/2021/06/25/matthew-west-removes-modest-is-hottest-video-christian-musician-purity-culture-abuse-youtube-pushback/.

4. Todd DeMitchell, Christine Kiracofe, Richard Fossey, and Nathan Fellman, "Genderized Dress Codes in K-12 Schools: A Mixed Methods Analysis of Law & Policy," *West's Education Law Reporter*, 376 Ed. Law Rep. 421, June 11, 2020, https://www.researchgate.net/publication/342502996_Genderized_Dress_Codes_in_K-12_Schools_A_Mixed_Methods_Analysis_of_Law_Policy.

5. "Allie Beth Stuckey in a Candid Conversation about Modest Is Hottest and the Controversy that Surrounded It," Episode 59, *The Matthew West Podcast*, August 11, 2021, https://www.matthewwest.com/podcast/60.

6. Dannah Gresh, *Secret Keeper Girl* (Chicago: Moody, 2004).

7. Gresh, *Secret Keeper Girl*, 24.

8. Dannah Gresh, *8 Great Dates for Moms and Daughters: How to Talk about True Beauty, Cool Fashion, and . . . Modesty!* (Eugene, OR: Harvest House, 2014), 38.

9. Dannah Gresh (@Dannah Kay), July 15, 2021, comment on Bare Marriage—formerly To Love, Honor and Vacuum, "Did anyone attend Secret Keeper Girl rallies as a preteen/teen? If so, what was your big feeling about your body afterwards?," https://www.facebook.com/Sheila.Gregoire.Books/posts/pfbid02caqVDxZze7pV9xcrSXF3PSxJVXGcm3XgiqKQmsKn4xtaTB9jzHaBfgQ19EW1RDzMl.

10. Kristen Clark and Bethany Baird, *Project Modesty: How to Honor God with Your Wardrobe while Looking Totally Adorable in the Process* (n.p.: Girl Defined, 2015), 11.

11. "Allie Beth Stuckey in a Candid Conversation about Modest Is Hottest."

12. Gresh, *8 Great Dates*, 69.

13. Clark and Baird, *Project Modesty*, 17.

14. Gabrielle Pickle, "Fall Fashion 101," *Brio*, 2007, https://web.archive.org/web/20080730085850/http://www.briomag.com/briomagazine/healthandbeauty/a0007516.html.

15. Shaunti Feldhahn, "A Letter to Our Teenage Daughters about How They Dress," April 10, 2019, https://shaunti.com/2019/04/a-letter-to-our-teenage-daughters-about-how-they-dress/.

16. Feldhahn, "Letter to Our Teenage Daughters."

17. Feldhahn, "Letter to Our Teenage Daughters."

18. https://hfrgroup.com/in-the-news/ shows a list of panels Feldhahn has participated in, including ones in which she excitedly shares her work with Brizendine. Additionally, as recently as 2016, Feldhahn allowed Brizendine's theories to be touted on her blog in a guest post by Emerson Eggerichs promoting his book, *Mother and Sons*, which also cites this disputed neuroscience. Shaunti Feldhahn, "Calling All Moms! Apply 'Respect Talk' to Your Sons," April 6, 2016, https://shaunti.com/2016/04/calling-all-moms-apply-respect-talk-to-your-sons/.

19. R. Young and E. Balaban, "Psychoneuroindoctrinology," *Nature* 443 (October 11, 2006): 634, https://doi.org/10.1038/443634a.

20. See, for example, Emily Bazelton's scathing *New York Times* book review of *The Male Brain*, March 28, 2010, https://www.nytimes.com/2010/03/28/books/review/Bazelon-t.html. To see another neuroscientist explain the problems with this book in a more accessible way for people who do not have formal neuroscience education, see Tal Yarkoni, "The Male Brain Hurts, or How Not to Write about Science," March 24, 2010, https://www.talyarkoni.org/blog/2010/03/24/the-male-brain-hurts-or-how-not-to-write-about-science/.

21. Ekaterina Mitricheva, Rui Kimura, Nikos K. Logothetis, and Hamid R. Noori, "Neural Substrates of Sexual Arousal Are Not Sex Dependent," *PNAS* 16, no. 31 (July 30, 2019): 15671–76, https://doi.org/10.1073/pnas.1904975116.

22. Mitricheva et al., "Neural Substrates of Sexual Arousal." This phenomenon is called *arousal non-concordance*, which women seem to experience more than men. Women's bodies physiologically become aroused from visual stimuli, but when asked if they're aroused, they're more likely to subjectively report that they aren't aroused, leading to less concordance between brain and body. Much of this is likely due to messages women are given about what is sexually arousing, and what is not arousing.

23. Lise Eliot, Adnan Ahmed, Hiba Khan, Julie Patel, 2021. "Dump the 'Dimorphism': Comprehensive Synthesis of Human Brain Studies Reveals Few Male-Female Differences beyond Size," *Neuroscience & Biobehavioral Reviews* 125 (June 2021): 667–97, https://doi.org/10.1016/j.neubiorev.2021.02.026.

24. Feldhahn, "Letter to Our Teenage Daughters."

25. "Dad Wants Me to Delete My Instagram," Open Christian, accessed August 26, 2022, https://www.reddit.com/r/OpenChristian/comments/sm9dod/update _dad_wants_mef16_to_delete_my_instagram/.

26. Current agreement with the statement that "girls who dress immodestly are worse than those who don't" was compared to current agreement with the statement that "girls talk too much." OR 3.99, p < 0.001. Agreement now with the statement that "boys can't help but lust after a girl who is dressed like she is trying to incite it" was compared with self-report on one's current marriage being abusive. OR 1.55, p < 0.001.

27. Shannon Ethridge and Stephen Arterburn, *Every Young Woman's Battle: Guarding Your Mind, Heart, and Body in a Sex-Saturated World* (Colorado Springs: Waterbrook, 2008). 91.

28. Bruna Nessif, "The Duggars Use Nike as a Code Word to Fight Lustful Thoughts—Plus, Jim Bob Steps Out Following Josh's Cheating Scandal," ENews, August 26, 2015, https://www.eonline.com/ca/news/690263/the-duggars-use-nike -as-a-code-word-to-fight-lustful-thoughts-plus-jim-bob-steps-out-following-josh -s-cheating-scandal.

29. Bob Gresh, quoted in Dannah Gresh, "What Advertisers Know about Your Body!," *Brio and Beyond* 2, no. 11 (Nov. 2002): 35.

30. Gresh, *Secret Keeper Girl*, 66. In her 2014 update of *Secret Keeper Girl*, called *8 Great Dates for Moms and Daughters*, the phrasing around intoxicating bellies remained the same (see p. 182); however, it has been removed for the 2021 updated edition of *8 Great Dates for Moms and Daughters*. The book is marketed to girls as young as eight years old.

31. Dannah Gresh, *8 Great Dates for Moms and Daughters: How to Talk About Cool Fashion, True Beauty, and Dignity* (Eugene, OR: Harvest House, 2021), 70.

32. Gresh, *8 Great Dates* (2021), 107.

33. Gresh, *8 Great Dates* (2021), 71.

34. Gresh, *Secret Keeper Girl*, 51–53.

## Chapter 10  She Deserves Permission to Be Big

1. Mark Gungor, Facebook, May 10, 2021, https://www.facebook.com/mark gungor/posts/335864871230803.

2. Mark Liberman, "Sex-Linked Lexical Budgets," August 6, 2006, http://itre .cis.upenn.edu/myl/languagelog/archives/003420.html.

3. In Karl S. Kruszelnicki, "'Talkative Women' Is Gender Gibberish," ABC Science, March 23, 2010, https://www.abc.net.au/science/articles/2010/03/23/2854143 .htm.

4. Claudia Hammond, "Prattle of the Sexes: Do Women Talk More Than Men?," BBC Psychology: Medical Myths, November 11, 2013, https://www.bbc.com/future /article/20131112-do-women-talk-more-than-men.

5. Susie Shellenberger, "Guy Talk," *Brio*, 2006, https://web.archive.org/web/2008 1011183930/http://www.briomag.com/briomagazine/relationships/a0007002.html.

6. Hammond, "Prattle of the Sexes"; Shellenberger, "Guy Talk."

7. T. Mendelberg, C. Karpowitz, and J. Oliphant, "Gender Inequality in Deliberation: Unpacking the Black Box of Interaction," *Perspectives on Politics* 12, no. 1 (2014): 18–44, https://doi.org/10.1017/S1537592713003691.

8. Brittany Karford Rogers, "When Women D̶o̶n̶'t̶ Speak," *Y Magazine*, Brigham Young University, spring 2020, https://magazine.byu.edu/article/when-women -dont-speak/.

9. Dannah Gresh, *8 Great Dates for Moms and Daughters: How to Talk about True Beauty, Cool Fashion, and . . . Modesty!* (Eugene, OR: Harvest House, 2014), 98.

10. Gresh, *8 Great Dates*, 99.

11. Gresh, *8 Great Dates*, 100.

12. Gresh, *8 Great Dates*, 99.

13. *The Princess Bride*, directed by Rob Reiner (Los Angeles: 20th Century Fox, 1987).

14. For more on the context of 1 Timothy 2:13–14, please see Marg Mowczko's work on cultural understandings of Adam and Eve in Ephesus at the time Paul was writing: Marg Mowczko, "Adam and Eve in Ancient Gnostic Literature and 1 Timothy 2:13–14," March 9, 2015, https://margmowczko.com/adam-and-eve-in -gnostic-literature/.

15. *Church Leadership: Explaining the Roles of Jesus, Elders, Deacons, and Members at Mars Hill*, Mars Hill Theology Series (Seattle: Mars Hill Church, 2004), 43.

16. John Piper and Wayne Grudem, eds., *Recovering Biblical Manhood and Womanhood: A Response to Evangelical Feminism*, rev. ed. (Wheaton: Crossway, 2021), 89.

17. Josh Pipa, "Leading in Worship," *The Log College* (blog), April 28, 2017, https:// web.archive.org/web/20220226045639/https:/thelogcollege.wordpress.com/2017 /05/03/4776/.

18. Nancy DeMoss Wolgemuth and Dannah Gresh, *Lies Young Women Believe: And the Truth that Sets Them Free*, updated ed. (Chicago: Moody, 2018), 22.

19. Dalia Fahmy, "Christian Women in the U.S. Are More Religious than Their Male Counterparts," Pew Research Center, September 10, 2020, https://www .pewresearch.org/fact-tank/2018/04/06/christian-women-in-the-u-s-are-more -religious-than-their-male-counterparts/.

20. Steven Lee, Benjamin F. Cummings, and Jason Martin, "Victim Characteristics of Investment Fraud," 2019 Academic Research Colloquium for Financial Planning and Related Disciplines, January 31, 2019, http://dx.doi.org/10.2139/ssrn .3258084.

21. Laura J. Kray, Jessica A. Kennedy, Alex B. Van Zant, "Not Competent Enough to Know the Difference? Gender Stereotypes about Women's Ease of Being Misled

Predict Negotiator Deception," *Organizational Behavior and Human Decision Processes* 125, no. 2 (2014): 61–72, https://doi.org/10.1016/j.obhdp.2014.06.002.

22. Shaunti Feldhahn and Lisa A. Rice, *For Young Women Only: What You Need to Know about How Guys Think* (Colorado Springs: Waterbrook, 2009), 167–68. Even though Feldhahn and Rice don't have "unconditional" in this sentence, the section of the book is about giving men unconditional respect, without requiring them to earn it. "If you are in a serious relationship with a guy, don't you want him to love you unconditionally, even when you're not being particularly lovable? Well, guys feel the same way about respect" (167).

23. Wolgemuth and Gresh, *Lies Young Women Believe*, 93.

24. Feldhahn and Rice, *For Young Women Only*, 31.

25. Feldhahn and Rice, *For Young Women Only*, 34.

26. Feldhahn and Rice, *For Young Women Only*, 29.

27. Feldhahn and Rice, *For Young Women Only*, 62.

28. The Editorial Board, "The Southern Baptist Convention Must Enact Tough Reform on Its Sexual Abuse Crisis," *Washington Post*, June 10, 2019, https://www.washingtonpost.com/opinions/the-southern-baptist-church-must-enact-tough-reform-on-its-sexual-abuse-crisis/2019/06/10/31160eb2-355a-11e9-af5b-b51b7ff322e9_story.html.

29. Kyle Swenson, "A Pastor Admitted a Past 'Sexual Incident' with a Teen, Saying He Was 'Deeply Sorry.' His Congregation Gave Him a Standing Ovation," *Washington Post*, January 10, 2018, https://www.washingtonpost.com/news/morning-mix/wp/2018/01/10/a-pastor-admitted-a-past-sexual-incident-with-a-teen-his-congregation-gave-him-a-standing-ovation/. In January 2018, Andy Savage, senior pastor at Highpoint Church in Memphis, admitted to his congregation that he had had a "sexual incident" with a youth group member when he was a youth pastor. They gave him a standing ovation. We want to stress that any sexual contact between a youth group leader and a youth group member is inherently coercive and is not an "incident" but instead an assault.

30. M. M. Kasumovic and J. H. Kuznekoff, "Insights into Sexism: Male Status and Performance Moderates Female-Directed Hostile and Amicable Behaviour," *PLOS One* 10, no. 7 (2015), https://doi.org/10.1371/journal.pone.0131613.

31. Ligon Duncan, "How Can Women Encourage Their Husbands to Be Spiritual Leaders in the Home?," The Gospel Coalition (@thegospelcoalition), Instagram, December 28, 2021, https://www.instagram.com/reel/CYCBRjioOc4/?utm_source=ig_web_copy_link.

32. Lucy Maud Montgomery, "The Strike at Putney," http://fullreads.com/literature/the-strike-at-putney/.

## Acknowledgments

1. To become a part of the Bare Marriage patreon, join here: https://patreon.com/baremarriage.

# CONNECT WITH SHEILA ONLINE

Find Sheila online for healthy, biblical, evidence-based help for your marriage and sex life.

Tune in to the *Bare Marriage* podcast through your favorite podcast streaming service.

Read the *Bare Marriage* blog at **BareMarriage.com**.

**f** Bare Marriage   🐦 📷 SheilaGregoire

# INVITE BARE MARRIAGE TO SPEAK

Are you interested in inviting Sheila, Keith, Rebecca, or Joanna to speak to your group or church, at your event, or on your podcast or radio show? Reach out to them at **BareMarriage.com/booking**.

## BareMarriage.com

 Bare Marriage      SheilaGregoire

# "This book is desperately needed in this moment."

—**Kristin Kobes Du Mez**, author of *Jesus and John Wayne*

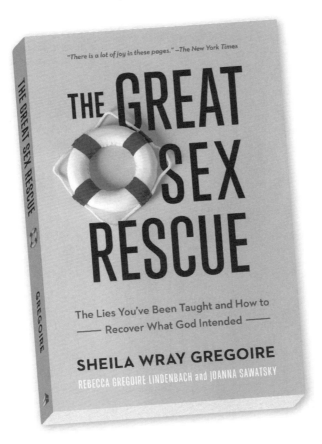

"There is a lot of joy in these pages." —*The New York Times*

# THE GREAT SEX RESCUE

### The Lies You've Been Taught and How to —— Recover What God Intended ——

## SHEILA WRAY GREGOIRE

REBECCA GREGOIRE LINDENBACH and JOANNA SAWATSKY

Based on a groundbreaking, in-depth survey of over twenty thousand women, *The Great Sex Rescue* pulls back the curtain on what is happening in Christian bedrooms, exposes the problematic evangelical teachings that wreck sex for so many couples, and points couples to what they should have been told all along.

a division of Baker Publishing Group
www.BakerBooks.com

Available wherever books and ebooks are sold.